The Buddha and His Teachings

The Buddha and His Teachings

Crystal Mirror Series
Volume Ten

Crystal Mirror Series

Library of Congress Cataloguing-in-Publication Data

The Buddha and His Teachings
p. cm. — (Crystal mirror series ; v. ten)
Includes bibliographical references and index.
ISBN 0–89800–272–9 (pbk.)
1. Buddhism I. Series
BQ 4012.B83 1995 294.3–dc20 95–46697

Director and general editor of the Crystal Mirror Series: Tarthang Tulku. Manuscript prepared by Elizabeth Cook under the auspices of the Yeshe De Project. Photograph on p. 84 courtesy of John C. and Susan L. Huntington.

Typeset in Adobe New Aster with New Aster Outline titles and initials. Printed and bound by Dharma Press, 2910 San Pablo Avenue, Berkeley, CA 94702.

10 9 8 7 6 5 4 3 2 1

NYINGMA

CRYSTAL MIRROR

ANCIENTONES

The Crystal Mirror Series

Introductions to Buddha, Dharma, and Sangha
created by Tarthang Tulku
for Western Students of the Dharma

1–3
Footsteps on the Diamond Path

4
Guru Padmasambhava and Buddhism in Tibet

5
Lineage of Diamond Light

6
The Three Jewels and History of Dharma Transmission

7
Buddha, Dharma, and Sangha in Historical Perspective

8
Light of Liberation: A History of Buddhism in India

9
Holy Places of the Buddha

10
The Buddha and His Teachings

11
Masters of the Nyingma Lineage

Dedicated to the Future of
Buddhism in the West

Homage to the Light of the World, the Victorious Buddha

Light of the World
The Victorious
Buddha

Homage to the Tathāgata Buddha Śākyamuni

The Path of the Perfect Buddhas

Through the centuries, accounts of the Buddha, the Perfectly Enlightened One, have been expressed in Sūtra, in poetry and art, and in historical works by masters of the Dharma traditions that flow from the Buddha's teachings. These accounts express two major approaches to the nature of the Buddha and his quest for enlightenment. In one view, the Buddha Śākyamuni is seen as an ordinary man who attained supreme realization after innumerable lifetimes dedicated to meritorious action. In traditions that emphasize this aspect of the Buddha, the Jātakas—accounts of the Buddha's previous births—are viewed as reflecting a steady progression from lower to higher forms of life, each offering greater scope for meritorious actions than the one before.

While many may be inspired to follow a spiritual path, only rarely in the stream of existence does a being awaken the aspiration to become a Buddha. Few are capable of accumulating the inconceivable virtue and wisdom that give rise to the thought of such a transformation, and fewer still can make the necessary effort to follow the path to its end. Lama Mi-pham explains in the Grub-mtha'-bsdus-pa that it is almost impossible for ordinary people to work on such a deep level for the benefit of others, since "they cannot endure the suffering of samsara, nor can they tame its wild negativity." But from time to time, under conditions made possible by the actions of a Buddha in the world, a rare individual generates the thought of enlightenment and begins to deliberately cultivate actions that will in time produce on his body the thirty-two major and eighty accessory marks of a Great Being.

At some point, by virtue of accumulated merit, this person is blessed with the rare good fortune of meeting and honoring a Buddha. Perceiving the incomparable beauty and value of a fully awakened one, he conceives the wish to become such a being and receives a prediction that in aeons to come, he too will join the lineage of Buddhas. From that time forward, he is always born in conditions that support his vow to become enlightened for the sake of all beings: His faculties are complete, he remembers his past lives, and he does not falter from his purpose. As a Bodhisattva, he acts with pure compassion, free from the taint of selfish concerns, bearing ill-treatment with patience and joyfully undertaking exhausting and painful labors. In successive aeons, he hears the Dharma from numerous Buddhas and works tirelessly on behalf of all living beings.

In all Buddhist traditions, Śākyamuni, the Buddha of our age, is seen as one in an endless procession of Buddhas that illuminate the primordial darkness of time and space. Inspired by an earlier Buddha also named Śākyamuni, he awakens the thought of enlightenment and begins to accumulate merit and wisdom. In the first great aeon, he venerates seventy-six thousand Enlightened Ones; in the second great aeon, seventy-seven thousand; and in the third, seventy-eight thousand. At the end of the second great aeon, in the northwestern city of Nagarahāra, the Bodhisattva as a young Brahmin spreads his cloak upon muddy ground for the Buddha Dīpaṁkāra, and receives from the Giver of Light his prediction to complete, perfect enlightenment. In the Bhadrakalpa, our present great aeon that will be blessed by the enlightenment of a thousand Buddhas, he serves the Buddhas Krakucchanda, Kanakamuni, and Kāśyapa.

Accumulating merit and wisdom in innumerable lifetimes, the Bodhisattva predicted to become Śākyamuni progresses through the stages of the Bodhisattva path and practices the six perfections—giving, morality, patience, vigor, meditation, and wisdom. When these qualities are developed to their fullest extent, they transcend by far the level of ordinary virtues and become "pāramitā," or perfected. (Descriptions of how these qualities are perfected are found in the Jātakas and detailed in the longer Prajñāpāramitā Sūtras.) The Bodhisattva then masters four additional perfections—skillful means, vow, powers, and primordial wisdom—that extend his capacities and empower him to genuinely benefit others.

When the Dharma of the Buddha Kāśyapa is exhausted, the Bodhisattva, with his compassion and wisdom fully developed, enters upon his final birth, in which he attains the perfect enlightenment of a Buddha. Upon enlightenment, he becomes a Tathāgata, a "Thus-gone One," defined in the Vajracchedikā-prajñāpāramitā as synonymous with true suchness: reality as it is, free of any taint of illusion. As the Buddha Śākyamuni, he rekindles the light of the Dharma. With his sweet and melodious voice he fulfills the ancient prediction and sets in motion the teachings that put an end to illusion and pain. Shaped to the needs and capacities of all manner of beings, the teachings of the Enlightened One resound once again throughout the three thousand great thousands of worlds.

In the Mahāyāna view, the Buddhas are not separate from universal truth: They are not really born and cannot really die. Their birth, life, and passing away is a compassionate enactment of how to attain liberation, performed for the sake of beings unable to perceive the truth of their nature. The forms in which they manifest as Bodhisattvas do not necessarily follow a linear progression from lower to higher forms of life, as enlightened compassion knows no limits of time or place. Called into existence by the suffering of sentient beings, the Bodhisattva appears in whatever form necessary to heal distress and turn the minds of beings toward enlightenment. The Buddha's past lives demonstrate this quality of selfless response, and his last life, in which he performs the twelve great acts of a Buddha, reveals the culmination of the play of enlightened being.

As described in the Lalitavistara and other Mahāyāna Sūtras, the Bodhisattva embarks on his final birth out of supreme compassion for the sufferings of sentient beings. From the outset his purpose is to awaken humanity and enable them to realize their potential for enlightenment. He speaks not only to the rare individual capable of full understanding, but to all beings, for all have the capacity to engage the path of the perfect Buddhas. Rich in imagery and symbolism that communicate meaning on multidimensional levels of consciousness, the Enlightened One's voice penetrates the heart directly. For those fortunate ones attuned to its profound and vast significance, the Buddha's speech resounds like a lion's roar, calling forth the aspiration to free all beings from sorrow and lead them to the great bliss of nirvana.

Seen from either perspective—as the spiritual development of a person striving for enlightenment or as the demonstration by an already enlightened being of the way to liberation, the Buddha's life is the culmination of aeons of preparation, and his nature is sublimely different in ways ordinary beings cannot understand. Whether one follows his teachings to mitigate suffering in this present life or aspires to emulate his realization in future aeons, the life of the Buddha is a unique religious biography, a guide to the view, resolve, and path to enlightenment. The Bodhisattva's actions can be emulated by all who sincerely wish to follow in his footsteps, improve the quality of their lives, and bring into the world the inconceivable blessings of enlightened knowledge.

Awakening Wisdom and Compassion

The Teaching of Vimalakīrti describes the root of human difficulties as ignorance and the thirst for existence. Habituated to patterns rooted in a fundamental not-knowingness, beings act from a dualistic discernment of self and other, solidifying faith in a separate self and perpetuating a dualistic view of all existence. This mistaken view has given rise to a pervasive illness that poisons life with the manifold sufferings resulting from desire, hatred, and confusion. Although the wisdom of the Bodhisattva penetrates the error of this view, the Bodhisattva shares in the suffering of others as if they were his children. Recognizing in his own suffering the full extent of their pain and the price they must pay for ignorance and denial, the Bodhisattva generates the wish to liberate all beings.

Inspired by the Buddha, the householder Vimalakīrti manifests as if suffering from illness. To the Bodhisattvas who ask after his welfare, Vimalakīrti explains that where the sickness of ordinary beings arises from ignorance, the sickness of the Bodhisattva arises from great compassion. Since he is ill because beings are ill, his sickness will last as long as beings remain mired in confusion. (VMK ch 5)

To be effective, the Bodhisattva's compassion must go beyond the compassion of parents for their children, which is hindered by entanglement with sentiment and emotion. Where compassion based on emotion would exhaust the Bodhisattva and limit his exercise of insight, compassion free of sentiment empowers him to work tirelessly and effectively on behalf of all beings. This is possible only when the Bodhisattva comprehends the emptiness (śūnyatā) of all existence and realizes that all manifestations— including suffering and beings that suffer—are essentially unreal. Compassion that lacks this knowledge, and wisdom that lacks compassion, are merely extensions of human bondage to the eight worldly dharmas—gain and loss, fame and disgrace, slander and praise, pleasure and pain. When both compassion and wisdom merge in a consciousness freed from concepts of self and other, liberation is possible, not only for the Bodhisattva, but also for all beings touched by the rays of his compassion. (VMK ch 1)

The Bodhisattva engages the Buddha's teachings on a deep level, constantly mindful of his intention to benefit all beings by developing the qualities of a Buddha. As he breaks the bonds of sentiment and emotionality, internal dialogues and external conflicts no longer interrupt his practice. Whatever obstacles arise only intensify his efforts; he will even engage in practices that provoke obstacles in order to bring subtle hindrances to light, where they can be seen and overcome.

With a clear understanding of the nature of mind, he is not deceived or led astray by its shifting currents. Focused on the complete enlightenment of a Buddha, he does not settle for lesser results. He progresses steadily by following clear guidelines for theory and practice, by full devotion to the path, and by skillfully applying vision and discipline. Refraining from self-centered judgments, he engages impartially in all experiences that arise and abandons all forms of hostility toward self and others. Deeply nourished and satisfied by the practice of the perfections, the Bodhisattva engenders enjoyment, fulfillment, and self-knowledge in himself and others.

TEN GREAT VOWS OF THE BODHISATTVA The Arhats, the perfect monks, the saints of the Buddhist traditions, attain nirvana by following the eightfold path that develops genuinely pure view, conceptualization, speech, conduct, livelihood, effort, mindfulness, and concentration. The Saddharmapuṇḍarīka Sūtra relates that, attaining the fruit of this path, Arhats are freed from emotionality and the passions. Comparable to great elephants in nobility, strength, and endurance, they have done their duty, accomplished all that was to be done, laid down their burden, and achieved their aim: They may enter nirvana at will.

The Bodhisattva's vow to liberate all sentient beings sets aside the goal of personal nirvana to embrace the liberation of all sentient beings. Only when all beings have entered into nirvana will the Bodhisattva reap the rewards of his efforts. In purpose and in field of activity, the Bodhisattva is unique among the Buddha's spiritual sons. As The Teaching of Vimalakīrti states, "Not the domain of ordinary beings and not the domain of the saint, this is the domain of the Bodhisattva."

The Large Sūtra on Perfect Wisdom relates that the Bodhisattva intent on the welfare of others takes on ten great vows: to worship the Buddhas, to praise the Tathāgatas, to make offerings to all the Buddhas, to confess past transgressions, to rejoice in the virtues and happiness of others, to request the Buddhas to preach the Dharma, to request that the Enlightened Ones not enter nirvana, to study the Dharma in order to teach it, to benefit all beings, and to transfer all merit of one's actions to others. Queen Śrīmālā, as related in the Śrīmālādevīsiṁhanāda Sūtra, pronounces ten similar vows: not to violate appropriate moral conduct, to respect Buddhist masters, not to bear anger or ill will toward others, not to indulge in jealousy or covetousness, not to accumulate wealth for personal use, to benefit sentient beings without taint of self-interest, to relieve the sufferings of beings, to put an end to what perpetuates suffering and support what leads to liberation, and to be always mindful of the Dharma.

The Saddharmapuṇḍarīka Sūtra adds that Bodhisattvas will roll the wheel of the Dharma that will never reverse its course; they will demonstrate friendship towards all beings, and aid all to attain liberation and happiness.

Great thoughts support the Bodhisattvas' aspiration and empower the fulfillment of the vows to benefit all beings:

May I someday be able to alleviate
the suffering of all sentient beings!
May I someday be able to provide great fortune
for sentient beings who suffer from poverty!
May I someday be able to benefit sentient beings
by means of my own flesh and blood!
May I someday be able to help all beings in hell,
abiding there for a very long time!
May I someday be able to fulfill the yearnings
of sentient beings by providing them with great wealth,
both worldly and spiritual!
May I someday become a Buddha,
able to destroy all traces of the suffering of sentient beings!

In all lifetimes, may I refrain from everything
that is not of benefit to sentient beings.
May I experience the ultimate.
May I never speak words that do not invigorate all beings.
May I never engage in a livelihood that does not help others.
May I never harm others by means of my body, friends,
wealth, or power!

May the fruit of the wrongs of others ripen upon me,
and may the fruit of my own virtue ripen upon others.

—Zhechen Gyaltsab, *Path of Heroes* 324–25

ལམ་ལྔ་

THE FIVEFOLD PATH

ཚོགས་ལམ་

sambhāra-mārga
Path of Preparation

སྦྱོར་ལམ་

prayoga-mārga
Path of Linking

མཐོང་ལམ་

darśana-mārga
Path of Seeing

སྒོམ་ལམ་

bhāvanā-mārga
Path of Meditation

མི་སློབ་པའི་ལམ་

aśaikṣa-mārga
Path of No More Learning

THE FIVEFOLD PATH The Bodhisattva's vision of universal enlightenment reveals an extensive path that culminates after lifetimes of cultivation in the perfect realization of a Buddha. The Abhidharma-samuccaya describes the way to this supreme attainment as fivefold: the Path of Preparation, Path of Application, Path of Seeing, Path of Meditation, and Path of No More Learning. This text inspires the descriptions given below.

Path of Preparation An individual enters the Path of Preparation by formulating the intention to become enlightened and taking to heart the Bodhisattva's vow to work for the enlightenment of all sentient beings. On this path he listens to the instructions of a spiritual teacher and works to develop all that is good and wholesome. As spiritual awareness awakens, he engages in practices appropriate for the ordinary person, consisting of the four foundations of mindfulness, the four genuine restraintss, and the four bases of supernormal powers.

sGam-po-pa explains that the four foundations of mindfulness (mindfulness of body, feeling, mind, and mental events) are practiced on the initial stage of the Path of Preparation. The four genuine restraints (not to initiate nonvirtuous actions not yet generated; to give up nonvirtuous actions already generated; to bring about virtuous actions not yet generated; not to allow virtuous actions already arisen to degenerate) are practiced on the middle stage. The four bases of supernormal powers (meditative experience based on willingness, mind, effort, and analysis) are practiced on the final stage.

Path of Linking The momentum generated by developing these skills leads the individual to the Path of Linking, in which he applies these skills diligently to cultivate the roots of meritorious action and concentrates on the meaning of the Four Noble Truths. (AS 104ff) On this stage the practitioner attains the highest worldly realization. Arousing meditative heat, he develops the five spiritual faculties (confidence, sustained effort, attentive inspection, meditative experience, and appreciative discrimination), and strives to transform them into the five strengths that overcome obstacles to entering the Path of Seeing.

Path of Seeing Obtaining profound insight, the aspirant generates the genuine or ultimate mind of enlightenment (bodhicitta), bringing to maturity the relative mind of enlightenment associated with first taking the Bodhisattva vow. He now perceives clearly the meaning of the Four Noble Truths and enters upon the Path of Seeing. From this point onward his course is set; he abides in joy that no adversity can erode, and he is always reborn in circumstances that favor his practice of aiding all living beings. The Bodhisattva exercises the seven limbs of enlightenment (attentive inspection, investigation of meanings and values, sustained effort, joy, refinement and serenity, meditative experience, and equanimity). When these qualities mature, he enters the Path of Meditation.

Path of Meditation On the Path of Meditation, the Bodhisattva perfects understanding of mind, beginning with insight into the inner meanings of the qualities practiced on previous stages. These qualities, mentioned above, are collectively known as the thirty-seven wings of enlightenment: the four foundations of mindfulness, the four genuine restraints, the four bases of supernormal powers, the five spiritual faculties, the five strengths, and the seven limbs of enlightenment, culminating in the noble eightfold path of the Arhat. Upon fulfillment of the Path of Meditation, the Bodhisattva attains the vajropama-samādhi, the unshakable adamantine samādhi that courses like a swift-flowing river to the complete, perfect enlightenment of a fully-awakened Buddha. (AS 128)

Path of No More Learning The Bodhisattva coursing in vajropama-samādhi dwells on the Path of No More Learning, in full awareness that all causes of suffering have lost their power and will never rise again. sGam-po-pa explains that this stage is known as the Path of No More Learning since the Bodhisattva's training is now complete and the path to nirvana has been followed to its end. The Bodhisattva has fully matured ten great attainments, traditionally classified into four perfectly pure groups: right speech, action, and livelihood, grouped under ethics and morality; right attentiveness and meditation, grouped under meditative absorption; right view, conception, and exertion, grouped under discriminating awareness; and right liberation, grouped under freedom. To right liberation is added the sub-group known as seeing in the illuminated knowledge of liberation. (JOL 234–35)

ས་བཅུ་གཅིག་

ELEVEN STAGES OF THE PATH TO ENLIGHTENMENT

རབ་ཏུ་དགའ་བ་

pramuditā

The Joyous

དྲི་མ་མེད་པ་

vimalā

The Immaculate

འོད་བྱེད་པ་

prabhākarī

The Illuminating

འོད་འཕྲོ་ཅན་

arciṣmatī

The Radiant

ཤིན་ཏུ་སྦྱང་དཀའ་བ་

sudurjayā

The Difficult to Conquer

མངོན་དུ་གྱུར་པ་

abhimukhī

The Manifest

རིང་དུ་སོང་བ་

duraṁgama

The Far-Reaching

མི་གཡོ་བ་
acalā
The Immovable

ལེགས་པའི་བློ་གྲོས་
sādhumatī
The Excellent Intelligence

ཆོས་ཀྱི་སྤྲིན་
dharmamegha
The Cloud of Dharma

ཀུན་ཏུ་འོད་
samantaprabhā
Universal Light

ELEVEN STAGES OF THE PATH TO ENLIGHTENMENT In the Daśabhūmika Sūtra, the Buddha describes ten bhūmis or stages of realization that unfold within the five paths. Prior to attaining the first of these stages, the individual aspiring to become a Bodhisattva matures his intention while traversing the Paths of Preparation and Linking. On these two paths he performs ten preliminary actions: accumulating merit and wisdom, applying knowledge with diligence, making the necessary preparations, revering the Buddhas, developing positive qualities, meeting with spiritual friends, purifying intention, developing resolve, generating great faith, and awakening compassion. (DB I) Reflections and practices that support this development form the substance of *Path of Heroes* (Dharma Publishing, 1995)

The Joyous At some point, the practitioner experiences a profound spiritual awakening that enables him to conceive of the possibility of becoming a Buddha. This awakening, known as the rising of ultimate Bodhicitta, the mind of enlightenment, ushers the aspirant onto the Path of Seeing, where he traverses the first of ten stages that culminate in Buddhahood. Since this awakening confers the ability to benefit both self and others, this stage is known as the Joyous. (MS V)

From this point onward, the full meaning of the vow to work for the enlightenment of all beings begins to manifest in the Bodhisattva's every act of body, speech, and mind. On this stage the Bodhisattva practices the perfection of giving. Intent on benevolence and good will, he experiences the ten forms of joy: great delight, faith, gladness, cheer, exaltation, aspiration, energy, freedom from agitation, freedom from injury, and absence of wrath.

The Bodhisattva dwelling on the stage of joy usually manifests as ruler of Jambudvīpa, the realm of human beings, able to demonstrate the value of the Dharma through the magnitude of his renunciation. He brings to maturity a hundred beings, opens a hundred doors to the Dharma, and manifests a hundred times, attracting at each time a following of a hundred Bodhisattvas. (DB I)

A Bodhisattva abiding on this first stage generates ten pure intentions: honesty, gentleness, skill, restraint, tranquility, goodness, non-defilement, non-attachment, noble-mindedness, and greatness of spirit. These qualities mark entrance to the second stage of the Bodhisattva, known as the Immaculate. (DB II)

The Immaculate On this stage he removes impurities that would hinder the development of Bodhisattva discipline. (MS V) Here the Bodhisattva practices the perfection of moral purity: He manifests ten meritorious paths of action, abstaining from taking life, taking what is not given, wrong desires, lying, spreading dissension, harsh words, idle talk, envy, malicious thought, and practices and views that distract one from enlightenment. Bringing forth all positive virtues, the Bodhisattva purifies the ten meritorious paths of action with immeasurable wisdom, great compassion, and skillful means, mindful at all times of the needs of living beings and relying on the vision and knowledge of the Buddhas. In this the Bodhisattva surpasses the ten meritorious paths practiced by the Śrāvakas, those who recognize only the literal meaning of the Buddha's teaching, and by the Pratyekabuddhas, those who attain enlightenment through their own efforts. (DB II)

The Abhisamayālaṁkāra names eight preparations that characterize this stage: the perfection of moral purity, gratitude for compassionate actions received, grounding in the power of patience, the cultivation of joy, manifestation of great compassion, respect for spiritual teachers, reverence for spiritual teachers, and vigorous practice of the perfections. (AA 23)

The Bodhisattva on the stage of joy is usually born as a universal monarch, lord of the four world-continents, skillful in turning beings from evil ways and establishing them in the ten meritorious paths of action. He brings to maturity a thousand beings, opens a thousand doors to the Dharma, and manifests a thousand times, attracting at each time a following of a thousand Bodhisattvas. (DB II)

The Illuminating Having completely purified intention, the Bodhisattva enters the third stage of development. Since the Bodhisattva, relying on unwavering concentration and contemplation, now supports the light of the Mahāyāna, this stage is known as the Illuminating. (MS V)

On this level the Bodhisattva engages in ten concentrations of mental intention and examines the impermanence of all conditioned things in the light of ultimate reality. Directing the mind toward the knowledge of the Buddhas, he observes that living beings lack leaders; that they are impoverished and consumed by the three fires of passion, hatred, and ignorance; that they are enclosed in the prison of existence; that they are asleep, covered by a forest of passions; that they lack the power of correct observation; that they are separated from desire for the Dharma; that they are distracted from the teachings of the Enlightened Ones; that they are carried along the stream of becoming; and that they have lost the means of liberation.

Seeing clearly the plight of beings, the Bodhisattva generates heroic vigor and willingness to enter the flames of samsara on their behalf. Abandoning all thought of pleasure and pain, the Bodhisattva dwells without attachment and works without expectation of reward. As a result, satisfaction and discouragement no longer arise to disturb his mind. Manifesting supernormal abilities and perfecting the practice of patience, he brings forth the splendor of peacefulness, friendship, and sweetness. Purified from all imperfections, his merits can be fully utilized to heal the afflictions of beings and free them from sources of sorrow. (DB III)

The Abhisamayālaṁkāra describes the Bodhisattva on this stage as manifesting five factors, each marked by the absence of self-centered concerns: an insatiable desire to learn; giving the Dharma without thought of reward; purifying the Buddhafield and turning over merit generated to others; tirelessly working for the welfare of beings; and a sense of shame and a dread of blame (arising from concern for the welfare of others).

A Bodhisattva on this stage usually becomes king of the gods of the Trāyastriṁsa Heaven, able to turn beings away from sensual desires and remove them from the grip of passions. He brings to maturity a hundred thousand beings, opens a hundred thousand doors to the Dharma, and manifests a hundred thousand times, attracting at each time a following of a hundred thousand Bodhisattvas. (DB III)

The Radiant From the third stage, the Bodhisattva engages the ten entrances to the light of the Dharma: living beings, the world, dharma, emptiness, consciousness, desire, form, formlessness, altruistic intention and faith, and fullhearted intention and faith. Carefully considering these ten, the Bodhisattva enters the fourth stage, known as the Radiant, where the virtues that support awakening burn away all obstacles. (MS V)

Here the Bodhisattva has attained ten maturations: irreversible intention; fully developed faith in the Buddha, Dharma, and Sangha; inquiry into the nature of conditioning; inquiry into the non-origination of self-nature; inquiry into the arising and ceasing of the world; inquiry into the origination of being; inquiry into becoming and nirvana; inquiry into living being; inquiry into past and future; and inquiry into non-existence and decay. On this stage the Bodhisattva practices the perfection of vigor. Having destroyed the roots of wrongdoing, the Bodhisattva effectively activates the thirty-seven wings of enlightenment (enumerated on page 15). (DB IV)

Bodhisattvas on this fourth stage manifest love for all living beings: Supported by adherence to their vows, they demonstrate supreme good will; they yearn to develop omniscient knowledge, to ornament the realm of enlightened ones, and to obtain the powers, confidences, and unique qualities of a fully enlightened Buddha. Yearning for the realization of a Buddha, they persevere in the Dharma, enlarging their knowledge of liberation and developing the power of skill in means. Having abandoned all wasteful pursuits and engaging always in meritorious actions, the Bodhisattva becomes a matchless hero, worthy of reverence from both humans and gods. (DB IV)

The Abhisamayālaṁkāra summarizes the ten factors to be adhered to by a Bodhisattva on this stage: living in a forest, having few desires, contentment, cultivation of ascetic practices, non-abandonment of moral training, aversion to sensuality, disgust for samsara, renunciation of personal possessions, uncowed (attitude of mind), and detachment from all things. (AA 24) The Bodhisattva who succeeds on this stage usually becomes Suyāma, king of gods, empowered to remove from beings false belief in a self and establish them in correct views. He brings to maturity a billion beings, opens a billion doors to the Dharma, and manifests a billion times, attracting at each time a following of a billion Bodhisattvas. (DB IV)

Difficult to Conquer The Bodhisattva enters the fifth stage, Difficult to Conquer, with ten qualities of purified intention: intention relating to the Dharma of past, future, and present Buddhas; intention relating to morality, mind, and removing doubt and incorrect views; intention relating to knowledge of favorable and unfavorable paths, good conduct, and ever-higher levels of practicing the factors that support enlightenment; and intention relating to maturing all living beings. (DB V)

sGam-po-pa explains that this level presents two major difficulties: The Bodhisattva makes strong effort to bring beings to spiritual maturity while maintaining emotional stability when these same beings become confused and fall into error. The Mahāyāna-saṁgraha states that here conventional and ultimate truth are seen in sharp contrast and are difficult to unify. For this reason this level is named Difficult to Conquer. (MS V)

On this stage Bodhisattvas penetrate the full meaning of the Four Noble Truths: the truth of suffering, its origin, its cessation, and the path to liberation from suffering. They come to understand the full meaning of conventional and ultimate truth and comprehend through faith the numerous forms of truth perfected in the enlightenment of the Buddhas. Attaining this knowledge, Bodhisattvas become supremely mindful. Forgetting nothing, they test and refine all the merits developed earlier in their practice, purify them, and cause them to shine ever more brilliantly.

Bodhisattvas on the fifth stage put on the armor of the five faculties: Wielding the bow of mindfulness and the arrows of the senses, mounted on the chariots of supernormal powers drawn by the horses of strenuous application, they do not turn back, nor can they be defeated. They practice the perfection of meditation; they exercise excellent wisdom, honor a million Buddhas, and listen tirelessly to their teachings. (DB V) The Abhisamayālaṁkāra attributes these accomplishments to the Bodhisattvas' avoidance of ten things: social intimacy, jealousy, places where people congregate, promoting self and deprecating others, the ten paths of unwholesome action, conceit, arrogance, wrong views, doubt, and giving in to defilements.

Bodhisattvas who stand on this stage usually become chief of the gods of the Tuṣita Heaven, able to turn beings away from false views and point out the way to truth. They bring to maturity a trillion beings, open a trillion doors to the Dharma, and manifest a trillion times, attracting at each time a following of a trillion Bodhisattvas. (DB V)

The Manifest The Bodhisattva engages the sixth stage, the Manifest, by comprehending the ten equalities of all things: equality because all things are without marks, without characteristics, non-originated, unborn, serene, pure from the beginning, and beyond verbal designation; because all things have nothing to do with acceptance or rejection; because all things are without acceptance and constructs; because all things are illusory and free from dualistic existence or non-existence.

Bodhisattvas on this stage consider the nature of ignorance: Perceiving that everything arises in dependence on conditions, they understand the full meaning of śūnyatā and know beyond all doubt that all things have no independent existence. Motivated by compassion for living beings, Bodhisattvas on the sixth stage accomplish the perfection of wisdom and apply this wisdom to perfecting still further all factors supporting enlightenment. (DB VI) The Mahāyāna-saṁgraha explains that this stage is known as the Manifest because herein the Bodhisattva relying on knowledge of pratītyasamutpāda (interdependent cooperation) is able to manifest the perfection of wisdom. (MS V)

The Daśabhūmika states that Bodhisattvas on this stage usually become kings among the Sunirmita gods. They are able to discourage beings from arrogance and pride; unperturbed by the questions of Śrāvakas, they become supremely skilled in presenting to beings the teaching of interdependent cooperation. They bring to maturity a hundred trillion beings, open a hundred trillion doors to the Dharma, and manifest a hundred trillion times, attracting at each time a following of a hundred trillion Bodhisattvas. (DB VI)

Far-Reaching Having developed profound knowledge and comprehended ultimate truth, the Bodhisattva enters upon the seventh stage. Here the Great Being perfects the practice of skill in means: He comprehends the realms of living beings and understands the great acts by which the Buddhas instruct them. Having accumulated great knowledge, Bodhisattvas on this stage are blessed with wisdom and skill in means, and characterized by most excellent conduct. Merit increases with their every act: Every moment they draw closer to full and perfect enlightenment.

Bodhisattvas on the seventh stage emphasize the perfection of skillful means and fulfill all ten perfections in a limited way. By offering merit to all, they fulfill the perfection of giving. By subduing passions, they fulfill the perfection of morality. By non-harming of beings, they fulfill the perfection of patience. By working to attain ever higher states of perfection, they fulfill the perfection of vigor. By becoming unshakable in the path, they fulfill the perfection of meditation. By comprehending the non-origination of undefiled existence, they fulfill the perfection of wisdom. Through transformation, they fulfill the perfection of skill in means. In wishing for greater blessings, they fulfill the perfection of vow. Through indestructibility, they fulfill the perfection of power, and by thorough investigation, they fulfill the perfection of omniscience. (DB VII)

Here Bodhisattvas become king of the Vaśvavartin gods, tireless in teaching the Dharma. They bring to maturity a quadrillion beings, open a quadrillion doors to the Dharma, and manifest a quadrillion times, attracting at each time a following of a quadrillion Bodhisattvas.

Activating knowledge, Bodhisattvas on the seventh stage accomplish all merits and vows. The splendor of their wisdom dries up the thirst of living beings like the light of the sun, and they become powerful and skilled in communicating their knowledge. Since the Bodhisattva arrives at this point of culmination, this stage is known as Far-Reaching. (MS VII) From this point onward Bodhisattvas proceed without effort into the eighth, ninth, and tenth stages, spontaneously obtaining the results of their meritorious action. (DB VII)

The Immovable Completely free from false constructs, proceeding with full understanding of the emptiness and nonarising of all things, the Bodhisattva enters the eighth stage, known as Immovable, for here the Bodhisattva cannot be moved by any image or mental activity. (MS V) He experiences joyful acceptance of the unoriginatedness of the whole of reality and attains two masteries: absence of habit-making forms of thought and pure Buddhafields. With this he develops the ten faculties of a Bodhisattva: power over life, mind, necessities, karma, birth, and manifestations, and power in vow, supernormal abilities, knowledge, and Dharma. (DB VIII, JOL 248–49)

Bodhisattvas on this stage course in effortlessness; performing no action of body, speech, or mind, they transcend the realm of concepts and abide in perfect wisdom. Here they emphasize the perfection of vow and become unshakable in calm and tranquility. Having overcome subtle passions, they attain the highest degree of receptivity and stand at the door to complete awakening. (DB VIII)

Perfectly balanced between samsara and nirvana, they do not manifest the behavior of the perfect Buddhas, nor do they manifest the behavior of Bodhisattvas, Pratyekabuddhas, or Śrāvakas. The splendor of their attainments extinguishes for living beings the darkness of the passions and opens the way of knowledge. Their course is now irreversible, and they will never fall back from their purpose. (DB VIII)

On this stage, where vow, compassion, and wisdom have been completely purified and fully developed, the Buddhas empower Bodhisattvas to engage the final stages of their journey. Calling to mind the condition of ordinary people who, enmeshed in passions and concepts, cannot abide in calm or tranquility, the Buddhas remind the Bodhisattvas of their vow to save all beings and exhort them to bring it to completion by bringing forth the special qualities of a Buddha. By means of an incomparable act of knowledge, the Buddhas reveal the inconceivable qualities of the Tathāgatas and open the doors to full omniscience. Their compassion saves Bodhisattvas on the Immovable stage from losing sight of their purpose to liberate all beings. Lacking this intervention, Bodhisattvas who have reached this stage would easily slip into nirvana. (DB VIII)

The Bodhisattva now undergoes a profound transformation. As a result of immovability, all acts of body, speech, and mind have taken on immeasurable dimensions, magnifying all qualities and perfections and enabling him to receive the full teachings of the Buddhas. Having with great effort rowed out of the harbor of samsara and reached the ocean of great conduct, the Bodhisattva crosses over into omniscience in an instant, carried by the blessings of the Buddhas as if a ship under full sail speeded by the power of wind and sea. Upon this attainment, the Bodhisattva's body emits radiant light; all living beings rejoice, and innumerable realms tremble. (DB VIII)

The Bodhisattva dwelling on this stage usually becomes a Brahmā, lord of thousands of worlds, unsurpassed in serving the needs of Arhats and Pratyekabuddhas. His every action is taken with mind fully concentrated upon the Three Jewels, Bodhisattva, the conduct of Bodhisattvas, the perfections, the stages, the powers, the unique Buddha-qualities, and the knowledge of omniscience. In an instant he can enter into as many samādhis as there are atoms in a million billion world-systems; he can bring to maturity this number of beings, enter into this number of realms, manifest this number of times, and attract a following of this number of Bodhisattvas. (DB VIII)

Excellent Intelligence Entering the ninth stage, Excellent Intelligence, which is profound, subtle, and difficult to comprehend, the Bodhisattva attains knowledge known only to the supremely Enlightened Buddhas. Well-prepared for his task, he has acquired infinitely devoted resolve and knowledge of the language of the gods. Realizations come in a continuous stream; among other qualities he has the power to direct his rebirth in a good family, to be in a spiritually supportive environment, to have good attendants, to sit under the Bodhi tree, and to perfect all virtues. (AA I:68–69) Equipped with knowledge of the dhāraṇīs, the samādhis, and the supernormal abilities, knowing the hearts, minds, destinies, and propensities of beings, the Bodhisattva can now enter all realms to work for the salvation of others. (DB IX)

The Bodhisattva has now accomplished ten great feats: He has investigated the enumerations, developed all positive qualities, fulfilled the limitless preparations, acquired great merit and knowledge, realized great compassion, developed skill in the manifold world-systems, engaged the activity of the realms of living beings, concentrated mind for the purpose of entering the sphere of the Buddhas, worked to acquire the special powers and characteristics of a Buddha, and obtained the coronation stage of omniscience. (DB IX)

The Bodhisattva on the ninth level emphasizes the perfection of power. He usually becomes a Brahmā, lord of two chiliocosms, able to prevail over all restraints to answer all questions in the minds of living beings. In an instant he can produce as many samādhis as there are atoms in countless Buddhafields. He can bring to maturity this number of beings and manifest this number of times, attracting at each time a following of this number of Bodhisattvas. (DB IX)

Cloud of Dharma Upon entering the tenth stage, the Bodhisattva concentrates on the perfection of omniscience and engages in meditations that arise spontaneously. These meditations culminate in the samādhi known as Coronation of Omniscient Knowledge. Here the Bodhisattva takes his place on the great lotus named King of Jewels, while all Bodhisattvas on the ninth stage, seated on jewel-lotuses, gather around him from the ten directions. The merit of their thousands of meditations removes all forms of negativity and purifies all world-systems. (DB X) This stage is known as Cloud of Dharma, for herein awareness of all doctrines silently permeates meditative concentration. As a cloud covers the sky, so the Bodhisattva now removes obstacles from view and brings into being the perfect Dharmakāya. (MS V)

A Bodhisattva on this level lets the Dharma fall like rain, cooling the passions that perpetuate misery for living beings. Thousands of rays of light emanate from specific parts of the Bodhisattva's body, relieving the suffering of beings in the six realms of existence, illuminating the Dharma for the Śrāvakas, empowering tranquil meditation for the Pratyekabuddha, and awakening wisdom and skillful means in Bodhisattvas on the first through ninth stages. Abiding on the tenth stage, the Bodhisattva upholds the power of the vow: He produces the cloud of compassion, the roar of profound Dharma, the lightning of supernormal faculties, the stirring up of the great rays of light, and the cloud-net of incomparable merit and knowledge, cooling the flames of the passions by raining down on all beings the nectar of great merit. (DB X)

A Bodhisattva coursing within the Cloud of Dharma becomes Maheśvara, king of the Śuddhavāsin gods, capable of manifesting innumerable forms and instantly attaining innumerable and unlimited samādhis. From the pores of his skin he can produce a continuous stream of Buddhas and Bodhisattvas, and can appear in any form necessary to teach the Dharma to living beings. (DB X, JOL 251)

Universal Light To the ten stages of the Bodhisattva path is added the stage of culmination known as Universal Light, the unique accomplishment of a Buddha. Here the vajropamāsamādhi has completely transformed the most subtle obscurations, releasing the Great Love, Great Knowledge, and Great Power of the Supremely Enlightened Ones.

The Infinitely Detailed Path of Awakening Throughout the Daśabhūmika Sūtra, the Buddha relates that all he has said concerning the stages of the path is only a brief indication of the way to perfect enlightenment, and expressing every detail of the path would require innumerable kalpas. Although the path is long and requires strenuous application, the Bodhicaryāvatāra reminds us that "Buddhahood is obtained by a fraction of the effort required to survive millions of years of suffering in samsara." (BCA VII:83)

Eighty Inexhaustible Buddha-Qualities

The Mahāyāna-sūtrālaṁkāra summarizes eighty inexhaustible qualities that begin to emerge on the Path of Seeing, when, heated by aspiration and effort, wisdom and compassion unite, producing a Bodhisattva. Within these eighty factors, Bodhicitta and the perfections form the foundation of the path, and the remaining factors are ways of developing and refining them. While Bodhisattvas cultivate these qualities as they progress through the stages of enlightenment, all eighty qualities of are brought to full maturity in the perfect enlightenment of a Buddha.

The Mind of Enlightenment Bodhicitta, translated as the mind or thought of enlightenment, is evoked in a relative sense by the aspiration to gain enlightenment for the sake of all beings. As it matures, this initial impulse becomes a mind "turned toward enlightenment," in which all thought, speech, and action arise from wisdom and compassion, and are focused solely on what fosters the enlightenment of others. The ultimate mind of enlightenment arises after many years or even

མི་ཟད་པ་བརྒྱད་ཅུ།

EIGHTY INEXHAUSTIBLE QUALITIES OF A BUDDHA

བྱང་ཆུབ་སེམས།

bodhicitta
mind of enlightenment

ཕར་རོལ་ཏུ་ཕྱིན་པ་བཅུ།

daśa-pāramitā
ten perfections

ཚད་མེད་བཞི།

caturapramāṇa
four immeasurables

མངོན་པར་ཤེས་པ་དྲུག

ṣaḍ-abhijñā
six superknowledges

བསྡུ་བའི་དངོས་པོ་བཞི།

catvāri-saṁgraha-vastūni
four means of conversion

སོ་སོ་ཡང་དག་པར་རིག་པ་བཞི།

catuḥ-pratisaṁvid
four exact knowledges

རྟོན་པ་བཞི།

catvāri-pratisaraṇāni
four reliances

The Four Immeasurables Loving-kindness (maitrī), compassion (kāruṇā), joy (muditā), and equanimity (upekṣā) are known as the four immeasuables. Contemplation on these qualities is a path of practice that has immense and immediate benefits, since it calms the emotions and leads to deeper states of awareness and understanding. Each of the four immeasurables pacifies a particular negative emotion. Loving-kindness, which arouses wishes for the happiness and well-being of all who live, pacifies anger. Compassion, the wish that there be freedom from suffering, counteracts malice. Joy in another's happiness and good fortune counteracts envy. Equanimity, which values all living beings equally, counteracts attachment. The practice of these four states becomes immeasurable when it is linked to the path of liberation. As manifested in the enlightenment of a Buddha, the four immeasurables become infinitely beneficial to all beings.

The Six Superknowledges The six superknowledges comprise clairvoyance, or the divine eye; clairaudience, or the divine ear; knowledge of the minds of others; supernormal abilities; knowledge of past lives; and knowledge of the cessation of all affliction and obscuration. The divine eye enables the Bodhisattva to see how beings are born and pass away according to their good and bad actions. The divine ear allows the Bodhisattva to hear sounds near and far. With the knowledge of the minds of others, the Bodhisattva can penetrate the thoughts of all beings; with supernormal abilities, his capacity to help others is vastly increased.

While practitioners of many spiritual paths can develop the first five superknowledges, only Bodhisattvas can aspire to the sixth: knowledge of the cessation of all afflictions and obscurations. The Prajñāpāramitā explains that after perfecting the superknowledges, the Bodhisattva travels from Buddhafield to Buddhafield, honoring the Buddhas, hearing them teach the Dharma, purifying the Buddhafields, and contributing to the maturation of living beings. (LSPW 135)

Four Means of Conversion Giving, kind words, actions that benefit others, and consistency between words and deeds are known as the four means of conversion. Even if one can not yet give on a spiritual level, giving even material gifts exercises detachment and stimulates a process of growth. Performed with joy and abundance, giving inspires emulation, enabling Bodhisattvas to offer to beings the incomparable gift of the Dharma. Kind words attract the mind and demonstrate the teachings of the perfections, and actions that benefit others accomplish the purpose of the perfections. Consistency between words and deeds inspires confidence and faith. To establish beings in the practice of the perfections, the Bodhisattva practices these four means of conversion. (LSPW 578ff)

Four Exact Knowledges The four exact knowledges are genuine awareness of the Dharma and genuine awareness of meaning, explanations, and eloquence. Genuine awareness of the Dharma is unimpeded knowledge of all of its forms, based on realization of the teachings of the three vehicles. Genuine awareness of meaning is unimpeded knowledge of the characteristics and the intentions of different types of teachings. Genuine awareness of explanations is unimpeded knowledge of how to adapt language to accord with regional expressions and connotations. Genuine awareness of brilliance is unimpeded knowledge of diverse doctrines: Unobstructed and untiring, it knows how to present the vastness and depth of the teachings.

The Four Reliances The Bodhisattva relies on the actual meaning of Dharma, rather than on the literal meaning of words that express it. He relies on primordial wisdom, not on ordinary consciousness. He relies on definitive teachings, not on those of provisional meaning, and he relies on the teachings, not on the personality of the teacher. Joined with the mind of enlightenment, these four reliances have royal power, allowing him to understand the deep and extensive Mahāyāna.

The Two Accumulations The Bodhisattva advances along the path by virtue of the two accumulations: the accumulation of merit and the accumulation of wisdom. The Bodhisattva accomplishes this by continuous action and repeated practice, which leads to mental concentration. The two accumulations are closely connected to the perfections: The perfections of giving and morality foster the accumulation of merit, and the perfection of wisdom supports the accumulation of wisdom. The perfections of patience, vigor, and meditation nurture the accumulation of both merit and wisdom. The accumulation of merit takes place in the sphere of ordinary reality, while the accumulation of wisdom takes place in the sphere of ultimate reality.

Thirty-seven Wings of Enlightenment The thirty-seven wings of enlightenment comprise the four foundations of mindfulness, the four genuine restraints, the four bases of supernormal powers, the five spiritual faculties, the five strengths, and the seven limbs of enlightenment, culminating in the noble eightfold path of the Arhat. See also pages 14–15.

Calm and Insight In the Abhidharma-samuccaya, Asaṅga defines śamatha (calm) as close contraction or binding of the mind, tranquility, unification, and composure. The qualities associated with vipaśyana (insight) are inquiry, search, complete thought, and investigation of mind and mental activities.

"By the power of calm, thought becomes unshakeable
in relation to its own object, like a lamp in still air.
By the power of insight, the light of right knowledge arises
as a result of understanding the reality of dharmas as they are.
All obstructions are thereby removed, just as darkness is
removed by the appearance of light."

—Kamalaśīla, Third Bhāvanākrama (BK 26)

Empowered Syllables and Empowered Inspiration Empowered syllables inspire deep remembrance of the teachings. Empowered inspirations arise from memory that does not fail, from intelligence that discriminates the Dharma, and from the realization of the meaning of the Dharma. Empowered realizations are of different kinds, associated with fearlessness, clarity, profundity, extensiveness of knowledge, alacrity of understanding, and uninterruptedness. (KJ 90a.1)

The Prajñāpāramitā Sūtras extol the virtues of the empowered syllables, the dhāraṇī-doors that open to complete, perfect enlightenment. Bodhisattvas who listen to this teaching, who bear it in mind, study, and practice it, will be mindful and clever, steadfast, wise, modest, and inspired. They will easily acquire the doors of the dhāraṇīs. They will not be assailed by doubts and will have no uncertainties. They will not be won over by sweet words or upset by harsh words. They will be neither dejected nor elated.

They will act appropriately in accord with circumstances; they will manifest skill in sounds, in the skandhas, elements, and sense-fields; in truths and in interdependent cooperation; in the root cause, in conditions, and in the true nature of the elements of reality. They will be skilled in cognizing the higher and lower faculties of others, the thoughts of others, the supernormal abilities, the divine ear, the recollection of former births, the nature of death and rebirth, and the ceasing of the outflows. They will become skilled in explaining what is possible and impossible, in going out, and in coming back. They will acquire the sense of shame and dread of blame necessary for great attainments on behalf of others. (LSPW 162)

The Four Laws of the Dharma The four laws of the Dharma express the condensed essence of the Buddha's teaching: All compounded things are impermanent; all that is corrupt is suffering; all conditioned things are without self; and nirvana is peace.

Going Alone The Bodhisattva realizes that the fulfillment of his vow depends on his efforts alone. "I must care for all beings by myself alone, lead them, protect them, and teach them. Even should there be no one else to help, I myself will accomplish this." Depending on no one else, relying on no supporters, the Bodhisattva is prepared to train all beings and bring each to maturity and enlightenment. For this reason the Bodhisattva is known as a shelter, a refuge, a place of rest, an island, a bringer of light, and a leader of the world.

Skillful Means The Bodhisattva's skill in means manifests in ten ways: skill in overcoming hostile forces; skill in dwelling in emptiness; skill in dwelling without support; skill in carrying out the Bodhisattva vows; extraordinary skill in perseverance; skill unattached to personal enlightenment; skill that is without basis in self or dharmas; skill that is signless; skill free of wishes for the future; skill in irreversibility; and skill which is unlimited in its objective range. (LSPW 424–30)

From *Samantabhadra's Prayer for Enlightened Practice:*

Immersed in the practices of enlightenment,
may I remember all past lives.
In all lifetimes, when I take rebirth,
may I always renounce the world.

May I perform the actions of all the Buddhas
and wholly perfect enlightened practice.
May I lead a faultless life, never regressing,
my moral practice pure and undefiled.

I will teach the Dharma in all tongues:
I will teach the Dharma in the language of the gods,
in the languages of the nāgas and the yakṣas,
in the languages of men and kumbhandas,
and in as many languages as there are types of beings.

May I be steadfast, striving to apply the six perfections,
never forgetting my resolve for enlightenment,
and may all my misdeeds, the cause of obscuration,
be completely washed away.

Free from karma and emotionality,
free from all evil influence,

I will act for beings in the world:
like the lotus in water, unsullied;
like the sun and moon in the sky, unhindered.

In all directions and throughout the Buddhafields,
I will alleviate the sufferings of the lower realms.
Establishing all beings in bliss, I will benefit all beings.

While perfecting the Bodhisattva's enlightened actions,
I will serve sentient beings in harmony with their needs,
demonstrating enlightened practice in all ways
throughout all future aeons. . . .

I will counter the strength of karma;
subdue the strength of the emotions;
nullify the strength of evil influences;
and perfect the strength of enlightened practice.

I will purify oceans of Buddhafields;
I will liberate oceans of sentient beings,
experience oceans of dharmas,
and realize oceans of wisdom.

Practicing resolutely for oceans of aeons,
I will purify oceans of practices;
I will fulfill oceans of aspirations
and honor oceans of Buddhas. . . .

May my practice be boundless,
may my attributes be without limit.
Abiding in immeasurable practice,
may I be all things to all people.

Should there be an end to space;
should there be an end to sentient beings;
should there be an end to karma and kleśas;
only then will I end my aspiration.

—Samantabhadra-praṇidhāna-rāja[1]

1. *World Peace Ceremony, Bodh Gayā,* pp. 162–175. (Berkeley: Dharma Publishing, 1994).

Manifesting Enlightened Being

Soon to become a Buddha, the Bodhisattva dwelling on the tenth stage of the path manifests throughout the realms of existence the inconceivable qualities of enlightened being. Crown prince among all the Buddha's spiritual sons, he teaches the gods in the Tuṣita Heaven, who delight in his words and broadcast them widely. Innumerable Bodhisattvas, well-advanced on their way to attaining the state of a Buddha, congregate from the ten directions for instruction and inspiration.

Looking down from the Tuṣita Heaven, the Bodhisattva perceives the miseries of human beings. Compassion for their sufferings awakens in him the resolve to be born a final time. In human form, the Bodhisattva will now perform the twelve great acts of a Buddha to demonstrate the path that puts an end to suffering. In the course of his teaching, he will lift the aspirations of many to engage the path of the perfect Buddhas and will give them, as in past aeons the Buddha Dīpaṁkāra gave him, the prediction to full enlightenment. Beneath the Bodhi tree he will shatter the force of illusion and enable the qualities of enlightenment to shine forth unhindered in the world.

སྐུ་གསུམ་

THREE BODIES OF THE BUDDHA

ཆོས་ཀྱི་སྐུ་

Dharmakāya
body of Dharma

ལོངས་སྤྱོད་རྫོགས་པའི་སྐུ་

Sambhogakāya
body of perfect enjoyment

སྤྲུལ་པའི་སྐུ་

Nirmāṇakāya
apparitional body

THREE BODIES OF THE BUDDHA The Uttaratantra lists six qualities of a Buddha: The Buddha is changeless, centerless, and endless, without beginning or end, dwelling in no place, and no longer subject to cycles of birth and death. All good qualities appear spontaneously, without effort; there is no need to rely on external conditions. The Buddha is omniscient, and his knowledge manifests in two forms: knowing things as they really are and comprehending the multitude and variety of appearances. The Tathāgata, the fully awakened Buddha, exhibits the most perfect form of compassion, and he has the power to help others free themselves from suffering and the causes of suffering. (UT 4, CN 16–17)

Tathāgata, literally "thus-gone" or "thus-come," refers to the perfectly enlightened Buddha. Whereas tathatā (suchness) is often used to indicate absolute reality, the Tathāgata is viewed within the Mahāyāna traditions as the direct manifestation of absolute reality. As such, the form of the Tathāgata is not limited to a body perceived by human senses.

The works of Maitreya and Asaṅga explicate the nature of a Tathāgata in terms of three "bodies," or kāya: Dharmakāya, Sambhogakāya, and Nirmāṇakāya. The Buddha briefly describes these terms in the Trikāya Sūtra:

The Blessed One, the Tathāgata, has three bodies:
the body of Dharma (Dharmakāya),
the body of perfect enjoyment (Sambhogakāya),
and the apparitional body (Nirmāṇakāya).
O son of good family, of the three bodies of the Tathāgata,
Dharmakāya is a perfectly pure nature;
Sambhogakāya is a perfectly pure samādhi;
and the Nirmāṇakāya of all Buddhas is a perfectly pure life.
The Dharmakāya of the Tathāgata is the capacity
of being without svabhāva, like space;
Sambhogakāya is the capacity of being visible like a cloud;
Nirmāṇakāya, being the object of all Buddhas, is the capacity
of permeating all things as does a rain.

DHARMAKĀYA Dharmakāya refers to undifferentiated openness from which all forms arise, represented by the Ādibuddha, the primordial principle of enlightenment. Dharmakāya is the ultimate nature of a Buddha —unlimited, inconceivable, and inexpressible. According to the Uttaratantra of Maitreya, Dharmakāya is unfathomable because of its vastness, immeasurable because of its qualities, inconceivable because it transcends intellect, incomparable because it is unique, and immaculate because all obscurations are abandoned. (UT 201–205, CN 87)

Undifferentiated, radiant, pure, and profound, free from all limitations, Dharmakāya is the result of great knowledge, inherently ungraspable by the senses of body and mind. Lists of the characteristics of Dharmakāya can be found in such authoritative works as the Abhisamayālaṁkāra, Mahāyāna-saṁgraha, and Abhidharmasamuccaya. The list below follows the order given in Lama Mi-pham's mKhas-'jug, a comprehensive manual of Abhidharma.

ཟག་པ་མེད་པའི་ཆོས་སྐེ་ཚན་ཉེར་གཅིག
TWENTY-ONE CHARACTERISTICS OF DHARMAKĀYA

བྱང་ཆུབ་ཀྱི་ཡན་ལག་གསུམ་བཅུ་རྩ་བདུན
saptatriṁśa-bodhipakṣa
thirty-seven wings of enlightenment

ཚད་མེད་བཞི
caturapramāṇa
four immeasurables

རྣམ་ཐར་བརྒྱད
aṣṭa-vimokṣa
eight deliverances

སྙོམས་འཇུག་དགུ
navānupūrva-samāpatti
nine concentrations

ཟིལ་གྱིས་གནོན་པའི་སྐྱེ་མཆེད་བརྒྱད
aṣṭāvabhibhvāyatana
eight dominant fields

ཟད་པར་གྱི་སྐྱེ་མཆེད་བཅུ
daśakṛtsnāyatana
ten all-encompassing fields

ཉོན་མོངས་མེད་པ
araṇā
freedom from emotionality

སྨོན་ནས་མཁྱེན་པ་

praṇidhijñāna

knowledge resulting from resolve

མངོན་ཤེས་དྲུག་

ṣaḍabhijñā

six superknowledges

སོ་སོ་ཡང་དག་པར་རིག་པ་བཞི་

catuḥ-pratisaṁvid

four exact knowledges

རྣམ་པ་ཐམས་ཅད་དག་པ་བཞི་

catuḥ-sarvākāraviśuddhi

four complete purities

དབང་བཅུ་

daśendriyā

ten faculties

སྟོབས་བཅུ་

daśabala

ten strengths

མི་འཇིགས་པ་བཞི་

catur-vaiśāradya

four fearlessnesses

སངས་རྒྱས་ཀྱི་ཆོས་མ་འདྲེས་པ་བཅོ་བརྒྱད་

aṣṭadaśa-āvenika-buddhadharma

eighteen special Buddhadharmas

བསྲུང་བ་མེད་པ་གསུམ་

tri-arakṣya
three unprotected things

དྲན་པ་ཉེ་བར་གཞག་པ་གསུམ་

tri-smṛtyupasthāna
three foundations of mindfulnesses

བསྙེལ་བ་མི་མངའ་བ་

asaṁmoṣatā
never-bewildered nature

བག་ཆགས་ཡང་དག་པར་བཅོམ་པ་

vāsanāsamudghāta
subtle residues completely removed

ཐུགས་རྗེ་ཆེན་པོ་

mahākāruṇā
great compassion

རྣམ་པ་ཐམས་ཅད་མཁྱེན་པ་

sarvākārajñāna
omniscience

TWENTY-ONE CHARACTERISTICS OF DHARMAKĀYA The following summaries of the twenty-one characteristics are based on the Abhidharmasamuccaya and the Mahāyāna-saṁgraha.

Thirty-seven Wings of Enlightenment Transformed by the primordial wisdom of a Buddha, mind as conceived of by ordinary beings no longer operates. Buddha-activity operates solely to empower the awakening of living beings. (See description of the elements of the thirty-seven wings on pp. 14–15.)

Four Immeasurables The Buddha manifests the four immeasurables practiced by the Bodhisattva—loving-kindness, compassion, joy, and equanimity—as perfections that surpass all ordinary conception.

Eight Deliverances The primordial wisdom that arises as the result of enlightenment delivers beings from all forms of suffering: the eight miseries endured by beings of the realm of desire, and the more subtle miseries that taint even the celestial realms of the gods.

Nine Concentrations Nine great samādhis that arise in succession liberate the awakened ones from all obscurations associated with the form and formless realms.

Eight Dominant Fields Complete domination over the six governing fields of perception, the first formless attainment, and the second formless attainment. Also called the Eight Bases of Overcoming. (LSPW 654)

Ten All-encompassing Fields Complete penetration of all appearance in the ten fields: earth, water, fire, wind, blue, yellow, red, white, space, and consciousness.

Freedom from Emotionality The ability to evoke freedom from emotionality in others. The Arhat accomplishes this in a temporary way by not arousing emotion in others. A Buddha can actually enable others to sever the roots of emotionality.

Knowledge Resulting from Resolve Knowledge resulting from resolve arises from the Bodhisattva's vow to know all that is knowable. Objects hidden from all other realized beings are clear to the fully awakened Buddha, who can answer any kind of question asked by others.

Six Superknowledges To the five superior knowledges developed earlier on the Bodhisattva path (divine eye, divine ear, knowledge of the minds of others, supernormal abilities, and knowledge of former lives), the Buddha uniquely develops a sixth: knowledge that the afflictions and obscurations—even the most subtle—are completely extinguished.

Four Exact Knowledges The four exact knowledges of the Buddha are knowledge of all forms of the Dharma, knowledge of all characteristics and intention, knowledge of language and interpretations used in all regions, and knowledge of eloquence.

Four Complete Purities The four complete purities of a Buddha are purity of body, purity of object, purity of mind, and purity of primordial wisdom. These purities confer the ability to attain whatever body is needed, to create whatever objects are required, to enter into any samādhi as desired, and to know all that is knowable.

Ten Faculties A Buddha manifests as perfections the ten faculties developed by Bodhisattvas: power over lifespan; power over mind, the result of perfect samādhi; power regarding all necessities, the result of giving; power regarding karma and power regarding birth, the result of perfect discipline; power of faith, the result of patience; power of vow, the result of effort; power regarding supernormal abilities, the result of samādhi; and power regarding wisdom and power regarding Dharma, both the result of wisdom.

Ten Strengths The ten strengths of a Buddha manifest as ten broad categories of knowledge: knowledge of what is possible and what is impossible; knowledge of the consequences of actions; knowledge of the different propensities of beings; knowledge of the constituents of being; knowledge of faith and all other higher and lower faculties of beings; knowledge of the causes and effects of all actions; knowledge of meditation, liberation, concentration, absorption, emotion, purification, and acquisition; knowledge of past lives; knowledge of the transference of consciousness at death and birth; and knowledge of the cessation of corruption. (AK VII:28–32, MN I:69–71) While other beings may possess some of these knowledges in a limited manner, only a Buddha possesses them all, as infinite powers free of all hindrances whatsoever.

Four Fearlessnesses The four fearlessnesses arise from four knowledges: knowledge that all factors of existence are understood; knowledge that the obstacles are correctly known and the way to stop them can be taught to others; knowledge that the path of renunciation, through which all the virtuous qualities are obtained, has in fact been accomplished; and knowledge that all corruption has come to an end. As a result of possessing the four fearlessnesses, Buddhas have the power to help others know all that is knowable, to enable others to abandon what must be abandoned, to teach what ought to be taught, and to help others attain the most pure and supreme enlightenment. (UT 248–49, CN 106–7)

Eighteen Special Buddhadharmas Eighteen special qualities are demonstrated only by a Tathāgata, a fully awakened Buddha: A Buddha never makes a mistake, is never boisterous, and never forgetful. The concentration of an Enlightened One never falters. He does not make distinctions, and his impartiality in all matters arises from knowledge (not from lack of caring). At all times the Buddha demonstrates undiminishing aspiration, effort, mindfulness, concentration, and wisdom, and his quality of liberation does not degenerate. His every action—physical, verbal, or mental—is preceded and followed by wisdom, and his knowledge and vision concerning the past, present, and future is unobstructed.

Three Unprotected Things The body, speech, and mind of a Buddha are known as the three unprotected things. Since the Enlightened Ones are completely faultless, there is nothing about them that needs to be concealed or protected in any way.

Three Foundations of Mindfulness The three foundations of mindfulness of a Buddha relate to profound equanimity in the three possible circumstances attendant on teaching the assembly of disciples: All the disciples may hear, accept, and practice the teachings; none of the disciples may hear, accept, and practice the teachings; and some of the disciples may hear, accept, and practice the teachings while others do not. The Buddha experiences no joy or satisfaction when disciples fully engage the teachings, and he experiences no displeasure or impatience when they do not. In all cases the Buddha dwells in equanimity, fully mindful and aware. While Arhats may also be indifferent to the responses of their disciples, only the Buddha's supreme equanimity, grounded in full knowledge of all consequences, operates from complete mindfulness and awareness. (AK VII:32, MN 1:140–42)

Never-bewildered Nature When the Buddha teaches others, there is no confusion; one action follows another with perfect clarity and appropriateness, like waves on the ocean. There is never anything inharmonious or out of rhythm.

Subtle Residues Completely Removed The Buddha has completely removed all traces of obscurations to knowledge and all emotional tendencies, even on the most subtle levels.

Great Compassion The great compassion of a Buddha is, like ordinary compassion, completely free from avarice or hatred. But unlike ordinary compassion grounded in dualistic views of self and other, great compassion arises from enlightened knowledge illuminated by omniscience. While ordinary compassion applies itself unevenly, turning only toward beings who are suffering, great compassion applies itself evenly, turning its warmth upon all beings equally. (AK VII:33) It watches and protects all sentient beings at all times.

Omniscience The omniscience of a Buddha is self-arisen primordial wisdom, nondual suchness, complete direct understanding of all aspects of reality.

SAMBHOGAKĀYA For the benefit of sentient beings, the formless Dharmakāya manifests in two forms: Sambhogakāya and Nirmāṇakāya. Sambhogakāya, the body of perfect enjoyment, arises as the creative communication of the potential for enlightenment. This association with bliss is said to reflect the

and to others worthy of offerings. He has given to them baths and ointments and clarified butter, liniments of sesame oil, warm water in cold weather, cool water and shade in the heat, soothing amusements, good clothing smooth to the touch, soft beds and soft chairs. He has offered to the caityas of the Tathāgatas silken banners and cords, and sprinklings of perfumed oil.

"He is called the Golden One, because he has long made a practice of love, setting aside harshness, taking up patience, encouraging all to endure, praising and encouraging those free from malice, adorning the caityas of the Tathāgatas with golden objects of all kinds, golden flowers and vases, inlaid carvings, banners and golden vestments, sprinkling gold dust all around.

"He is called the one with each hair rising distinctly, because he has long attended on paṇḍitas, asking about virtue and non-virtue, about failings in practice and what to depend on, examining what is bad or fair or fulfilling, weighing the teachings with unconfused care, clearing away debris from the caityas of the Tathāgatas, removing the spiders and worms, the dirt and faded flowers, the cobwebs and weeds.

"He is called the one with the seven lofty parts, because he has long shown respect to parents and teachers, to masters and superiors, to śramaṇas and Brahmins, to those worthy of respect, to unfortunate beggars, and to all who approached, giving enjoyment to all, offering whatever they desired: food and drink, bedding, clothes, lamps, shelter, utensils, and medicine, and ponds and wells of fresh water.

"He is called the one whose upper body resembles the lion, because he has long offered obedience, speaking words of welcome and security, and words of peace to parents and teachers, to śramaṇas, Brahmins, and all those deserving offerings, upholding the weak, sheltering those seeking refuge, and never scorning or abandoning them.

"He is called the one with broad shoulders, because he has long weighed his own faults carefully, not seeing weakness in others as failings, giving up the source of divisiveness and argument, reciting mantras, and guarding well against extremes of speech and action.

"He is called the one with the well-turned shoulder, because he has long offered welcome and peace, rising in the presence of those deserving offerings, parents and teachers, śramaṇas and Brahmins. Assured in the śāstras, he cuts short debate; completely trained, he sets ministers and kings on the path of virtue; through meditation, he has comprehended and upheld all the precepts of the Tathāgatas; he has total grasp of all virtuous action.

"He is called the one with the lion's jaw, because he has long given up everything, like a beggar, addressing sweet words to all who approach, despising none, deceiving none, turning no one away, fulfilling their desires with gifts and firm support.

"He is called the one with forty even teeth, because he has long given up harsh words and chants which foster divisiveness, eager to bring all into accord, speaking against slander and argument, reciting mantras of conciliation.

"He is called the one with the white teeth, because he has long abandoned the dark side and accumulated the white roots of virtue, giving up the growth of dark deeds while encouraging the white, painting the caityas of the Tathāgatas with a mixture of chalk and milk, giving milk, cooked food, white garments, garlands of sumana, vārṣika, and dhanuṣkarī flowers, and beautiful bouquets of white flowers.

"He is called the one with firm and good teeth, because he has long left off mocking and teasing, giving only joy, guarding his speech, using words which delight, not looking for the weakness and faults of others, greeting all with impartiality and equanimity, teaching the Dharma to the sick, giving firm support to all beings, and never giving them up.

"He is called the possessor of the best elixir, because he has long harmed no sentient being, never scoffing at anyone, caring for the sick, caring for travelers, the deprived, and the weak, giving medicines and remedies, never sad to give, giving all he can.

"He is called the one with the voice like Brahmā's, because he has long given up false speech, cruel, sharp words that wound others, as well as biting and disparaging words. His words are loving and compassionate, joyous, pleasant, sweet, and sympathetic, welcoming and encouraging; they go straight to the heart, delighting all the senses.

"He is called the one with the blue-black eyes, because he has long gazed upon beings benevolently, like a father, giving love to beggars as to an only son, regarding all with compassion, completely free of jealousy, having gazed at the caityas of the Tathāgatas without blinking, with the power of faith, having shown the Tathāgatas to others, welcoming them, upholding them firmly.

"He is called the one with the eyelashes of a heifer, because he has long abandoned base thoughts and feelings, his brow never wrinkled, his face ever smiling, concerned with accomplishing generous intentions, guiding all beings with faith in the best Dharma, seeking continually the presence of teachers, never hesitating to accumulate virtue.

"He is called the one with the very long tongue, because he has long abandoned erroneous speech, singing instead the praises of the Śrāvakas, Pratyekabuddhas, and Teachers of the Dharma, requesting the Sūtras taught by the Tathāgatas, reciting and reading and comprehending them, skillfully conveying the meaning of the Dharma to all beings.

"He is called the one with the unseen diadem, because he has long bowed his head to the feet of his parents, to the feet of śramaṇas, Brahmins, and spiritual teachers, to all worthy of offerings. To the wandering monks he has

spoken with just words, giving sweet-smelling oils
and shaving their heads, giving beggars colored powders,
garlands, and head ornaments.

"He is called the one who has between his brows the circle
of hair curling to the right, and the one with the pure and
brilliant complexion, because he has long given offerings
of all sorts, guiding beings in virtue, not obscuring the rules,
and following the teachings of the friends of virtue,
encouraging the traveling teachers of the Dharma,
honoring the Buddhas, Bodhisattvas, and Pratyekabuddhas,
noble Śrāvakas, Dharma Teachers, parents, and all worthy
of homage, honoring and giving gifts of sweet-smelling oils
and butter, lamps and torches to dispel darkness,
adorning the images of the Tathāgatas
with all the most beautiful things.

"He bears the tuft of milk-white hair between his eyebrows;
distinguished by his immense accumulation of virtue,
he has encouraged beings to manifest
the Thought of Enlightenment."

—Voice of the Buddha II: 645–52

The Vajracchedikā-prajñāpāramitā clarifies that since the thirty-two marks also appear on the body of a universal monarch, the supreme form of worldly being, one cannot identify the Tathāgata solely on the basis of the physical evidence of these thirty-two marks.

From the Dharma should one see the Buddhas,
from the Dharmakāya comes their guidance.
Yet the Dharma's true nature cannot be discerned,
and no one can be aware of it as an object.

—Vajracchedikā-prajñāpāramitā

In addition to the thirty-two major signs of a Great Being, there are eighty accessory marks. The following list is based on the Mahāvyutpatti.

དཔེ་བྱད་བཟང་པོ་བརྒྱད་ཅུའི་མིང་མཚན།
EIGHTY ACCESSORY MARKS OF A GREAT BEING

སེན་མོ་ཟངས་ཀྱི་མདོག་ལྟ་བུ

ātāmranakha

copper-colored fingernails

སེན་མོའི་མདོག་སྣུམ་པ

snigdhanakha

glossy fingernails

སེན་མོ་མཐོ་བ

tuṅganakha

elevated fingernails

སོར་མོ་རྣམས་ཟླུམ་པ

vṛttāṅguli

round fingers

སོར་མོ་རྣམས་རྒྱས་པ

citāṅguli

full fingers

སོར་མོ་བྱིན་གྱིས་ཕྲ་བ

anupūrvāṅguli

tapered fingers

རྩ་མི་མངོན་པ

nirgūḍhaśira

veins not visible

རྩ་མདུད་མེད་པ་
nirgranthiśira
no knots in the veins

ལོང་བུ་མི་མངོན་པ་
gūḍhagulpha
ankle-joints not visible

ཞབས་མི་མཉམ་པ་མེད་པ་
aviṣamapāda
no disproportion of the feet

སེང་གེའི་སྟབས་སུ་གཤེགས་པ་
siṁhavikrāntagāmī
walking in the manner of a lion

གླང་པོ་ཆེའི་སྟབས་སུ་གཤེགས་པ་
nāgavikrāntagāmī
walking in the manner of an elephant

ངང་པའི་སྟབས་སུ་གཤེགས་པ་
haṁsavikrāntagāmī
walking in the manner of a swan

ཁྱུ་མཆོག་གི་སྟབས་སུ་གཤེགས་པ་
vṛṣabhavikrāntagāmī
walking in the manner of a bull

གཡས་ཕྱོགས་སུ་ལྡོག་ཅིང་གཤེགས་པ་
pradakṣiṇavartagāmī
turning to the right in walking

མཛེས་པར་གཤེགས་པ་

cārugāmī

walking in an elegant manner

མི་གཡོ་བར་གཤེགས་པ་

avakragāmī

walking uprightly

སྐུ་འབྲིལ་བག་ཆགས་པ་

vṛttagātra

a chosen body

སྐུ་བྱི་དོར་བྱས་པ་ལྟ་བུ་

mṛṣṭagātra

body well cleansed

སྐུ་རིམ་པར་འཚམ་པ་

anupūrvagātra

well-proportioned body

སྐུ་གཙང་བ་

śucigātra

clean or pure body

སྐུ་འཇམ་པ་

mṛdugātra

delicate body

སྐུ་རྣམ་པར་དག་པ་

viśuddhagātra

purified body

མཚན་ཡོངས་སུ་རྫོགས་པ་

paripūrṇa-vyañjana
perfect characteristic signs

སྐུ་བོ་ལག་ཡངས་ཤིང་བཟང་བ་

pṛthucāru-maṇḍalagātra
ample and sound-complexioned body

གོམ་པ་སྙོམས་པ་

samakrama
taking even paces in walking

སྐུ་ཤིན་ཏུ་གཞོན་མདོག་ཅན་

sukumāragātra
a youthful body

སྐུ་ཞུམ་པ་མེད་པ་

adīnagātra
body showing no distress

སྐུ་རྒྱས་པ་

utsadagātra
developed body

སྐུ་ཤིན་ཏུ་གྲིམས་པ་

susaṁhitagātra
well-controlled body

སྐུ་ཡན་ལག་དང་ཉིང་ལག་ཤིན་ཏུ་རྣམ་པར་འབྱེད་པ་

suvibhaktāṅgapratyaṅga
well-proportioned body and limbs

གཟིགས་པ་རབ་རིབ་མེད་ཅིང་རྣམ་པར་དག་པ་
vitimira-viśuddhāloka
sight clear, free from dimness

དཀུ་ཟླུམ་པ་
vṛttakukṣi
rounded hip

དཀུ་སྐབས་ཕྱིན་པ་
mṛṣṭakukṣi
cleansed hip

དཀུ་མ་རྙེངས་པ་
abhugnakukṣi
not crooked hip

ཕྱལ་ཕྱང་ངེ་བ་
kṣāmodara
belly somewhat pendulous

ལྟེ་བ་ཟབ་པ་
gambhīranābhi
with a deep navel

ལྟེ་བ་གཡས་ཕྱོགས་སུ་འཁྱིལ་བ་
pradakṣiṇāvartanābhi
navel turning to the right side

ཀུན་ནས་མཛེས་པ་
samantaprāsādika
handsome from all sides

ཀུན་ཏུ་སྤྱོད་པ་གཙང་བ

śucisamācāra

pure in conduct of life

སྐུ་ལ་སྨེ་བ་དང་གནག་བག་མེད་པ

vyapagata-tilakakālagātra

no dark spots on his body

ཕྱག་ཤིང་བལ་ལྟར་ཤིན་ཏུ་འཇམ་པ

tūlasadṛṣa-sukumārapāṇi

hand soft like cotton

ཕྱག་གི་རི་མོ་མདངས་ཡོད་པ

snigdhapāṇilekha

glossy lines on his palms

ཕྱག་གི་རི་མོ་ཟབ་པ

gambhīrapāṇilekha

deep lines on his palms

ཕྱག་གི་རི་མོ་རིང་བ

āyatapāṇilekha

long figures on his palms

ཞལ་ཧ་ཅང་ཡང་མི་རིང་བ

nāyāyata-vadana

face not too long

ཞལ་ལ་གཟུགས་ཀྱི་གཟུགས་བརྙན་སྣང་བ

bimbapratibimba-darśanavadana

reflections of the bimba-fruit seen in his face (= red lips)

ལྗགས་མཉེན་པ་

mṛdujihva

pliant tongue

ལྗགས་སྲབ་པ་

tanujihva

thin tongue

ལྗགས་དམར་བ་

raktajihva

red tongue

གླང་པོ་ཆེའི་ང་རོ་དང་འབྲུག་གི་སྒྲ་དང་ལྡན་པ་

gajagarjita-jīmūtaghoṣa

thunderous voice like the trumpeting of an elephant

གསུང་སྙན་ཅིང་མཉེན་ལ་འཇམ་པ་

madhuracāru-mañjusvara

speech sweet, elegant, and soft

མཆེ་བ་ཟླུམ་པ་

vṛttadaṁṣṭra

round eye-teeth

མཆེ་བ་རྣོ་བ་

tīkṣṇadaṁṣṭra

sharp eye-teeth

མཆེ་བ་དཀར་བ་

śukladaṁṣṭra

white eye-teeth

མཆེ་བ་མཉམ་པ་

samadaṁṣṭra

uniform eye-teeth

མཆེ་བ་བྱིན་གྱིས་ཕྲ་བ་

anupūrvadaṁṣṭra

tapered eye-teeth

ཤངས་མཐོ་བ་

tuṅganāsa

a prominent nose

ཤངས་གཙང་བ

śucināsa

clean nose

སྤྱན་རྣམ་པར་དག་པ་

viśuddhanetra

clear eyes

སྤྱན་ཡངས་པ་

viśāla-netra

eyes wide like a deer's

རྫི་མ་སྟུག་པ་

citapakṣma

thick eyelashes

སྤྱན་དཀར་ནག་དབྱེས་ཤིང་པདྨའི་འདབ་མ་རངས་པ་ལྟ་བུ་

sitāsita-kamaladala-śakala-nayana

black and white of the eyes bright like lotus petals

སྨིན་ཚུགས་རིང་བ་

āyatabhrū

long eyebrows

སྨིན་མ་འཇམ་པ་

ślakṣṇabhrū

soft eyebrow

སྨིན་མ་སྤུ་མཉམ་པ་

samaromabhrū

uniform eyebrow hairs

སྨིན་མ་སྣུམ་པ་

snigdhabhrū

glossy eyebrows

སྙན་ཤལ་སྟུག་ཅིང་རིང་བ་

pinayatakarṇa

thick and long earlobes

སྙན་མཉམ་པ་

samakarṇa

uniform ears

སྙན་གྱི་དབང་པོ་མ་ཉམས་པ་

anupahatakarṇendriya

undiminished power of hearing

དཔྲལ་བ་ལེགས་པར་འབྱེས་པ་

supariṇatalalāṭa

well-defined forehead

དཔྲལ་བ་དབྱེས་ཆེ་བ
pṛthulalāṭa
broad forehead

དབུ་ཤིན་ཏུ་རྒྱས་པ
suparipūrṇottamamāṅga
head well-developed

དབུ་སྐྲ་བུང་བ་ལྟར་གནག་པ
bhramarasadṛṣakeśa
hair of the head black as a bee

དབུ་སྐྲ་སྟུག་པ
citakeśa
hair of the head luxuriant

དབུ་སྐྲ་འཇམ་པ
ślakṣṇakeśa
fine hair

དབུ་སྐྲ་མ་འཛིངས་པ
asaṁlulitakeśa
hair not tangled

དབུ་སྐྲ་མི་གཤོར་བ
aparuṣakeśa
hair of the head not tousled

དབུ་སྐྲ་དྲི་ཞིམ་པ
surabhikeśa
hair of the head sweet-smelling

ཕྱག་དང་ཞབས་དཔལ་གྱི་བེའུ་དང་
བཀྲ་ཤིས་དང་གཡུང་དྲུང་འཁྱིལ་བས་བརྒྱན་པ་

śrīvatsa-svastikanandyā-varttalalita-pāṇipāda

hands and feet adorned with auspicious emblems
of prosperity, plenty, and good fortune

THREE COMPLETE ATTAINMENTS Buddhas exhibit three complete attainments: the attainment of cause, the attainment of result, and the attainment of service. Reflecting on these attainments and appreciating their value awakens profound respect for the Enlightened Ones, a quality that develops aspiration to follow in their footsteps. (AK VII)

The Abhidharmakoṣa explains the attainment of cause as the cultivation of the accumulation of all qualities and all knowledge. This cultivation intensifies in four stages, from the initial cultivation to prolonged, uninterrupted, and strongly energetic cultivation.

The attainment of result is the realization of the Dharmakāya. This realization results in four attainments: the attainment of four kinds of knowledge, four kinds of power, four perfections of removing (obstacles), and four perfections of the material body.

The four kinds of knowledge are untaught knowledge, omniscience as regards the characteristics of things, omniscience as regards all aspects of being, and spontaneous knowledge that arises simply through the desire to know.

The attainment of powers is mastery of the power of creating, transforming, and sustaining an external object; mastery of the power of the length of life; mastery over movements such as flying through space, moving through objects, traveling at great speeds; and mastery of miraculous powers.

The attainment of the four perfections of removing consists of perfecting the removing all defilements, perfecting definitive and irreversible removing, perfecting the removing of the most subtle traces of all defilements, and perfecting the removing of all obstacles to samādhi and the absorptions.

The attainment of the four perfections of the material body includes obtaining the thirty-two marks and the eighty accessory marks of a Great Being; the possession of great strength; the development of the body so that internally the bones are adamantine, like diamond; and externally, light radiates forth.

The attainment of service is also fourfold: perfecting the abilities to deliver beings from the suffering of each of the three realms of rebirth into the three vehicles of deliverance; and fourth, to deliver them from the suffering of passage into painful realms into favorable realms of rebirth. (AK VII)

The Mahāyāna-saṁgraha gives reasons why, having attained power over the duration of life, the Buddha does not remain in this world in his Nirmāṇakāya form: His action is complete; his departure encourages others to aspire higher than the nirvana of the Arhat for the sake of living beings; in departing he removes the basis for disrespect of the Buddha and his teachings and nourishes understanding of suchness and the doctrine. Knowing that the Buddha is no longer in the world, beings longing for him are encouraged to develop the aspiration for enlightenment and to put forth great effort to persevere.

While the Nirmāṇakāya form of the Buddha has vanished, the activity of enlightenment never ceases. The Mahāyāna-saṁgraha explains that from the aspect of Dharmakāya the Buddha has neither entered nor not entered nirvana, because Buddhas are liberated from all obstacles and their action is without end.

Praising the Qualities of the Buddha

The qualities of a Buddha extend so far beyond ordinary understanding that even naming them requires special insight. Yet pronouncing the the attributes of enlightened being stimulates the mind and heart, arousing awareness of the inestimable value of the Buddha and evoking these qualities in one's experience. The Abhidharmakoṣa explains:

"The foolish, who lack spiritual understanding
and judge others by their own impoverished qualities,
cannot conceive of the value of praising the qualities
of a Buddha and thus cannot develop affection
for the Buddha or the Dharma.

"But the wise understand the value
of extolling the qualities of the Buddha;
the wise develop faith in the Buddha and the Dharma
that penetrates to the marrow of one's bones." (VII:34)

Out of great compassion for ordinary beings, the Buddha teaches the words and phrases that can be recited and held in the heart to accumulate merit and awaken the aspiration to attain the enlightenment of a Buddha. From "The Praise of the Qualities of the Tathāgata" in the Lalitavistara Sūtra:

"He is called the perfect and complete Buddha; Svayambhū, self-arising; Lord of the Dharma; the Guide and the Leader; Guide in all things; Driver of the caravan; Master over all dharmas; Master of the Dharma.

"He is the one who turns the Wheel of the Dharma;
the Benefactor of the Dharma; the Lord of Offerings;
the one who makes the best offerings;
the being whose practices are fulfilled;
the being whose intentions are carried out.

"He is the Teacher; the one who consoles; the one who reassures; the Hero; the one who has abandoned emotionality; the complete Victor in battle; the one who opens the parasol and unfurls the standard and the banner.

"He is the One who creates light; the being bringing forth clarity; the one who dispels obscurity; the Torch-bearer.
He is known as the Great King of Physicians; the Genuine Healer; the one who withdraws the arrow of misery.

"He has the unobscured vision of wisdom; he sees all;
his eyes see everywhere; he illuminates everything.
He is called the Gate to Everything, and the Completely Good.

"He is known as the one in all ways like the moon;
all-gracious, rejecting nothing and accepting nothing
in the unstable world.

"He is known as the one like the earth, because his mind is never inflated, never depressed. He is known as the one like a mountain, because he is unshakable. He is known as the most glorious in all the world, because he is endowed with every good quality. He is known as the one whose head disappears from sight, because he is the most exalted in all the worlds.

"He is known as the one like the ocean, because his depth cannot be fathomed. He is known as the source of the jewels of the Dharma, because he has perfected all facets of Enlightenment.

"He is known as the one like the wind, because he has no abode. He is known as the one whose thought is unattached, because his wisdom is unbound and free from limitations. He is known as the unswerving Dharma, because he has completely understood all dharmas.

"He is known as the one like a flame, because he has burned away all fetters, abandoned all pride, and reached a state difficult to attain. He is known as the one like water, because he is free from all conceptions, spotless in body and mind, and clear of all defilements.

"He is known as the one like the sky, because he has obtained omniscient understanding and knowledge of the sphere of action of the Dharmadhātu—without center and without limits—boundless sphere of wisdom.

"He is called the one who dwells in complete deliverance and unhindered knowledge, because he has abandoned obscured teachings. He is called the one with the body which has completely entered the Dharmadhātu, because he has passed from sight and is the same as space. He is called the Highest of Beings, because he is untouched by the fettering passions of the world.

"He is known as the Being of immeasurable intelligence, Teacher of a Dharma Beyond the World; Teacher of the World; Caitya of the World; Physician of the World; raised above the world; not clothed in worldly dharmas; Protector of the World; finest of the World; Most Perfect of the World; Lord of the World; Honored One of the World; the Friend of the World; the one who has reached the shore beyond the world; Lamp of the World; the one who has passed from the world; Spiritual Teacher of the World; the one who renders service to the world; the one who knows the world; the one who has attained mastery over the world. . . .

"He is known as the one who possesses pure attentiveness, realization, intelligence; the one who possesses mindfulness, complete renunciation, the degrees of supernatural abilities, the powers and strengths, the branches of awakening, the path, calm abiding, and intense insight. He is called the one who has crossed the sea of rebirth; the one who has arrived at the other shore; the one who stands on firm ground; the one who is full of joy; the one who has obtained fearlessness. . . .

"He is known as the destroyer of dark ignorance; the one who sees distinctly with the great light of knowledge; the one free of conceptualization; the one illuminating an immeasurable domain with love, kindness, and great compassion; the one shining equally for each living being; the possessor of the maṇḍala difficult to envision, difficult to attain, and profound in transcendent wisdom. . . .

"He is known as the one endowed with the thirty-two signs of a great man; the Great Being; the one endowed with the eighty accessory marks; the Leader of Men; the one endowed with the ten strengths; possessor of the four fearless affirmations; the eminent Guide of those to be trained; the Teacher; the one who is replete with all the eighteen Buddhadharmas; the one above reproach in body, speech, and mind. He is called the possessor of the maṇḍala of completely purified knowledge, because he is endowed with the best of signs.

"Because he understands the connections and balance of interdependent cooperation, he is called the dweller in emptiness. Because he realizes absolute truth, he is called the dweller in signlessness. Because he is unsullied by emotional entanglements, he is called the dweller in wishlessness.

"Because he halts the stream of conditionality, he is called the one who does not manifest conditioned responses. Because he is unconfused about the wisdom of true reality, he is called the speaker of the genuine reality. Because he abides in the domain of knowledge, described as the sky, the Dharmadhātu, having the nature of Thatness as its characteristic, he is called the speaker of the essence of the nonmistaken. . . .

"Because he causes complete deliverance to arise, he is called the one meaningful to hear and see. Because he strives to train living beings, he is called the one with meaningful stride.

"Because he has ended the thirst for existence, cutting off ignorance completely, he is called the one who has crossed the fire pit of hell. Because he points out the path to the certain exit, he is called the solid bridge. Because he is unsullied by the deeds of the demon, and has surmounted the obtacles of Māra and the fetters of passion, he is called Jina, Victorious. . . .

"He is called the one who welcomes the Bodhisattvas, the one who causes the Bodhisattvas to celebrate and makes them happy; the harmonious Teacher of the Dharma; the Teacher of the Dharma which bears fruit. He is known as the one who wastes not a single word, who teaches the Dharma which is always timely."

—Voice of the Buddha II:639–59

The Abhidharmakoṣa relates that "There is no end to the perfections of the Buddhas . . . Only the Buddhas, the Blessed Ones, if they were to prolong their existence for numerous kalpas, would be capable of knowing and enumerating all their virtues." (AK VII)

The knowledge of the Buddha is unending
like the vast expanse of space. One could
speak for an aeon and not come to the end
of the qualities of the Buddha.

—Voice of the Buddha II: 663

The Life of the Buddha

Homage to Ārya Śākyamuni, Buddha of our time.

Life of the Buddha

In all schools of Buddhism, dates are calculated from the time of the Buddha's Parinirvāṇa. Historical events derive their meaning from their relationship to this central act of the Enlightened One. Since these relationships carry nuances of meaning that are important to preserve, this account of the life of the Buddha follows the traditional form of dating.[1] However, throughout the long history of the Dharma, the Buddhist traditions have applied different methods of determining the date of the Parinirvāṇa and have arrived at different dates. In the Tibetan tradition alone, there are numerous ways to calculate the date of the Buddha's passing from life. The dates given below rely on three major traditions: the Tibetan, as calculated by 'Phug-pa-lhun-grub (P); the Theravādin schools (T); and the Chinese tradition (C).

1. B.N. Before Nirvana
   A.N. After Nirvana
   A.E. After Enlightenment
   C.E. Common Era (= A.D.)
   B.C.E. Before Common Era (= B.C.)

Information presented in the timeline below relies on the Lalitavistara Sūtra, accounts in the 'Dul-ba (Tibetan translation of the Mūlasarvāstivādin Vinayavastu and Kṣudrakavastu), Sūtras in the Tibetan bKa'-'gyur and the Pāli Canon, and the ancient Sinhalese chronicles (Mahāvaṁsa and Dīpavaṁsa). While the timing of some events in the Buddha's life after the enlightenment can be traced in the Vinaya accounts, most are difficult to establish with certainty. This timeline presents a possible sequence, anchored by the dates and places of the rainy season retreats, on which the Buddhist traditions generally agree. The Buddha's major acts are numbered 1–12.

93 B.N. Five hundred Pratyekabuddhas residing at the Deer Park of Sārnāth enter nirvana upon hearing that within twelve years a Buddha, a fully awakened being, will be conceived. Rising together into the air, they vanish in fire and their ashes rain upon the ground. The place where they pass into nirvana becomes known as Ṛṣipatana, the place where the sages fell.

81 B.N. Pravrata, Resolve to Be Born in the World After three great aeons of lifetimes devoted to practicing generosity, virtue, and compassion, the Bodhisattva takes birth in the Tuṣita Heaven, where he is known as Svetaketu. After teaching the Dharma to the inhabitants of that realm, the Bodhisattva perceives the plight of human beings who remain entrapped by desire and illusion. Moved by compassion, he resolves to be born in this Sahaloka (world of endurance) to demonstrate the way to liberation.

1. Bhagavato utrāṁti, The Descent from Tuṣita P: 962 B.C.E. T: 621 B.C.E. C: 567 B.C.E. Considering the most favorable conditions for accomplishing his purpose, the Bodhisattva selects the continent of Jambudvīpa; he determines to be born amongst the Śākyas, a warrior clan descended from the sage Gautama of the ancient Īkṣvaku lineage. His mother will be the virtuous Queen Māyā and King Śuddhodana will be his father. Placing his crown upon the head of Maitreya, the next of the lineage of Buddhas, the Bodhisattva departs from Tuṣita and descends into the world accompanied by a great host of celestial beings.

2. Garbha-avakrāṁti, Entering the Womb P: 962 B.C.E. T: 621 B.C.E. C: 567 B.C.E. On the fifteenth day of the month of Āṣāḍa (Chu-stod), which roughly corresponds to July/August, the Bodhisattva descends from Tuṣita. At that time King Śuddhodana and Queen Māyā are residing in Kapilavastu, capital of the Śākyas, located in the Nepalese terai, the sloping plain abutting the Himalayan foothills. The land and the people are prospering under King Śuddhodana's protection: The fields are well-tended, and the land around the city walls is adorned with forested parks where flowers surround pools of sweet water.

Having withdrawn from palace life to observe a fast of purification, Queen Māyā dreams that a white elephant, richly adorned, descends from the heavens and enters her body through her right side. Assured by seers that the dream is auspicious and indicates she will bear a most well-favored son, the queen awaits the birth. The Bodhisattva spends ten months in the womb, which he transforms into a dwelling free from impurities.

3. Janma, Birth P: 961 B.C.E. T: 620 B.C.E. C: 566 B.C.E. The Buddha is born on the seventh day of Vaiśākha, the fourth lunar month (Sa-ga), corresponding to May/June of the Western calendar. While journeying to the city of Devadaha to visit her mother, Queen Māyā rests a while in the Lumbinī Garden, about six miles east of Kapilavastu. As she grasps the branch of a plakṣa tree with her right hand, the Bodhisattva emerges from her right side. The Lalitavistara Sūtra describes the miracles that attend the birth of the Great Being:

"All beings felt their skin shiver with pleasure. A great frightening earthquake made their hair stand on end, and the musical instruments of gods and men sounded without being touched. Simultaneously, everywhere in the three thousand great thousands of worlds, trees of all seasons brought forth perfect flowers and fruits. Thunder was heard in the heavens, and rain fell from a cloudless sky. From the land of the gods came forth all sorts of flowers, garments, ornaments, and perfumed powders; soft fragrant winds began to blow. Every place took on a serene and luminous appearance, free from shadows, dust, smoke, and fog.

"Sweet and prolonged, the great sounds of Brahmā were heard from the heights of the sky. All the splendors of Candra and Sūrya, of Indra, Brahmā, and the Guardians of the World were eclipsed by a light which spread throughout the three thousand great thousands of worlds, sparkling with a hundred thousand colors, producing well-being and joy in the body and mind of each being touched by its rays.

"As soon as the Bodhisattva was born, great pleasure filled all beings. All were delivered from desire, hatred, and ignorance, pride, sadness, depression, and fear. They were freed from attachment, jealousy, and greed, and ceased all actions contrary to virtue. The sick were cured; the hungry and thirsty were no longer oppressed by hunger and thirst. Those maddened by drink lost their obsession. the mad recovered their senses, the blind regained sight, and the deaf once more could hear. The halt and the lame obtained perfect limbs, the poor gained riches, and the prisoners were delivered from their bonds. For beings thrown into the Avīci and the other hells, for beings reduced to the condition of beasts devouring one another, and for hungry and thirsting beings in the realm of Yama, there was relief from suffering and misery."

—Voice of the Buddha I: 132–33

A host of gods appears to attend his birth; Śakra and Brahmā welcome the child and lower him gently to earth, while nāgas, powerful serpentine beings who govern the watery realms, shower him with warm and cool streams of water. The Bodhisattva takes seven steps in each of the four directions and proclaims the fulfillment of his ancient vow: "The destroyer of old age and death has come forth, the greatest of physicians . . .

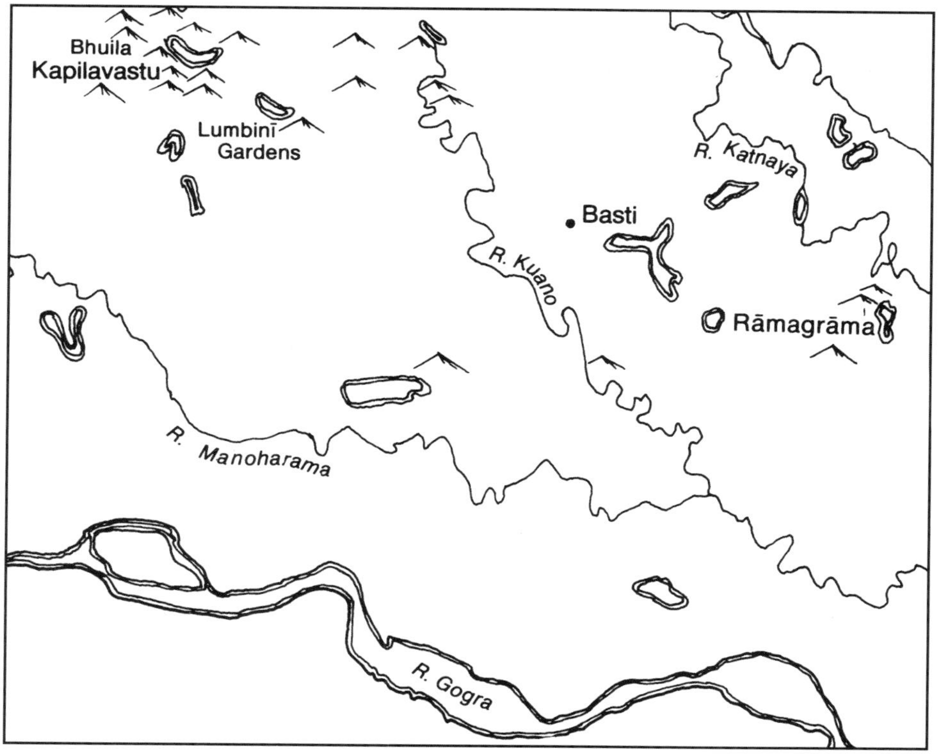

I am the leader of the world; I am the guide of the world; this is my final birth." Where his feet touch the ground, lotuses spring from the earth. The earth shakes, a brilliant light shines forth, and flowers burst into bloom.

Simultaneously, four princes—Bimbisāra, Prasenajit, Udāyana, and Pradyota—are born in northern India. They will rule the four kingdoms where the teachings of the Buddha will first become widely known.

Seven days after giving birth, Queen Māyā dies and is reborn in the Trāyastriṁśa, the Heaven of the Thirty-three Gods. King Śuddhodana brings the Bodhisattva to his palace in Kapilavastu and entrusts his care to Mahāprajāpatī, Queen Māyā's sister. Assisted by thirty-two attendants, Mahāprajāpatī looks after the prince and fulfills his every wish with great love and devotion. Śuddhodana names the child Sarvasiddhārtha, he who has accomplished all purposes. Seeing that the child bears the marks of a great being, the sage Asita predicts that he will become the most powerful of rulers if he follows a worldly path, but should he renounce the world, he will become a Buddha, a fully enlightened one, able to free countless beings from illusion and pain.

4. Kalā, Education and Sports P: 954 B.C.E. T: 616 B.C.E. C: 559 B.C.E. So well does the king protect the prince from distress of every kind that the child has no opportunity to perceive even the possibility of illness, pain, or a life bereft of love, wealth, and beauty. At the age of seven years he begins the education befitting a future king. Effortlessly mastering languages, mathematics, philosophy, logic, and science, the young prince demonstrates such extraordinary intelligence that he astounds the greatest masters of the realm. On a visit to the countryside, he enters so deeply into meditation under a Jambu tree that his spiritual power attracts the reverence of passing sages. Even his father bows down to the young prince in wonder.

Mindful of the sage's prophecy, the king seeks to bind the prince more firmly to worldly life through luxury and pleasure. When Prince Gautama reaches the age of nineteen (in some sources, sixteen), the king pressures him to marry and offers him his choice of the realm's most beautiful maidens. Acquiescing to his father's request, the prince chooses the virtuous Gopā, daughter of the Śākya warrior Daṇḍapāṇi, who will allow her to marry only one skilled in the physical arts of a warrior. In a contest attended by all the youths of the Śākya clan, the prince demonstrates great physical strength and surpasses all others in every sport.

60 B.N. About this time Bimbisāra, a future patron of the Buddha, becomes king of Magadha at the age of fifteen and begins to strengthen and enlarge his kingdom. He conquers Aṅga to the east, marries daughters of the ruling families of Kosala and Vaiśālī, and befriends King Pukkasāti of Takṣasilā.

5. Krīḍāmuda, Life of Pleasure 61–51 B.N. After his marriage to Gopā, the prince lives a life of leisure in the three palaces built for him by the king. Surrounded by wealth, luxury, and beauty, with all the resources of the kingdom at his command, for ten years he passes his days in delightful ease. But one day the sound of cymbals recalls his earlier meditation, and the prince turns inward in reflection. Concerned, the king grants the prince's wish to visit the royal gardens and orders the road to be cleared of anything that might disturb his pleasure or turn his mind to renunciation.

But when Prince Siddhārtha travels outside the palace, the king's orders fail to prevent the prince's awakening. For the first time Siddhārtha observes the suffering of illness, old age, and death. With growing horror he hears his charioteer relate that these sufferings come to all, rich and poor alike. All beings in all realms of existence must yield to the law of impermanence, from which ultimately there is no appeal; not even the gods can free themselves from decline, death, and decay. The dreams, wishes, and plans of sentient beings unfold against unbearable uncertainty: Every moment holds the potential for catastrophe. Not for one instant are beings truly secure.

The shock of seeing this unending torment unfold in life after life penetrates all thought of self and awakens profound compassion in the young prince. The first to seriously question the unquestionable facts of existence, he gazes unflinchingly into the great abyss of human despair: How can one live in happiness, knowing that all love ends in separation, all beauty in old age, and life itself in death? The serenity of a passing mendicant monk stirs memories of his earlier meditation. Could this be a path to liberation?

In the palace the prince continues to penetrate the illusions that bind human beings to a dream world of their own making. The promise of pleasure and happiness attracts mind and body to sources of suffering, as honey on a razor blade attracts the tongue with its sweetness. Drawn to pleasures, with senses fixated on objects of desire, beings cannot see clearly where their actions are leading. The fleeting pleasures gained only intensify thirst for more; opportunities pass unseen, while time and energy run their course, inviting frustration and despair.

As the prince contemplates how blindly beings are drawn into endless cycles of suffering, pain enters the whole of his being: He sees that he is burning; his wife and father are burning, as are his countrymen. Throughout worlds of beings of the six realms and the three times, all are burning, trapped in a net of illusion from which there is no escape.

6. Abhiniṣkramana, Home-Departure P: 933 B.C.E. T: 594 B.C.E. C: 537 B.C.E. Sensing that there must be some solution, the prince resolves to find it. There can be no choice, no postponement, no question of returning to a life of leisure. While the sorrow of leaving his loved ones rends his heart, he resolves to depart from the palace.

Worried that the prince is about to renounce worldly life, Śuddhodana places guards outside the palace grounds and orders that the prince be continuously entertained. Although Siddhārtha expresses his intention and receives his father's permission to depart, the king, unable to bear the consequences of his promise, intensifies the guards and fortifies the palace gates. That same night, on the eighth day of the month of Kārttika (smin-drug), everyone in and around the palace falls into a deep sleep, save the prince and Chandaka, his loyal charioteer. Asking Chandaka to bring his horse Kaṇṭhaka, the prince directs Kaṇṭhaka at full gallop toward the bolted doors of the eastern gate. His passage is swift but soundless; protecting his purpose, the devas accompany his flight, cushioning the horse's hooves in their hands. As he reaches the gate, the massive doors swing open of their own accord, and the prince and Chandaka pass through them into the night.

At dawn, Siddhārtha and Chandaka reach the Stūpa of Kāśyapa, the previous Buddha. Giving Chandaka his ornaments of royal rank, the prince sends his charioteer back to Kapilavastu with his horse. Abandoning all symbols of worldly position, he cuts his long hair, exchanges his garments for those of a passing hunter, and makes his way to the city of Vaiśālī. Here, at the age of twenty-nine years, he masters the teachings of the renowned philosopher Ārāda Kālāma; then traveling south, he crosses the Ganges River and enters Magadha, the kingdom ruled by Bimbisāra.

7. Duṣkarācārya, Practice of Hardships 51–45 B.N. Nearing the royal city of Rājagṛha, the Bodhisattva dwells alone in a mountainside retreat a short distance from the capital. King Bimbisāra, having seen the Bodhisattva making his begging rounds in the city, travels to the mountain to meet him, and requests that he continue to bless the kingdom with his presence. The Bodhisattva gives his word that he will return upon fulfilling his purpose. In the hills of Rājagṛha he studies with Rudraka Rāmaputra, who, like Ārāda Kālāma of Vaiśālī, is one of the most respected masters of his time. Finding that Rudraka's teachings offer no lasting relief for the problem of suffering, the Bodhisattva resolves to continue his search.

Traveling west, the Bodhisattva and five of Rudraka's disciples arrive at the banks of the Nairañjanā River near Uruvilvā, where they practice hardships, a traditional route to spiritual growth, for a period of six years. Fasting to the point of emaciation, the Bodhisattva enters the Āsphānaka contemplation and traverses the celestial realms and the six realms of existence. From this meditation he perceives the whole of samsara; understanding the workings of consciousness, he now sees how the patterns of samsara interlock, forming a prison where all actions lead to sorrow. Although the great samādhis could open the gates of the heaven realms, even this would be no permanent solution.

8. Bodhimaṇḍa-kramaṇa, Proceeding to the Seat of Enlightenment 45 B.N. Recalled to his purpose by the knowledge that his passing into the higher realms would not benefit beings struggling in samsara, the Bodhisattva ends his austerities and accepts rice and milk from the maiden Sujātā, who later, in some accounts, along with her servant Pūrṇā becomes the first laywoman to take refuge in the Buddha, Dharma, and Sangha. Seeing him abandon the practice of hardships, his five companions desert him. Alone, the Bodhisattva makes his way to the Bodhi tree near the Nairañjanā River. This tree marks the site of the Vajrāsana, the Diamond Seat, the only place in the world capable of sustaining the energy released through the enlightenment of a Buddha.

Through the aeons, this holy place has attracted a steady stream of sages and renunciates, who draw upon its power to illuminate their contemplations. Here, seated on the Vajrāsana at Bodh Gayā, the three previous Buddhas of our aeon had experienced their great transformation at the foot of a spreading Bodhi tree. Following in the footsteps of all the Buddhas before him and renewing the path for Buddhas to come, Gautama approaches the Diamond Throne.

9. Mārajit, Victory over Māra 45 B.N. Accepting a handful of kuśa grass from a laborer tending the area, the Bodhisattva fashions it into a meditation mat and takes his seat on the Vajrāsana, as had all Buddhas before him. With firm resolve he makes this vow:

"Here on this seat my body may shrivel up,
my skin, my bones, my flesh may dissolve,
but my body will not move from this very seat
until I have obtained Enlightenment,
so difficult to obtain in the course of many kalpas."

—Voice of the Buddha II:439

Rays of light emanate from his body; perceiving this light, Māra, lord of illusion, knows his power is now seriously threatened. Summoning his demon armies, he hastens to the Bodhi tree. Hurling trees, lightning bolts, clubs, hammers, chains, arrows, and sharp weapons, the fearsome horde approaches. But before their weapons strike the Bodhisattva, they are transformed into flowers by the power of his concentration. Meditation offers a parallel to this attack of the demons: Just as the bright light of awareness is about to penetrate the darkness of ordinary mind, images of aggression, fear, revulsion, or desire arise like demons to distract the mind and confine it firmly within samsara.

Seeing the Bodhisattva fearless and unperturbed, Māra challenges his preparation and worth. The Bodhisattva touches the earth, calling it to witness his countless lifetimes dedicated to perfecting virtue and compassion. The earth shakes in six ways, and the earth goddess Sthavarā affirms the truth of the Bodhisattva's word. Then Māra tempts the Bodhisattva with power and sends his lovely daughters Rati, Aratī, and Tṛṣṇā (Delight, Discontent, and Thirst) to seduce him, but the Bodhisattva's steady gaze reveals the true ugliness of their nature. Although Māra's demons mount a last desperate effort, the Bodhisattva deepens his concentration, and Māra and his armies flee in confusion and disarray.

10. Abhisambodhi, Enlightenment P: 927 B.C.E. T: 588 B.C.E. C: 531 B.C.E. As night falls and the great turmoil fades, the Bodhisattva brings forth into the world the perfect clarity that arises when all forms of illusion are transcended. During the watches of the night the Bodhisattva passes through increasingly deep levels of samādhi. In the first level of meditation, he attains detachment from desire, abandons observation and reflection, and purifies concentration, merging it into a single stream. Entering the second level of meditation, he maintains steady concentration as joy and pleasure arise. Letting go of attachment to pleasure, he enters the matchless equanimity of the third level of meditation and dwells in great joy and mindfulness. Abandoning joy, he abides in the fourth level of meditation where there is neither suffering nor pleasure, where equanimity and mindfulness are completely pure.

On each level the Bodhisattva finds the samsaric patterning of identity and mind that separates the subjective world of consciousness from the objective world of existence. Wherever the realms of subject and object persist, there is no bridge from samsara into nirvana, no way to escape the dualistic mind that perpetuates the manifold sufferings of samsara.

Around midnight, the demon Rāhu seizes the moon, precipitating an eclipse. In the darkness, the Blessed One unfolds the full potential of consciousness and understands with fully awakened omniscience how all that has ever existed comes into being and passes away. Seeing the rise, duration, and cessation of all beings throughout countless lifetimes, he observes the connection between cause and effect and formulates the Four Noble Truths: All life is imbued with suffering; suffering has a cause, and can therefore be brought to an end. Cessation of suffering comes about by means of the eightfold path: developing right view, conceptualization, speech, conduct, livelihood, effort, mindfulness, and meditative concentration focused on the attainment of enlightenment.

On the fifteenth day of the month of Vaiśākha (Sa-ga), as Rāhu releases the moon and the sun begins to rise, the cosmos opens; the Bodhisattva's realization illuminates the three thousand great thousands of world-systems and warms all the beings who dwell in them. The rays of the rising sun reveal the perfect form of a Buddha, a fully enlightened being.

The Avataṁsaka Sūtra relates that, at the time of the enlightenment, the ground surrounding the Vajrāsana is adorned with brilliant jewels and every tree is festooned with banners of precious gems and garlands of fragrant flowers. Jewels spontaneously take form in the air and fall on the earth like rain. Through the power of the realized Buddha, the whole area is ablaze with light magnified by infinite reflections in rows of trees made of jewels. The Bodhi tree, its trunk transformed into diamond and its branches into lapis lazuli, spreads its leaves in all directions like clouds. Radiant light emanates from the Tree of Enlightenment, and sublimely beautiful sounds directly communicate truth.

Here an immeasurably great host of enlightened beings, numerous as the atoms in ten Buddhafields, gathers around the

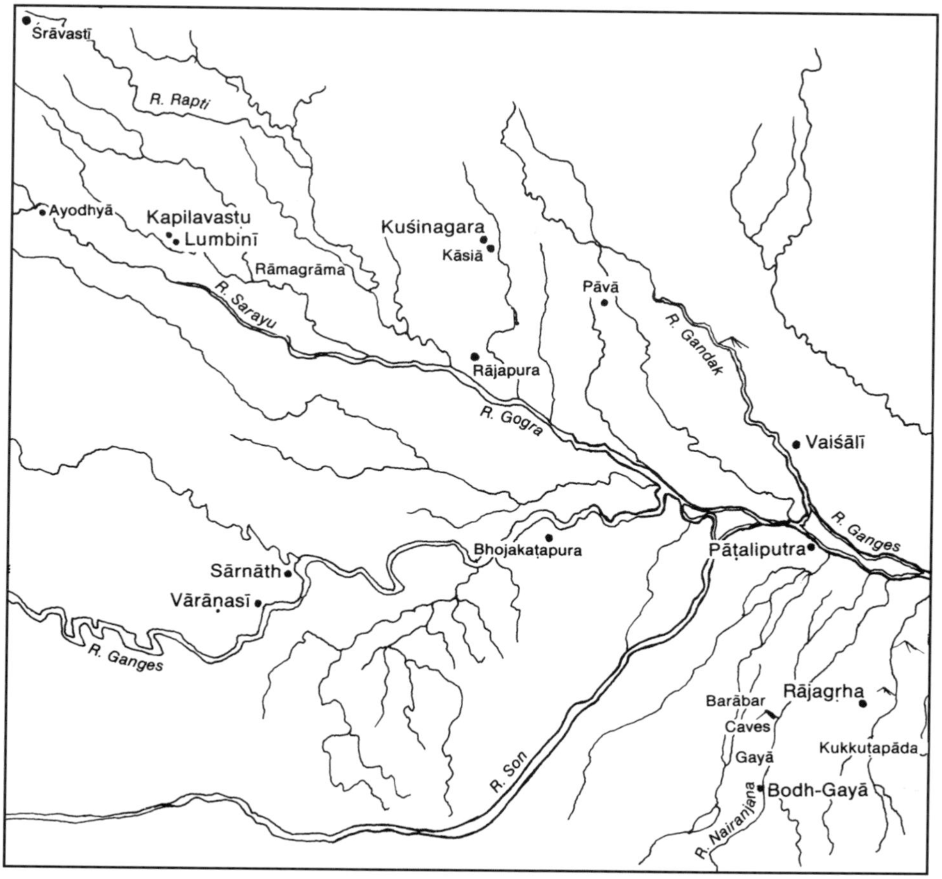

Buddha, whose body extends throughout the ten directions and whose light illuminates the world. To this host of great beings, born from the Buddha's ocean of virtue and illumined by brilliant light, the Buddha expounds all truths. Thus the Dharma, the whole spectrum of enlightened knowledge, is completely manifest in the world from the first instant of the enlightenment.

45 B.N. In the weeks after the enlightenment, the Buddha dwells in peace of such depth and clarity that no words can convey the experience. For seven days he remains motionless in the profound samādhi named Prītyāhāravyūha, Assimilating the Food of Joy. In the second week, continuing in meditation, he visits the three thousand great thousands of worlds; during the third week he gazes steadily upon the Bodhi tree.

During the fourth week the Buddha walks from the Eastern Sea to the Western Sea. When a great tempest arises in the fifth week, Mucilinda, lord of the nāgas, wraps the Buddha in his coils to protect him from wind and rain. The sixth week the Enlightened One rests under a banyan tree on the banks of the Nairañjanā River; the seventh week he meets the merchants Trapuṣa and Bhallika, who offer him honey and cakes.

Then the Blessed One withdraws into the forest, pondering how it might be possible to teach this realization to living beings. Are there ways to express such subtle meanings? Can language convey what lies beyond the grasp of the dualistic mind? Who might hear his teaching, and, hearing it, who would understand? Perhaps it would be better to live in solitude in the forest rather than allow this precious teaching to be disregarded or misunderstood. Then Brahmā, lord of the gods, knowing the Buddha's thoughts, petitions the Enlightened One to teach the view and path to liberation:

"Point out clearly the path of peace, happiness,
and prosperity, free of sickness and far from sorrow.
Without a protector, beings stray from the path of nirvana.
O Guide, have compassion for them."

—Voice of the Buddha II:597

Three times Brahmā calls upon the Buddha to teach for the sake of beings struggling in Māra's net of illusion. Knowing that while many will not comprehend the profound meaning of the Dharma, there will be others for whom his effort will make the difference between enlightenment and endless pain, the Buddha decides to teach the Dharma.

11. Dharmacakrapravartana, Turning the Wheel of Dharma P: 927 B.C.E. T: 588 B.C.E. C: 531 B.C.E. Perceiving that his five former companions are most likely to benefit from hearing the teachings of liberation, the Buddha travels to the Deer Park of Sārnāth where the five are residing. Here he first turns the wheel of the Dharma, stating the view, reflections, and path that lead to enlightenment. The Vinayavastu describes how, as the Buddha's first five disciples hear this teaching, first Kauṇḍīnya, then Vāṣpa, Bhadrika, Mahānāman, and Aśvajit in turn awaken to full understanding. Their realization confirms that the Buddhadharma can be transmitted to human beings and gives rise to the Ārya Sangha, the community that implements the Buddha's teaching in action and realization. The Three Jewels—the Buddha, Dharma, and Sangha—are now manifest in the world.

"When delusive mental activity is understood,
this complex of production is no more.
The ignorance which brings it forth does not arise:
There is nothing for it to come from.
When the cause of karmic dispositions is removed,
there is no driving influence
drawing one thing after another. . . .

There is no conceptual activity, no conceptualization;
there is only the expression of the way things are.
Knowing the way things are,
there is no more ignorance.
When there is no more ignorance,
all the branches of existence are extinguished;
they do not arise."

—Voice of the Buddha II:633–34

45 B.N. The Buddha teaches the Dharma for forty-five years, from his enlightenment at the age of thirty-five until his eighty-first year, when he passes away near the town of Kuśinagara. Wherever he travels, thousands gather to hear his teachings, from practiced ascetics to householders bound to the lay life. The Sūtras describe the human and non-human beings that come to hear the Dharma: nāgas, celestial beings, gods of the heavenly realms, and hosts of Bodhisattvas, representing the most developed levels of consciousness. All hear the teachings according to their capacities for understanding.

Three Turnings of the Dharma Wheel In his physical embodiment as Śākyamuni, the Sage of the Śākyas, the Buddha reveals the Dharma to human beings in three major phases known as the Three Turnings of the Wheel of the Dharma. Emanating directly from the heart of enlightenment, such teachings have never before been heard in our age. For all sentient beings, they extend the limits of knowledge and open the way to liberation.

Tradition holds that for the first seven years after enlightenment, the Buddha teaches the foundation of the Dharma, known as the First Turning. (Although the years in which the Buddha imparts each of the Three Turnings have also been calculated, sources vary, and the Three Turnings do not necessarily follow a chronological order.) During this time the Buddha emphasizes the Four Noble Truths, the chain of interdependent cooperation, and the path of the Arhats, the saints whose realization stops the production of karma and frees them from bondage to samsara. As the disciples are able to comprehend the all-pervasive nature of suffering, the Buddha explains exactly how suffering arises. When the disciples see how the chains that entrap them are forged, the Buddha points out the path to liberation. While the Enlightened One can inspire and illuminate the way, those who wish to benefit from his experience must themselves follow the path to its end.

For the Brāhmanic tradition that relies on a priestly class skilled in rituals and propitiation of many gods, the Buddha's teachings of salvation through one's own efforts are truly revolutionary. Faith itself is not sufficient for liberation, for unless faith is tested and confirmed through direct experience, it cannot support the growth of knowledge. Uninformed by knowledge, faith is blind, and those who act out of blind faith can easily lose their way. Buddhism teaches the value of faith linked with wisdom, each in turn leading the other, as the feet do in walking. Thus faith, continually strengthened and verified through experience, transforms into knowledge, enabling practitioners to take responsibility for their spiritual education and participate actively in the process of liberation. Those who support unquestioning acceptance of religious dogma have sometimes opposed Buddhism for its emphasis on individual investigation and responsibility.

Through the years, the Buddha's interaction with his disciples forges the Sangha, the community dedicated to realizing in their own experience the truth of the Buddha's way. Their shared experience gives rise to the teachings of the Vinaya, the code of conduct for the Sangha; the Sūtras that support the Sangha's practice; and the more technical teachings that outline topics to be examined by the disciples in greater detail. These technical teachings, which will be further delineated for centuries after the Buddha's Parinirvāṇa, become the foundation of the Abhidharma.

12, 27, 30, or 31 years A.E. (Bu 52) Turning the Dharma Wheel a second time on the Vulture Peak near Rājagṛha, the Buddha reveals the profundity of omniscient knowledge in teachings given to multitudes of celestial beings, innumerable Bodhisattvas, and to assemblies of monks, nuns, laymen, and laywomen. The foundation of the Second Turning teachings is Prajñāpāramitā, the perfection of wisdom called the Mother of the Buddhas, omniscience that transcends all ordinary understanding. At its heart is the teaching of śūnyatā, the emptiness of all constituents of existence, and the path of the great Bodhisattvas, the spiritual heroes who forego the fruits of their realization to work for the enlightenment of others.

7, 9, 10, 12, 26, 27 years A.E. (Bu 54) Turning the wheel of the Dharma a third time, the Buddha reveals the unsurpassable teaching discriminating between provisional and ultimate reality. In the Sūtras that present the teaching of Tathāgatagarbha, the enlightened nature inherent in all beings, the Buddha removes the basis for the extreme views of nihilism and eternalism in order to guide beings to the view of the middle way. In these and in other Third Turning teachings he reveals the infinite breadth and beauty of the Enlightened Ones' field of activity, the vastness of the path, the purity of all experience, and the inexpressible wonder of being. Often classified among the Third Turning teachings are the Daśabhūmika and Gaṇḍavyūha Sūtras, chapters thirty-one and forty-five of the extensive Avataṁsaka Sūtra, together with the rest of this teaching and many of the forty-eight chapters of the Ratnakūṭa Sūtra.

Set in motion at Bodhimaṇḍa (the seat of enlightenment), at Mount Malaya, in Vaiśālī, and elsewhere, these teachings are accessible only to those whose spiritual capacities are well-developed, enabling them to realize the full implications of the Buddha's enlightenment. Entrusted to the great Bodhisattvas, the teachings of the Second and Third Turnings emerge over time, as the followers of the Buddha develop their practice of the First Turning teachings and deepen their understanding through meditation.

Through the centuries, the teachings of enlightenment are called forth in ever-widening cycles according to the changing needs and capacities of human beings. Whereas the Sūtras appear in various times and places, the teachings of the most sublime Atiyoga Tantras (also known as Mahāsaṁdhi, or the teachings of the Great Perfection) remain in the Dharmakāya realm at Vajrāsana imperceptible to ordinary beings. They are brought forth centuries after the enlightenment and imparted to the great Vidyādharas, bearers of realized knowledge who protect them and ensure their transmission.

1 A.E. Buddha's 36th year At Sārnāth, where the Buddha spends the first three-month rainy season in the Deer Park, the Sangha of monks expands to sixty: Kauṇḍīnya and the other four first disciples; Yaśas and his friends Pūrṇa, Vimala, Gavāṁpati, and Subāhu; and fifty more young men from the leading families of Vārāṇasī. The Buddha sends these early disciples to travel "no two by the same road" as they carry the Dharma throughout the land. Alone, the Buddha begins his journey east to Rājagṛha (modern Rajgir), as he had promised King Bimbisāra. On the way he stops at Uruvilvā, where he converts the

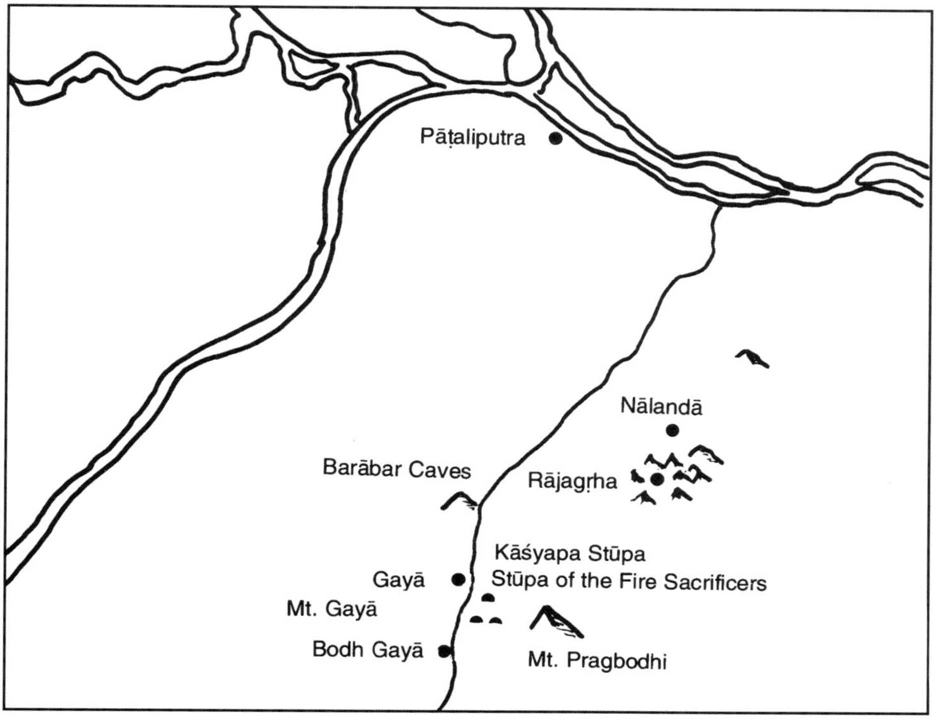

fire-worshipper Uruvilva Kāśyapa, then 120 years old, and his younger brothers Nadi and Gāya Kāśyapa. All three brothers, famous leaders of large groups of ascetics, join the Sangha together with their thousand disciples.(R 38–41)

At Gayāśīrṣa, or Mount Gayā, he teaches this assembly of one thousand monks the Aditta-pariyaya and the Gayāśīrṣa Sūtra, explaining how the fires of greed, anger, and attachment consume life and happiness and how the Dharma liberates beings from sorrow.

While resting at Uruvilvā, the Buddha visits the land of the Kurus in the northwest. Then, nine months after his enlightenment, he appears in Śrī Laṅkā, where he clears the island of yakṣas and prepares it for human habitation. A multitude of gods gathers to praise this act and to hear the Buddha speak the Dharma. The Buddha gives their leader Sumana a lock of his hair; Sumana builds the Mahiyaṅgama Thūpa (Stūpa) here and enshrines the hair-relic within. (MV I:1–43)

2 A.E. Buddha's 37th year As the Buddha approaches the southern gate of Rājagṛha, he stops to rest at the Supratiṣṭha shrine in the Sapling Grove. Hearing of his arrival, King Bimbisāra comes to greet the Blessed One, accompanied by a great throng of attendants. Welcoming the Buddha and the Sangha, Bimbisāra gives them his royal garden, the Bamboo Grove, as a dwelling-place near the city. (R 41–43) Here, in the fragrant flower-filled garden rimmed with graceful fronds of bamboo, the Buddha passes the second rainy season retreat with his disciples, now a thousand in number.

Passages in the Sūtras preserved in the bKa'-'gyur and in the Pāli Canon mention that in this grove the Enlightened One gives teachings on such topics as the Four Truths, impermanence, and the nature of conditioned existence, and speaks of the way of life that can ensure the well-being of the Sangha. Members of the royal family, ministers, and laymen come to the Bamboo Grove to hear the Buddha's words. Even the devas descend from the heavenly realms to question the Buddha on points of Dharma. In Rājagṛha alone the Buddha establishes the king, several hundred thousand disciples, and numerous inhabitants of the heavenly realms in the Dharma.

North of Rājagṛha are a number of small but prosperous villages where Bimbisāra's counselors and those who serve the royal court dwell. From Nālandā and other villages come three of the Buddha's most outstanding disciples, all of whom are highly educated Brahmins: Maudgalyāyana, the disciple foremost in intuitive understanding; Śāriputra, the disciple foremost in understanding the Abhidharma, and Mahākāśyapa, the great ascetic, from the village of Mahātiṣṭha.

Although married for several years, Mahākāśyapa and his wife have lived as brother and sister, both desiring to lead a religious life. The day after the Buddha's enlightenment, Mahākāśyapa, encouraged by his wife, leaves home to become a mendicant monk. Meeting the Buddha on the road between Nālandā and Rājagṛha, Mahākāśyapa immediately recognizes the Enlightened One as his master and casts himself down before him. The Buddha ordains him and honors the great disciple by exchanging outer robes with him.

Śāriputra and Maudgalyāyana, disciples of the skeptic philosopher Sañjāya, meet the Buddha's disciple Aśvajit in Rājagṛha and awaken faith upon hearing him recite a short summary of the Four Noble Truths known as the Ye Dharma: "All things arise from a cause. The Tathāgata has explained the cause. The cause has been completely destroyed. This is the teaching of the Great Śrāmaṇa."

Upon the death of their teacher Sañjāya, Śāriputra and Maudgalyāyana join the Sangha together with Sañjāya's two hundred and fifty disciples. With this the Sangha increases to 1,250 monks. A few weeks later, while residing in the Sukarakhata Cave on the Vulture Peak, the Buddha teaches the Dharma for the benefit of Śāriputra's uncle, the long-nailed skeptic Dīrghanākha. Hearing this teaching, both Śāriputra and Maudgalyāyana become Arhats and Dīrghanākha is freed from all doubt. (R 44–45)

At Rājagṛha the Buddha meets the philosopher Pūrṇa of Kosala, who in his pride comes to Rājagṛha to debate with the Enlightened One. Greeting Pūrṇa, the Buddha convinces him that debate is futile; only through dialogue can one open one's heart to the teaching of liberation. With this, Pūrṇa and his twenty-four students seek ordination and thereafter devote their talents to the study and practice of the Buddha's teaching. Pūrṇa, skilled in conveying the words of the Buddha to others, becomes one of the Blessed One's ten foremost disciples.

3 A.E. Buddha's 38th year Soon after the enlightenment, the Buddha returns to Kapilavastu at his father's request, as recorded in the teaching known as the Meeting of Father and Son. To the astonishment of the Śākyas, King Śuddhodana pays homage to the Buddha, as he had done years ago when his son, then a child, entered a deep meditation and manifested great spiritual power. The king now reminds his son of the beauty and pleasure of his former life, but falls silent upon hearing the Buddha contrast these worldly delights with the blessings of enlightenment.

At Kapilavastu, the Buddha ordains his cousin Nanda and asks Śāriputra to ordain his son Rāhula, who according to some accounts was born shortly before the Buddha left home and was then nine years old. (Other accounts relate that Rāhula was conceived before the home-departure and was born on the day of the Buddha's enlightenment. In these accounts the Buddha returns to Kapilavastu six years after the enlightenment, when Rāhula is six or seven years old.) While at Kapilavastu the Sangha dwells in the Nyagrodha (Banyan) Grove built for their use by the king. In this spacious grove the Buddha accepts three major lay conversions: first his uncle Śuklodana and seventy thousand Śākyas, then his former father-in-law Daṇḍapāṇi with sixty-six thousand Śākyas, followed by his kinsman Amṛtodana and seventy-five thousand Śakyas. Soon afterward, King Śuddhodana and the Buddha's former wife Gopā also become lay disciples.

While attending the Buddha in the Banyan Grove, Mahānāman, the Buddha's cousin, asks what quality in himself encourages the greed, aversion, and confusion that persist in taking hold of his mind. To Mahānāman and the assembled Śākyas, the Buddha gives the Cūḷadukkhakkhandha Sutta, a teaching of the way of the mendicant monk, by which one abandons attachment and dwells in happiness greater than that of kings.

After the Buddha departs from Kapilavastu and travels southeast to the kingdom of the Mallas, five hundred of his countrymen follow him to request ordination, including his cousins Ānanda, Aniruddha, and Devadatta. King Śuddhodana, hearing of their intention, sends his barber Upāli to shave their heads and beards. When Upāli completes his task, the young Śākyas give him their princely ornaments and send him back to Kapilavastu. But the low-caste Upāli, impressed by the Śākyas' willingness to abandon worldly riches, conceives a great desire to follow the Buddha's way; hanging the ornaments on the branches of trees for anyone to take, he follows the Śākyas to where the Buddha is residing.

At the Buddha's request, Upāli the barber is ordained first, before the noble sons of the Śākyas. So devoted is he to the Buddha's way that he becomes one of the ten great disciples, foremost in keeping the precepts. Ānanda becomes the disciple renowned for his having heard every word spoken by the Buddha, and Aniruddha becomes known as the disciple foremost in divine insight. Rāhula, the Buddha's physical son, becomes the very root of the Vinaya lineage, renowned as the disciple foremost in quietly doing good.

After a time, the Buddha returns with the Sangha to Rājagṛha, where he spends the third rainy season retreat in the Bamboo Grove. (R 52–59) The five hills that enclose the ancient city of Rājagṛha harbor numerous caves that have long served as meditation sites for sages and ascetics. The valley itself is watered by two rivers, the Tapodā, fed by hot springs, and the Sarpinī. The Sūtras record the names of places near Rājagṛha used by the Buddha and his disciples for meditation and teaching, including the Tapodā hot springs, the Saptaparṇī and Indraśaila caves, and the groves on Mt. Vaibhāra and on the Sarpaśuṇḍika-pragbhara. The Buddha and his disciples also stay at Jīvaka's Mango Grove, where the royal physician Jīvaka, a son of King Bimbisāra, attends the Sangha. Foundations of ancient vihāras can still be seen at this site today.

Of all Rājagṛha's spiritually powerful places, the most famous and enduring is Gṛdhrakūṭa, the Vulture Peak Mountain. Here, at the appropriate time (see page 103), the Buddha sets in motion the teachings of the Second Turning, including the Saddharmapuṇḍarīka (The Lotus of the True Law) and the profound Prajñāpāramitā.

When the Enlightened One teaches the Mahāratnakūṭa Sūtra on Vulture Peak, "Through the virtue of the Tathāgata, this monarch of mountains is bounteous and majestic and radiates splendor and beauty. Its slopes are adorned with a vast array of flowers and fruit trees. By the power of the Buddha, yakṣas and tribes of savages live here peacefully, as do birds and wild animals of every kind. On the mountain, streams, lakes, and ponds are covered with lotuses, their banks fragrant with a vast variety of herbs. The rain clouds crowning Vulture Peak are swept away by the mighty voices of the gods to reveal sparkling skies. High grasses the color of a peacock's throat cover the slopes, and the ground gives spring to the step. Lotuses the color of gold, crystal, and fire diffuse an incomparable fragrance throughout the ten directions."

From a promontory atop Vulture Peak, the Buddha and the Sangha can view the old city of Rājagṛha nestled in the bowl formed by the surrounding mountains, with King Bimbisāra's palace a short distance from the southern gate. Two and a half millenia later, pilgrims will still see and marvel at the massive rock walls that protected the city in the Buddha's time.

4 A.E. Buddha's 39th year After the third rainy season, while dwelling in Rājagṛha, the Buddha meets Anāthapiṇḍada, a wealthy merchant from Śrāvastī. Anāthapiṇḍada, who soon becomes one of the Sangha's most loyal and generous patrons, invites the Buddha to Śrāvastī and purchases Prince Jeta's royal garden to prepare a suitable dwelling.

The Vinaya relates that the Gandhakuṭi, the central structure of the vihāra, will eventually hold sixty large and sixty small halls ornamented according to the Buddha's instructions. The Acintyaprabhāsa-nirdeśa Sūtra records that, as the Enlightened One enters the city gates, the blind see, the deaf hear, and the naked are clothed. All beings in the city, filled with faith in the Dharma, pay homage to the Buddha.

The Buddha names the vihāra Anāthapiṇḍadārāma in honor of the devoted merchant and names the park Jetavana, Jeta's Grove, in honor of Prince Jeta. In the years that follow, the Buddha gives hundreds of teachings in Jeta's Grove and shapes the growth of the Sangha. Here the Buddha receives

Prasenajit, king of Kosala, the largest and most powerful kingdom of the time, who arrives with a great entourage of attendants, musicians, and townspeople. The Sūtras preserve specific teachings given to King Prasenajit and his wives, including the Prasenajid-gāthā (NE 322), verses enumerating the blessings that arise from honoring the Tathāgatas, shaping their images, and making specific types of offerings. The king, his wives, and his attendants all become lay disciples. The Buddha spends the fourth rainy season with the Sangha either in Jeta's Grove or in Rājagṛha. (R 47–49)

5 A.E. Buddha's 40th year The Pāli chronicles record that the Buddha visits Śrī Laṅkā a second time in the fifth year after his enlightenment, while residing in Jeta's Grove. In Śrī Laṅkā the Enlightened One pacifies warring groups of nāgas, converts them to the Dharma, and plants a rājāyatana tree to commemorate this event. (MV I:44–70)

After the fourth rainy season, while the Buddha is dwelling in the Bamboo Grove at Rājagṛha, he responds to a request to visit Vaiśālī, which is suffering from an epidemic that neither the doctors nor the spiritual masters there can relieve. The Buddha sends Ānanda to say prayers while circumambulating the city, and the epidemic subsides during the Buddha's visit. This action wins the hearts of the tribes that formed the Vṛjjian confederacy, who welcome the frequent visits of the Buddha and his disciples. The citizens of Vaiśālī build a vihāra in the Mahāvana, or Large Grove, where the Buddha spends the fifth rainy season retreat.

Some time later, the courtesan Āmrapālī joins the lay Sangha and donates the Āmrapālīvana, the Mango Grove, to the Buddha and Sangha. Both the Mahāvana and the Āmrapālīvana become sites of numerous teachings, including a teaching by the layman Vimalakīrti, who engages in a famous dialogue with Mañjuśrī, emanation of the Buddha's enlightened wisdom. Inspired by the Blessed One, Vimalakīrti speaks on the nature of sickness experienced by a Bodhisattva and teaches

Śāriputra and Maudgalyāna the nature of a Bodhisattva's power, knowledge, and skill in liberating others. From the teachings of Mañjuśrī and Vimalakīrti, a hundred thousand beings awaken the thought of enlightenment, and ten thousand Bodhisattvas advance to a higher stage of the path.

The Teaching of Vimalakīrti describes the splendors that precede this teaching, when the Licchavi Ratnākara comes forth from the city of Vaiśālī accompanied by five hundred Licchavi youths, all bearing parasols made from seven kinds of precious jewels. Approaching the seated Buddha, they circumambulate the Enlightened One and place before him their offering of parasols. By the miraculous power of the Blessed One, the parasols are transformed into a great canopy that arches over the entire great galaxy of a billion worlds. In its reflection, all present can clearly see the manifold realms of gods and men.

At this, the Licchavi Ratnākara praises the matchless qualities of the Buddha; in response to Ratnākara's question, the Awakened One explains the nature of a Bodhisattva's Buddhafield, which gives scope for a Bodhisattva's practice and attainments. This teaching alone liberates eight thousand monks from mental obscurations and clarifies the nature of perfect enlightenment for eighty-four thousand Bodhisattvas.

Once, when the Buddha visits the Mahāvana, a monkey offers him a gift of honey beside a pool; for this event Vaiśālī will become known as one of the eight great wonders. A century or more later, the Dharma King Aśoka will erect a lion-topped pillar at the site of this "monkey pool."

6 A.E. Buddha's 41st year From Vaiśālī the Buddha travels to Kapilavastu, where he attends his dying father and dwells in the Banyan Grove. After his father's death, his foster mother Mahāprajāpatī, Gopā, and five hundred Śākyan women seek full ordination into the Sangha, but the Buddha encourages them rather to seek fulfillment as laywomen. When he departs from Kapilavastu on his way to Śrāvastī, the women follow, and the disciple Ānanda repeats their request.

After three requests, the Buddha ordains the women, establishing the order of bhikṣuṇīs headed by his aunt and stepmother Mahāprajāpatī. (R 60–62) King Prasenajit builds the Rājakārāma, a large convent for the bhikṣuṇīs, near Jeta's Grove, and Śrāvastī becomes their central home. (Generations later, Sanghamittā, daughter of King Aśoka, will bring Mahāprajāpatī's bhikṣuṇī lineage to Śrī Laṅkā, where it continues today.) The Buddha returns to Rājagṛha the following year; the Vinaya records that he spends the sixth rainy season near Rājagṛha on Mt. Golāṅgula (Pāli: Mankuta or Makula Hill).

7 A.E. Buddha's 42nd year When the rains have passed, six famous spiritual masters known as the "six philosophers," jealous of the Sangha's success, challenge the Buddha to a demonstration of powers at Śrāvastī. Seeing that this event cannot be avoided, the Buddha travels to Śrāvastī and defeats the philosophers by demonstrating the Miracle of the Pairs.

After this display, the Buddha creates a wondrous array of Buddhas filling the vast extent of the heavens, and spectators behold the Blessed One walking through the sky on a golden pathway. Then the Enlightened One ascends to the Trāyastriṁśa Heaven, where he dwells for the seventh rainy season and teaches the Abhidharma for the benefit of his mother and many gods. (R 79–81) In the assembly hall at Jeta's Grove, a sandalwood statue of the Buddha remains in his place to remind the Sangha of his continuing presence.

When his sojourn in the Trāyastriṁśa Heaven comes to an end, the Buddha descends to earth on a celestial ladder at Saṁkāśya, an ancient city some distance southwest of Śrāvastī. A temple will later be built at the site of the ladder, which sinks into the ground after the Buddha's departure. The Sangha welcomes the Blessed One upon his return and accompanies him to Śrāvastī. (R 81)

Soon after the formation of the Sangha, disciples begin to carry the Buddha's teachings beyond the groves and cities of Magadha and Kosala. In Kauśāmbī, the capital of Vatsa, a kingdom west of Kosala, Piṇḍola Bharadvāja introduces the Dharma to the court of King Udāyana. Inspired by the teachings, the king's son Vajrīputra joins the Sangha. Later, with Piṇḍola, he becomes one of the Sixteen Great Arhats who pledge to forego entering nirvana in order to watch over the Sangha and preserve the purity of the Buddhadharma.

8 A.E. Buddha's 43rd year Pacifying King Udāyana's jealousy, Piṇḍola gains his trust and is permitted to teach the king's wives and their attendants. After meeting the Buddha in Jeta's Grove at Śrāvastī, three merchants of Kauśāmbī—Ghoṣita, Kukkuṭa, and Pāvārika—invite the Buddha to their city. Returning home, each of the merchants builds a place of retreat (ārāma) for the Sangha. (All three of these places—the Ghoṣitārāma, Kukkuṭārāma, and Pāvārikārāma—become important centers during the Buddha's lifetime.) On his way to Kauśāmbī the Blessed One passes the eighth rainy season in the Bhesakala Grove on Siśumāra Hill (Pāli: Suṁsumāra Hill).

At the invitation of the nāga-king Maṇikkhika, the Buddha appears a third time in Śrī Laṅkā accompanied by five hundred bhikṣus. The Blessed One leaves his footprints on Mt. Sumanakūṭa and visits the future sites of the Mahāmegha Monastery, the Bodhi tree that will be brought by Aśoka's daughter, the Great Thūpa of Anurādhapura, and the Thūpārāma, the monastery associated with the Great Thūpa. (MV I: 71–84)

9–11 A.E. Buddha's 44th through 46th years The Buddha dwells near Kauśāmbī for nearly a year. He passes the ninth rainy season here and gives teachings on the importance of maintaining harmony in the Sangha at the Ghoṣita Monastery. During the following season of rains, the Enlightened One, attended only by wild elephants, dwells alone in the Pārileyyaka Forest before beginning the long journey to Rājagṛha, where he spends the eleventh rainy season.

12 A.E. Buddha's 47th year Invited to Vairantī (Verañjana), a city west of Mathurā, the Buddha begins the long journey northwest to the land of the Kurus, a people strongly influenced by Brāhmanic traditions. The Vinaya records that this journey is difficult; famine is ravaging the land and alms are hard to obtain.

Near Mathurā, in answer to Śāriputra's question as to how the Buddha's teaching may prosper for a long time, the Blessed One speaks of the Prātimokṣa, the guidelines for the conduct of monks which in the times of previous Buddhas have ensured the integrity of the Sangha. Up to this time, Śākyamuni's Sangha has been formed of highly developed monks, and the need for the Prātimokṣa has not yet arisen. Although the Buddha does not return to this region, several of his disciples return to teach in Mathurā, and great patriarchs firmly establish the Dharma here after the Buddha's Parinirvāṇa. In time Mathurā becomes a strong center for Vinaya and Abhidharma studies as well as a major artistic center renowned for its stone images of the Buddha.

13–14 A.E. Buddha's 48th through 49th years During the thirteenth rainy season, the Buddha dwells with the Sangha on Caityagiri (Stūpa Hill), a name associated with Sāñcī, a major Buddhist center at the time of Aśoka. The next year he spends the fourteenth rainy season in Jeta's Grove near Śrāvastī.

15–17 A.E. Buddha's 50th through 52nd years Hearing that his kinsmen are engaged in a difficult border dispute with a neighboring land, Śākyamuni travels to Kapilavastu, where he spends the fifteenth rainy season in the Banyan Grove. The next year he dwells in the Atavaka (Pāli, Ālavi) Forest near Śrāvastī during the rains; the following year he returns to Rājagṛha, where he spends the seventeenth rainy season.

18–20 A.E. Buddha's 53rd through 55th years Traveling west, the Blessed One and the Sangha stop at Jvālinī Hill near Gayā for the eighteenth rainy season, and return to spend the nineteenth rainy season here as well. During the twentieth rainy season, the Buddha dwells at Rājagṛha (Śrāvastī in the Theravādin tradition).

Historical accounts preserved in the Vinaya texts describe how, for the first twenty years after his enlightenment, the Buddha travels nearly continuously. During this time he teaches in Śrāvastī, Vaiśālī, Rājagṛha, Kapilavastu, Sārnāth, in the vicinity of Gayā and other places in Magadha, traveling as far east as Campā, near the modern boundary between Bihar and West Bengal. At the age of fifty-five, the Buddha accepts Ānanda as his personal attendant and designates Śrāvastī as a permanent site for the rainy season retreat. Thereafter he appears to have spent much of his time in Śrāvastī, building a firm foundation for the Sangha and developing the Vinaya guidelines preserved in the Prātimokṣa.

Śrāvastī, the prosperous capital of the kingdom of Kosala, proves an ideal center for the Sangha. In the Buddha's day, fifty-seven thousand families live within its walls, surrounded by rich wheat fields nourished by the waters of the Achiravatī (modern Rapti) River. The town is bordered by thick forests: the Jālinī Forest where the Buddha converts Aṅgulimāla the murderer, notorious for wearing a garland of fingers, and the Ālavi Forest where he eases the suffering of a wild yakṣa.

Trade routes radiating out from Śrāvastī enable monks as well as merchants to travel throughout northern India. To the north, a road links Śrāvastī with Mathurā, gateway to the route west across the plains to Takṣaśilā and other cities in Gandhāra. To the southwest, another major route connects Śrāvastī with Saketa, Kauśāmbī, Vidiśa, Ujjain, and Paithana on the Godavarī River. A third route to the southeast links the countries of Kosala, Śākya, the Vṛjjian confederacy, and Magadha; passing through Kapilavastu and Kuśinagara to Pāvā, it continues through Vaiśālī and ends at Rājagṛha. It is this route the Buddha travels on his final journey.

In the course of the Buddha's life, Śrāvastī becomes the site of three major homes for the Sangha. As named in the Vinaya, they are Jeta's Grove and the Pūrvārāma, located near the city, and the Rājakārāma, the convent for nuns built inside the city walls. In Jeta's Grove is the Gandhakuṭi, the Hall of Fragrance, where the Buddha dwells and teaches the Dharma. To the north is the Blind Man's Grove, also known as the Wood of Recovered Sight, where five hundred men blinded for their misdeeds by King Prasenajit regain their vision upon hearing the Buddha teach the Dharma. Overcome with joy, the men drive their staffs into the ground and prostrate themselves before the Buddha in gratitude. The staffs take root and become a thick grove of trees, a favorite place for meditation by the disciples living in Jeta's Grove.

Close by the Pūrvārāma is the Ekasalakatinduka Grove of Queen Māllikā, King Prasenajit's wife, where monks and wandering ascetics can find shelter and meditate. These and other sites named in the Sūtras can be seen in the ruins of Śrāvasti at the twin archaeological sites known as Saheṭh-Maheṭh.

21–44 A.E. Buddha's 56th through 79th years As the Sangha expands and attracts people of diverse backgrounds to renounce the world for the wandering life, the Buddha gives clear rules for ordaining monks and nuns and explains the eight forms of Sangha: bhikṣu and bhikṣuṇī, fully ordained monks and nuns; śrāmana and śrāmaṇī, men and women who have taken the vows of the novice; śīkṣamāṇas, those not yet old enough to receive full ordination; upavasthas, laymen who assume temporary vows; and upāsakas and upāsikās, men and women who remain householders and follow the lay precepts.

At Śrāvasti, in Jeta's Grove, the Buddha explains to the monks the importance of ridding themselves of the five major impediments to realization: doubts about the teacher, the Dharma, and the training; and anger and displeasure with the Sangha. These five factors lead to the five bondages: attachment to sense-pleasures that create desire and lead to thirst and craving; attachment to body; attachment to material shapes; attachment to food; and aspiration to be reborn as a deva in the god-realms. In the teaching known as the Cetokhila Sutta (DN 16), the Buddha teaches that a monk who roots out these five mental bondages increases maturity and discipline and cultivates the four bases of supernormal powers.

At Śrāvastī, having heard monks praising the virtues of the disciple Pūrṇa, Śāriputra follows Pūrṇa into the Blind Man's Grove and meditates nearby until Pūrṇa rises from his meditation. Then, engaging Pūrṇa in a dialogue concerning the purpose of his practice, Śāriputra questions him on the connection between purity of moral purpose, mind, view, abandoning doubt, and the manner of entering into knowledge and insight. In response, Pūrṇa uses the image of a chariot relay to describe how purity of moral purpose becomes the basis of purity of mind, and purity of mind the basis for purity of view, and so forth until the purpose of attaining nirvana is completely fulfilled. So eloquently does Pūrṇa speak that Śāriputra hears as though listening to the words of the Buddha. For his clarity of speech and thought, and for his excellence in numerous other virtues, Pūrṇa becomes known as the disciple foremost in teaching the Dharma. (MN 24)

21 A.E. Buddha's 56th year The patroness Viśākhā, also known as "Mother Mṛgara," donates her jewels to build for the Sangha the magnificent Pūrvārāma, the Eastern Monastery, in Śrāvastī a short distance southwest of Jeta's Grove. According to the Vinaya, the Blessed One spends the twenty-first through twenty-fourth rainy seasons here.

While dwelling in the Pūrvārāma, the Buddha summarizes for the Sangha of monks and nuns the categories of his teachings to be held in mind, remembered, and illuminated through study and practice. Among the more detailed of these summaries is the Arthaviniścāya Sūtra, the Compendium of Categories, which lists and succinctly defines the five aggregates (skandhas), the five aggregates of clinging, the eighteen elements (dhātus), the twelve sense-fields (āyatānas), the twelve limbs of pratītyasamutpāda, the Four Noble Truths, the four meditations, the four formless attainments, the four sublime

The Ārya Sangha

Homage to the great Arhats, exemplars of the Dharma

Sixteen Great Arhats

While the Buddha lived, many thousands of disciples calmed body and mind and completely purified all karmic influences to attain the state of an Arhat. Liberated from the endless rounds of samsaric existence, Arhats were no longer subject to rebirth and could pass into nirvana at will. When Śāriputra and Maudgalyāyana passed away, their disciples, one hundred fifty thousand in all, immediately entered nirvana.

Knowing that most of his disciples would also choose to enter nirvana upon his passing from life, the Buddha asked sixteen great Arhats to remain in the world and watch over the Dharma as long as beings were capable of benefiting from the teachings. At that time, the sixteen Arhats vowed to remain until the coming of Maitreya, the future Buddha.

Over the centuries, the sixteen great Arhats have appeared upon occasion to encourage the devoted and support confidence in the Dharma. Their spiritual energy, still present in our world, continues to protect and guide the Sangha.

The artistic traditions of China and Tibet represent the sixteen great Arhats as bearing iconographic symbols that support the development of spiritual qualities. Meditation on the great Arhats and the symbols they carry strengthens aspiration and stimulates insight into the Buddhist teachings. Biographies of the sixteen Arhats preserved in the Tibetan tradition indicate their native lands, their current dwelling places, and the special qualities of their iconography. (See Loden Sherap Dagyab, *Tibetan Religious Art, Part I: Texts*. Wiesbaden, 1977.)

1. Aṅgaja A native of Rājagṛha, the great Arhat Aṅgaja now dwells on Mt. Kailāśa. Those who visualize Aṅgaja, see his flywhisk, or smell the fragrance of the incense he carries, obtain freedom from the six major and twenty minor emotions which bring misery to human beings.

2. Ajita Originally from Śrāvastī, the great Arhat Ajita now dwells on Drang-srong, the hermit-sage mountain. Those who pray to Ajita obtain protection from harm and develop steadfast determination to persevere in Dharma practice.

3. Vanavāsin Born in Kosala, the great Arhat Vanavāsin now dwells in the mountain cave of Saptaparṇi, site of the First Council. Those who pray to Vanavāsin protect themselves from distraction and obtain fulfillment of all their wishes.

4. Kālika The great Arhat Kālika, who joined the Sangha in Śrāvastī, now dwells in Tamradvīpa or Śrī Laṅkā. Those who pray to Kālika develop compassion and gain the power to set others on the path to enlightenment.

5. Vajrīputra Son of Udāyana, king of Kauśāmbi, the great Arhat Vajrīputra now dwells in Śrī Laṅkā. His flywhisk confers wisdom and mental discipline as well as infinite radiance that attracts others to the Dharma. Those who see and reflect upon the form of this great Arhat receive answers to their prayers.

6. Śrībhadra The great Arhat Śrībhadra, who came from the Śākyan kingdom, joined the Sangha in Kapilavastu. He now dwells on an island in the Yamunā River (Yamunādvīpa). His gestures enable one to discern wrong paths, overcome habitual patterns that lead to suffering, and acquire spiritual powers that attract others to the Dharma.

7. Kanakavatsa The great Arhat Kanakavatsa dwells on the Saffron Hill. Those who honor and pray to Kanakavatsa will never be separated from their teachers; dignified in bearing, honored and respected by all beings, they will enjoy the friendship of kings and sages alike.

8. Kanakabharadvāja A native of Śrāvastī, the great Arhat Kanakabharadvāja now dwells on Godānīya, the Western Continent. Those who pray to him obtain opportunities to view the face of a Buddha, practice the six pāramitās, and progress on the stages of the path.

9. Bakula The great Arhat Bakula of Śrāvastī now dwells in a mountain cave on the Northern Continent. The mongoose he holds empowers practitioners to refine the five senses, attain the six perfections, comprehend the meaning of śūnyatā, and manifest love and compassion for all sentient beings.

10. Rāhula The great Arhat Rāhula, the Buddha's son and a primary transmitter of the Vinaya lineage, now dwells in Prīyāṅgudvīpa, in the northern region of ancient India. Those who pray to Rāhula receive the protection of the Dharmapālas. Through his blessing one becomes able to vanquish passion, comprehend the teachings, and receive the blessings of the Buddhas and Bodhisattvas.

11. Cūḍapanthaka The great Arhat Cūḍapanthaka, native of Śrāvastī, now dwells on the Vulture Peak, together with sixteen hundred Arhats. Those who pray to him become able to free themselves from desire, hatred, and ignorance, ill-will toward others, and all views that lead to suffering.

12. Piṇḍola Bharadvāja The great Arhat Piṇḍola Bharadvāja perfected the practice of subsisting solely on alms; he scrupulously adhered to the Buddha's teachings and consistently worked to benefit others. Well-known as the Arhat who brought the Dharma to Kauśāmbī, he now dwells in a mountain cave on the Eastern or Western Continent. Those who pray to him become free of suffering and obtain the blessings of wisdom and virtue.

13. Panthaka A native of Śrāvastī, the great Arhat Panthaka dwells in the Trāyastriṁśa, the Heaven of the Thirty-three Gods. Those who visualize Panthaka and see the book of teachings he holds are liberated from unfavorable karma; they become able to understand the Dharma and have opportunities to hear and follow the Mahāyāna teachings.

14. Nāgasena Born a prince in northern India, the great Arhat Nāgasena dwells on Mt. Vipulaparśva. He holds a vase which removes poverty and spiritual deficiencies and a monk's staff. Those who pray to Nāgasena and hear the bells of this staff are cleansed of all defilements and filled with confidence in the Three Jewels.

15. Gopaka Healed of a painful karmic affliction through his practice, the great Arhat Gopaka is dedicated to the teachings and assists others through his knowledge. He dwells in a cave on Mt. Bihula; those who pray to Gopaka are blessed with knowledge of the arts and sciences and awaken the discriminating awareness that relieves suffering and confers wisdom.

16. Abheda The great Arhat Abheda, born in Rājagṛha, was renowned for his knowledge and compassion. He now dwells on Mt. Gangs-can near Shambhala, in the Himalayan region north of India. All who see and meditate on the stūpa he holds in his hands gain good fortune and merit, obtain freedom from ill-favored karma, and fulfill all wishes for realization.

Time of the Great Patriarchs

The Mūlasarvāstivādin Vinaya names seven patriarchs predicted to watch over the Dharma after the Buddha's departure from life: Mahākāśyapa, Ānanda, Śāṇavāsika, Upagupta, Dhītika, Kṛṣṇa, and Mahāsudarśaṇa.

1 A.N. Patriarch Mahākāśyapa Aware that thousands of Arhats are entering nirvana and concerned for the survival of the Buddhadharma, Mahākāśyapa convenes an assembly of five hundred Arhats at Rājagṛha under the sponsorship of King Ajātaśatru. In the Saptaparṇi Cave on Mt. Vaibhara, Upāli recites the Vinaya teachings, Ānanda the Sūtras, and Mahākāsyapa the Mātṛkā, the seeds of the Abhidharma. Exercising their power of total recall, the Arhats verify that every word is exactly as the Buddha had spoken.

Then, passing the care of the Dharma to Ānanda, the great disciple begins a pilgrimage to Lumbinī, Bodh Gayā, Sārnāth, and Kuśinagara, sites of the Buddha's birth, enlightenment, first teaching, and Parinirvāṇa, and worships at the eight great stūpas built over the Buddha's relics.

Returning to Rājagṛha, Mahākāśyapa climbs Mt. Kukkuṭapāda, puts on the Buddha's robe, seats himself in meditation, and enters nirvana. The three peaks of the mountain close over him, sealing his body inside. When the future Buddha Maitreya becomes enlightened, Mahākāśyapa's body will be shown to Maitreya's disciples as an example of the excellent ones who served the Dharma of the Buddha Śākyamuni. (R160–63)

1–40 or 1–26 A.N. Patriarch Ānanda The Sangha regains its strength and expands during the forty years Ānanda serves as patriarch. (Tār 21–25) Throughout this time Ānanda supports the development of the younger monks by his example and his knowledge of the Dharma's power. As the Buddha had predicted, Ānanda ordains Śāṇavāsika, a merchant's son, who becomes the third patriarch, as well as Madhyāntika, the Arhat destined to establish the Dharma in Kashmir. Ānanda enters nirvana on an island in the Ganges River; flames envelop his body, reducing it to ashes that spontaneously form two balls of jewels. These relics are carried by the river's waves, one to the shore of Magadha and the other to the land of the Vṛjjis. (Tār 25) The people of these lands enshrine Ānanda's relics in stūpas built in Vaiśālī and Rājagṛha. (R 163–67)

Some of the Buddha's disciples continue to propagate the Dharma during Ānanda's time: Pūrṇa in Sopāraka, on the western coast; Mahākātyāyana and Soṇakuṭikarṇa in the kingdom of Avanti; and Bavari and his disciples along the route south. While some monks tend to reside in specific areas, most remain wandering mendicants. Ancient inscriptions describe this Sangha of mendicant monks as "the Sangha of the Four Directions."

5 or 8 A.N. Birth of Padmasambhava Padmasambhava, spiritual son of the Buddha Amitābha, is born from a lotus in Oḍḍiyāna and raised as the son of King Indrabhūti. Exiled from his homeland, he travels to India, where he hears the Dharma from the Buddha's disciple Ānanda and receives the teachings of the Sūtras. Ordained by the master Prabhahasti, Padmasambhava disciplines himself in the Three Yogas of body, speech, and mind and becomes known as the monk Śākya Seng-ge. (LLP, LGS)

24 or 27 A.N. Death of Ajātaśatru. (MV) His son Udayabhadra (Udāyin) becomes king of Magadha. According to Pāli sources, his successors are Anuruddha, Muṇḍa, and Nāgadāsaka, whose reign ends c. 66 A.N. According to Tāranātha, Ajātaśatru dies a year after the Patriarch Ānanda, which would place his death in 41 A.N. Tāranātha names only four successors between Ajātaśatru and Aśoka: Subāhu, Sudhanu, Mahendra, and Camaśa, who collectively rule 71 years. This would place Aśoka's coronation around 112 A.N., without accounting for Aśoka's predecessors, Candragupta Maurya and Bindusāra, which Tāranātha locates among Aśoka's later descendants.

The account in the Annals of Li-yul, preserved in Tibetan translation, relates: "King Ajātaśatru, having become king, reigned thirty-two years; five years after his accession to the throne, the Buddha passed away, after which he reigned twenty-seven years. From Ajātaśatru to Dharmāśoka there were ten generations (of kings)." (R 233) This account places Aśoka's coronation as 234 A.N.

26–43 or 41–58 A.N. Ordained by Ānanda just before the great disciple enters nirvana, the Arhat Madhyāntika teaches the Dharma in Vārāṇasī. After a time he moves north to Mathurā accompanied by ten thousand Arhats and dwells on Uśīra Hill, where the householder Aja supports the Sangha for a year. Eventually Madhyāntika's community expands to forty-four thousand Arhats. (Tār 26–27)

26–c. 66 or 42–c. 82 A.N. Patriarch Śāṇavāsika Born in Mathurā near the end of Ajātaśatru's reign, Śāṇavāsika teaches the Dharma in Śrāvastī. About this time, Magadha annexes the western kingdom of Avantī, opening the way for the more rapid growth of the Dharma in the region of Ujjain and Vidiśa. (Tār 27–28) In 50 A.N. Śāṇavāsika arrives at Gurupāda (Kukkuṭapāda) near Rājagṛha and converts two yakṣas who are spreading disease. Blessed with total recall of all that he hears, Śāṇavāsika teaches the Dharma to the four classes of Sangha in the six cities. (Tār 31)

29 A.N. Guhyapati, Lord of Secrets, turns the wheel of the Dharma on Mount Malaya. Texts containing the esoteric Tantras fall onto the palace of Indrabhūti (King Dza), ruler of the land of Zahor.

41 or after 59 A.N. Fifteen years after his ordination (or during the reign of Subāhu —Tār), Madhyāntika travels to Kashmir, where he pacifies the nāgas and receives from them nine valleys in which to establish the Dharma. He brings five hundred Arhats and a multitude of laymen to settle in Kashmir, where the nāgas predict that the Dharma will abide for one thousand years. Madhyāntika teaches the Dharma in Kashmir for twenty years. (Tār 31)

59 A.N. Death of Subāhu, king of Magadha; his son Sudhanu becomes king. (Tār 29)

82 A.N. Death of Sudhanu, king of Magadha; his son Mahendra becomes king. Śāṇavāsika ordains two thousand of Sudhanu's attendants and spends the rainy season retreat with them at Śitavana, the cremation ground near Bodh Gayā. Śāṇavāsika ordains Upagupta, who becomes an Arhat in seven days. Entrusting Upagupta with the Dharma, Śāṇavāsika enters nirvana in the eastern city of Campā. In all, Śāṇavāsika guides ten thousand disciples in attaining the state of Arhat. (Tār 32)

c. 82–? A.N. Patriarch Upagupta Upagupta, the fourth patriarch, strengthens the Dharma from Videha on the northeast to Mathurā on the northwest. In Videha, he dwells in a monastery built by the patron Vasusāra. During his first rainy season retreat, a thousand disciples become Arhats. In Mathurā, the brothers Naṭa and Bhaṇṭa, anticipating that a great Arhat will establish the Dharma there, build the Naṭabhaṇṭa Monastery on Mt. Urumuṇḍa. Upagupta goes to Mt. Gandha to teach the Dharma. (Tār 35)

85 A.N. Upagupta arrives in Mathurā and resides in the Naṭabhaṇṭa Monastery. Here Upagupta serves the Dharma for many years, defeats Māra, lord of illusion, and converts thousands to the Buddha's way. As the Buddha had predicted, Upagupta attains such a high level of realization that he becomes known as a "Buddha without the marks," referring to the thirty-two major and eighty-four accessory signs of a Great Being. The Aśokāvadāna relates that his power is so great that eighteen thousand disciples become Arhats. While the Aśokāvadāna describes Upagupta as Aśoka's guide on the Dharma king's 256-day pilgrimage of the Buddhist holy places, Tāranātha places Upagupta during the reigns of King Mahendra and Mahendra's son Camasa. (Tār 34–44)

c. 85 A.N. Arhat Uttara serves the Dharma in Baṅgala, in eastern India, where laymen build the Kukkuṭārāma for Uttara and the Sangha. The Arhat Yaśas becomes Uttara's disciple. (Tār 39)

91 A.N. Death of King Mahendra. His son Camaśa becomes king. During his reign Jaya, Sujaya, and Kalyāṇa each build temples and have images of the Buddha made for them: Jaya at Sārnāth on the site of the Buddha's first teaching, Sujaya in the Bamboo Grove of Rājagṛha, and Kalyāṇa at Vajrāsana, where he has placed an image of the Buddha's enlightenment. The great patriarch Upagupta enters nirvana at the end of King Camaśa's reign, and the Arhat Dhītika becomes patriarch. (Tār 39–45)

c. 100 A.N.? Patriarch Dhītika Dhītika, son of a rich Brahmin, leaves home to become a mendicant and wanders in search of a teacher. He meets the patriarch Upagupta in Mathurā and generates faith in the Dharma. Together with his five hundred followers, Dhītika joins the Sangha and becomes an Arhat in seven days. As patriarch, Dhītika travels widely to propagate the Dharma among the eight types of Sangha, from Thogar, north of Kashmir, to Kāmarūpa (modern Assam) in the east, and to Kauśāmbī, where he inspires the people to rebuild Ghositā Monastery and spends his last years. (Tār 45–49)

110 A.N. The Second Council of the Sangha While the patriarch Dhītika lies ill in Kauśāmbī, ten monks of Vaiśālī relax their observance of the Vinaya discipline and indulge in ten kinds of prohibited actions. The Arhat Yaśas convenes a second general council of the Sangha in Vaiśālī at the monastery of Kusumapura, supported by the patronage of King Nandin. (Tār 68) (The Mūlasarvāstivādin Vinaya mentions Dharmāśoka and the Mahāvaṁsa gives Kālāśoka as patron.) The seven hundred Arhats who attend disavow the ten practices. Harmony is restored; after formally rehearsing the Buddha's teachings, affirming their accurate transmission for the second time after the Buddha's Parinirvana, the Arhats return to their home regions. (Tār 68, R 171–80)

In the years after the Second Council, differences in implementing the Buddha's teachings persist. Within the great stream of the Dharma, two main currents—the conservative Sthaviras, or elders, and the more expansive Mahāsaṁghikas—begin to develop, leading to the formation of two major Śrāvaka traditions. According to Klong-chen-pa, the Sarvāstivādin, Mahāsāṁghika, Sthavira, and Saṁmatīya schools arise at this time. Over the next few hundred years, as Arhats and monks continue to carry the Dharma throughout India and beyond, each of these four traditions gives rise to additional branches, collectively known as the eighteen Śrāvaka schools.

Patriarch Kṛṣṇa The Arhat Kṛṣṇa, the sixth Patriarch, is entrusted with the Dharma by Dhītika, who then enters nirvāṇa at Ujjain. Kṛṣṇa, son of a prominent merchant family, is known for guiding all four classes of disciples to realization. In Kashmir he counters the false view of self being promulgated by the monk named Vatsa, a leader or a member of the school known as Vatsīputrīyas.

Kṛṣṇa propagates the Dharma from Kashmir to Śrī Laṅkā, to which he travels at the request of King Āsanasiṁhakoṣa accompanied by five hundred Arhats. In Śrī Laṅkā he teaches, builds monasteries, and strengthens the Sangha, restoring the light of the Dharma to its full brilliance. Passing the care of the Dharma to Mahāsudarśana, Kṛṣṇa enters nirvāṇa in Kuśavana in northern India. (Tār 71–73)

Patriarch Mahāsudarśana Born into a prosperous family in the western seaport of Bharukaccha, Mahāsudarśana becomes an Arhat by hearing the Arhat Śukāyana teach the Dharma. He asks Śukāyana for ordination, but is told he must first obtain his father's permission. Distressed, his father restrains him, but is himself converted by seeing his son's display of wondrous powers. Mahāsudarśana becomes the disciple of the patriarch Kṛṣṇa, who later entrusts him with the Dharma.

As the seventh patriarch, the last of those renowned as the "Great Elephants," Mahāsudarśana works for the Dharma during the reign of Aśoka. He makes great efforts to end the widespread practice of animal sacrifice and tames remote wild places west of India. In the western province of Sindh, he uses his remarkable powers to awaken respect for the Dharma among the yakṣas, nāgas, and other powerful beings. He also works extensively in the south, propagating the Dharma in the southern islands, and in the north, beyond the Himalayas, possibly as far northeast as China. (Tār 72–75)

Although dating of the patriarchs presents numerous difficulties, Tāranātha relates an account by the Paṇḍita Indradatta, who describes the period of the patriarchs as lasting for one hundred and ten years and ending during the reign of King Aśoka. (Tār 75) From Tāranātha's account, based on the avadānas compiled by Kṣemabhadra, this period would have lasted somewhat longer than one hundred and ten years.

The Time of King Aśoka

The Mañjuśrī-mūlakalpa predicts that a great Dharma king will arise one hundred years after the Parinirvāṇa. Living in the same time and land as the great patriarchs, this king will be a true Dharmacakrin ruler, the first to apply the Dharma for the well-being of his subjects and the benefit of beings in all times and places.

Dates for the beginning of Aśoka's reign given in traditional sources range from 100 or 110 A.N. to 234 or 236 A.N. Buddhist sources offer two systems of dating, often referred to by modern historians as the short and long chronologies. The Sanskrit and Chinese traditions place Aśoka at approximately 100 or 110 years after the Parinirvāṇa, naming as many as twelve kings and five major patrons between Bimbisāra and Aśoka, while the Annals of Li-Yul gives Aśoka's date as 234 A.N.

Tāranātha follows the short chronology and names five kings between Bimbisāra and Aśoka. The Mahāvaṁsa and Dīpavaṁsa, histories of Śrī Laṅkā preserved in Pāli, place

Aśoka's coronation at 218 A.N., naming thirteen kings and five Vinaya masters (Upāli, Dāsaka, Sonaka, Siggava, and Mogalliputta Tissa) between Bimbisāra and Aśoka, and describing Aśoka's Council at Pāṭaliputra as occurring in 236 A.N. The Mahāvaṁsa records that the great Dharma king reigned thirty-seven years. Modern historians generally place the date of Aśoka's reign as c. 268–232 B.C.E. or 272–237 B.C.E. The account given below reports both the Parinirvāṇa-based dates of the Mañjuśrī-mūlakalpa and the 268–232 B.C.E. dating of modern historians. The order and timing of events in Aśoka's life vary among the sources.

100 A.N.; 268 B.C.E. Upon succeeding his father Bindusāra as king of the vast empire established by his grandfather Candragupta Maurya, Aśoka conquers the fiercely independent Kaliṅgas at great cost: One hundred and fifty thousand Kaliṅgans are captured, a hundred thousand slain, and many times more die in the aftermath of the war. (Rock Edict XIII)

The Aśokāvadana describes the young Aśoka as "The Cruel," a violent and passionate man who defends his right to succession and who executes many members of his court after he succeeds in ascending the throne. Traditional Buddhist sources relate that he creates a lovely garden to entrap unwary travelers and commands an executioner to torture and slay all who enter. When the monk Samudra enters the garden and observes the suffering inflicted there, he becomes an Arhat and no torture can harm him. Seeing this miracle, Aśoka abandons his violent ways and becomes a Buddhist. (Tār, Bu) In the Tibetan tradition, Samudra is considered a manifestation of the Oḍḍiyāna Guru Padmasambhava, who performs this act to effect Aśoka's transformation into a Dharma king.

108–110 A.N.; 256–254 B.C.E. Aśoka lives close to the Sangha and performs austerities for more than a year; he formally becomes a Buddhist on or shortly before the tenth year after his coronation and proclaims his adherence to the Dharma in a rock edict at Maskī. In a series of edicts carved on stone columns and large rocks throughout his empire, he encourages his people to regard nonviolence and compassion as the highest morality and to practice generosity, truthfulness, respect for parents, self-control, concern for the happiness of others, and devotion to teachers of the Dharma.

"In the past, kings used to go on pleasure tours. On these tours they hunted and indulged in other pastimes. But King Priyadarśī became enlightened in wisdom ten years after his coronation. Since then his tours have been Dharma-tours."

—Rock Edict VIII

113 A.N., 255 B.C.E. In the thirteenth year of his reign, Aśoka issues the edict of Bhābrā, proclaiming his faith in the Three Jewels and encouraging all who follow the Buddha's way to study a specific list of teachings: The Exaltation of Moral Discipline; The Modes of Ideal Life; Fears of the Future; The Song of the Hermits; Discourse on the Saintly Life; The Questions of Upatiṣya; and The Teaching Given to Rāhula.

"It is my desire, Revered Sirs, that many monks and nuns listen to these texts on Dharma frequently and meditate on them. The lay disciples, both men and women, should do the same."

—Bhābrā Rock Edict

The Aśokāvadana relates that, soon after Aśoka becomes a Buddhist, he undertakes a 256-day pilgrimage of the holy places in company with the great Arhat Upagupta. At the most sacred sites, Aśoka erects pillars and shrines. He opens seven of the eight stūpas holding the Buddha's relics, divides the relics into eighty-four thousand portions (corresponding to the eighty-four thousand atoms believed to make up a human body), and vows to enshrine them in eighty-four thousand stūpas throughout his empire.

According to the Mañjuśrī-mūlakalpa, Aśoka gives the relics to yakṣas, ordering them to adorn the whole of Jambudvīpa with stūpas and transform the earth itself into a monument to enlightenment. The yakṣas complete the task in half a night. Aśoka then loads his chariot with precious metals and jewels and makes generous offerings at these new relic stūpas.

Accounts of pilgrims through the centuries verify that many stūpas were erected during the time of Aśoka. Archaeologists have already identified numerous locations of Aśokan stūpas ranging from South India to the Indus River, and they continue to discover remains of these ancient monuments.

The Aśokāvadana specifically describes Aśoka building stūpas at Lumbinī, Bodh Gayā, Sārnāth, and Kuśinagara to commemorate the four most sacred sites, and he probably returns to worship at these sites more than once. So often does he visit Bodh Gayā to gaze upon the Bodhi tree that one of his queens grows jealous and has the tree cut down. Aśoka's sorrow is so great, however, that the queen restores the tree with the milk of a thousand cows. To protect the tree, Aśoka encloses it within a stone railing, then celebrates by sponsoring a ceremony and distributing an enormous quantity of alms.

Aśoka erects additional monuments that can still be seen today: the pillars that stand at Lumbinī and Vaiśālī; a now-broken pillar at Sārnāth; a shrine at Nālandā marking the place of Śāriputra's birth and nirvana; and the royal monastery built in the Kukkuṭārāma, the "Rooster's Park" of Pāṭaliputra, known as the Aśokārāma in his honor. The Arhat Yaśas serves as abbot of the monastery and as Aśoka's personal counselor.

In modern times, fragments of Aśokan pillars have been found in the plains of southern Nepal, at the birthplaces of the previous Buddhas Krakucchanda and Kanakamuni. A Nepalese tradition holds that during his pilgrimage Aśoka travels northeast from Lumbinī and founds the city of Patan, where he builds five shrines, four of which still exist today. This same tradition records that Aśoka's daughter Cārumatī marries Devapāla, a Nepalese noble who founds the town of Deopatan.

North of this town Cārumatī builds the Chabahil Stūpa. Aśoka is also associated with the Svāyambhū Stūpa in Nepal.

113 A.N., 255 B.C.E. Aśoka encourages transmission of the Dharma throughout his kingdom and beyond. Aśoka's fifth rock edict records the dispatch of royal envoys to introduce the Dharma among the kingdoms to the west and northwest, and south to Tāmraparṇī (Śrī Laṅkā). In each of these places he commands administrators to reward those who faithfully follow the path of Dharma.

The network of roads built for efficient administration of the empire stimulates commerce and provides safe passage for monks who travel west to the Buddhist centers arising in Bhārhut, Sāñcī, and Ujjain, and northwest to Mathurā, Kashmir, and Takṣaśilā. During Aśoka's reign, thousands of people of all castes and ways of life turn to the Buddha as a refuge and a path, donning the white robes of the Buddhist layman.

114 A.N., 254 B.C.E. In the fourteenth year of his reign, Aśoka travels to the village of Nigālīsāgar, in Nepal, where he enlarges the stūpa erected at the birthplace of Kanakamuni Buddha.

c. 116 A.N., 252 B.C.E. Aśoka builds the Dharmarājika Stūpa at Takṣaśilā, ancient capital of Gandhāra and a major crossroads of the ancient world. Monasteries established here continue to support Buddhist education and Dharma transmission in the northwest and to Central Asia until the fifth century C.E.

116 A.N., 252 B.C.E. Before Aśoka became king, he served as his father's viceroy in Ujjain, where he married Devī, who bore him a son and a daughter. Six years after Aśoka's conversion, Mogalliputta ordains Aśoka's son, known in the Mahāvaṁsa as Mahinda, and shortly after Mahinda's sister Sanghamittā also joins the Sangha. After his ordination, Mahinda resides in central India, in a monastery in Vidiśā (Vedisa, modern Bhīlsa) built by his mother, and Sanghamittā lives in the convent built for the Buddha's aunt Mahāprajāpatī in Śrāvastī.

During the reign of King Devānaṁpiyatissa (236–207 A.N., 247–207 B.C.E. in the Theravādin tradition), Aśoka's son Mahinda travels to Śrī Laṅkā from Vidiśā accompanied by five disciples, Mahinda's nephew Sumana, and the lay disciple Bhaṇḍuka. Soon after meeting Mahinda and his disciples, King Devānaṁpiyatissa and five hundred of his attendants take refuge in the Dharma, and Queen Anūlā and five hundred of her attendants also request ordination. In response, Mahinda sends for his sister Sanghamittā to ordain the women and establish the lineage of bhikṣuṇīs in Śrī Laṅkā. Sanghamittā brings with her a branch of the Bodhi tree from Bodh Gayā. Archaeological evidence found at Vidiśā verifies that Aśoka and Devānaṁpiyatissa were contemporaries and that monks traveled from Vidiśā to Śrī Laṅkā during their reigns.

118 A.N., 236 A.N. Aśoka highly values harmony in the Sangha and close adherence to the Buddha's central teachings. His generosity attracts many to join the Sangha, not all of whom are sincere in practicing Buddhism. The Sinhalese chronicles relate that in 236 A.N. he convenes a council in Pāṭaliputra to review the doctrines of the Buddhist schools and expels sixty thousand monks who hold heretical views. Although the Sinhalese tradition counts this event as the Third Council of the Sangha, texts of the northern traditions either do not mention it or do not regard it as involving the entire Sangha.

According to the Mahāvaṁsa, 236 years after the Parinirvana, during the reign of Aśoka and immediately after the council of Pāṭaliputra, the Arhat Mogalliputta Tissa sends nine missions of monks to the Himalayas and Kashmir in the north and northwest, to the land of the Greeks, to southwestern India, and to Śrī Laṅkā and Suvaṇṇabhūmi (probably Burma).

The mission led by Majjhantika is sent northwest to Kashmir and Gandhāra, where Majjhantika preaches the Āsīvisūpamā Sutta and converts eighty thousand people. Mahādeva is sent to Māhīṣamandala, probably in Mahārāṣṭra, south of the Narmadā River, where he teaches the Devadūtta Sutta and converts forty thousand. Rakkhita travels to Vanavāsī, in modern Karṇataka, where he teaches the Anamatagga Sutta, brings sixty thousand to the Dharma, and founds five hundred vihāras. Yonata (the Greek) Dhammarakkhita travels to Aparāntaka, in westernmost India, where he preaches the Aggikkhadhandopamā, converts thirty-seven thousand and ordains a thousand monks and a thousand nuns. Mahādhammarakkhita goes to the region of Mahārattha (Mahārāṣṭra), on the upper Godavarī River, where he teaches the Mahānāradukassapa Sutta and converts eighty-four thousand to the Dharma.

Mahārakkhita travels northwest to the country of the Yonas (Greeks), where he teaches the Kālakārāma Sutta, converts one hundred seventy thousand (or one hundred thirty-seven thousand), and accepts ten (or one) thousand into the order of monks. Majjhima is sent to the Himalayan region together with Kassapagotta, Dundubhissara, Sahadeva, and Mūlakadeva, where eight hundred thousand people enter the first stage of the path upon hearing the Buddha's first teaching (the Dhammacakkapavattana Sutta). Sona and Uttara travel to Suvaṇṇabhūmi, a name associated with lower Burma, where they teach the Brahmajāla Sutta; they convert sixty thousand and ordain five thousand people. Inscriptions at Sāñcī, a strong center of the Sthavira tradition, connect relics found in urns here with Majjhima and possibly also with Mogalliputta Tissa.

The Indian Buddhist texts do not mention these nine missions, but both the Mūlasarvāstivādin Vinaya and the Mahākarmavibhaṅga describe the dissemination of the Dharma by specific disciples of the Buddha, the great patriarchs, and by masters of Aśoka's time, including the Arhats Mahākāśyapa, in the western kingdom of Avanti; Madhyāntika, in Kashmir; Gavāṁpati in Suvarṇabhūmi (which usually refers to Burma); Piṇḍola Bhāradvāja in eastern India; Mahendra (Mahinda) in Siṁhāladvīpa (Śrī Laṅkā); and Pūrṇa in Sopāraka, on the western coast.

Some time after the council of Pāṭaliputra, Aśoka pacifies the inhabitants of Kashmir and founds Śrīnagara, its capital city. He dedicates the country to five hundred Sarvāstivādin Arhats from Pāṭaliputra who have taken refuge here and builds stūpas and monasteries at Vitastātra (Vethavutur) and Śuṣkalektra (Hukhalitar). The Dharma flourishes in Kashmir during his reign.

118 A.N., 250 B.C. The Mahāvaṁsa records that in the eighteenth year of Aśoka's reign, King Devānaṁpiyatissa performs twelve great actions on behalf of the Sangha in Śrī Laṅkā. He donates to the Sangha the Mahāmegha (Great Cloud) Garden, a place blessed by the visits of the four Buddhas of our aeon—the Tathāgatas Krakucchanda, Kanakamuni, Kāśyapa, and Śākyamuni. Here he plants the Bodhi tree branch brought by Aśoka's daughter Sanghamittā, which flourishes and gives rise to many great trees from its seeds.

In this same garden Devānaṁpiyatissa builds the Mahāvihāra, the Great Monastery, and erects a stone pillar. On Mt. Missaka, where Mahinda first alighted on the island, the king builds the Cetiyapabbata Vihāra for the Sangha's traditional rainy season retreat. He also builds the Issarasamaṇa and Vessagiri vihāras for monks and the Upāsikā and Hatthāḷhaka vihāras for nuns. His contributions to the Dharma include the building of the Tissa Pool and the Paṭhama Thūpa, where he enshrines the Buddha's collarbone relic.

120–200 A.N. Dharma Centers Expand Aśoka's activities and policies widely support the expansion of the Buddhist Sanghas. Large monasteries are built near Pāṭaliputra, Aśoka's capital city, and major centers arise along the trade routes that radiate in all directions throughout the vast empire. On the route west are the ancient Buddhist centers of Bhārhut and Sāñcī, which develop into veritable cities of stūpas and temples. Somewhat later, the Sanghas begin to carve the magnificent cave temples of Ajaṇṭā, Ellora, and Kārlī out of the living rock of the Western Ghats. On the route northwest to the Silk Road that traverses Central Asia to connect China and the Middle East, Dharma centers begin to thrive in Mathurā, Kashmir, Takṣa-śilā, and Oḍḍiyāna, and beyond the Indus River in Gandhāra and Bāmiyān (ancient Afghanistan).

By the second century A.N., and perhaps even earlier, Buddhist communities are taking form along the road leading south from Sāñcī and between the lower valleys of the Godāvarī and Kṛṣṇā rivers. The great stūpa of Amaravatī may have been erected in the time of Aśoka, then successively enlarged and ornamented to reach its full beauty centuries later. Amaravatī, located in modern Andhra near the mouth of the Kṛṣṇā River, is associated with the Mahāsāṁghika tradition and with the great Mahāyāna master Nāgārjuna. From this time, emerging Buddhist Sanghas in South India build stūpas and monasteries in the port cities of India's eastern seacoast, opening channels of transmission with Śrī Laṅkā and Burma and facilitating the travel of monks from Tāmralipti at the mouth of the Ganges to Kāñcī in the South.

126 A.N. Twenty-six years after his coronation, Aśoka has this inscription carved on a pillar:

"Twelve years after my coronation I began ordering edicts on Dharma to be inscribed for the welfare and happiness of the people, in order that they might give up their former ways of life and grow in Dharma in the particular respects set forth. Since I am convinced that the welfare and happiness of the people will be achieved only in this way, I consider how I may bring happiness to the people, not only to my relatives or residents of my capital city, but also to those who are far removed from me. I act in the same manner with respect to all. I am similarly concerned with all classes."

—Pillar Edict VI

130 A.N., 238 B.C.E. Aśoka worships at the stūpa of the Buddha Kanakamuni at Nigālīsāgar on a second journey to the Lumbinī Garden.

130–132 A.N., 238–236 B.C.E. With so many people of diverse backgrounds now entering the Sangha of monks and nuns, harmony is sometimes difficult to maintain, especially in certain regions. Toward the end of his reign Aśoka issues the Edict of Kauśāmbī, stating restrictions on who may enter the order, emphasizing the importance of unity within the Sangha, and prohibiting dissension. Those monks and nuns who demonstrate that they are uncommitted to the Dharma, lax in their Vinaya observances, or who violate Aśoka's injunctions are forced to return to lay life. Aśoka succeeds in these reforms.

137 A.N., between 236–231 B.C.E. Aśoka dies at Pāṭaliputra. Traditional accounts relate that Aśoka's son and heir Kuṇāla, who had become a monk and an Arhat, abdicates the throne in favor of his own son Vigatāśoka. According to Tāranātha, Aśoka is succeeded by his son Vigatāśoka, who is succeeded by his own son Virasena.

"I have supported righteousness,
that it may endure as long as the moon and the sun,
and that my sons and my great grandsons may
support it; for by so doing they will gain
both this world and the next."

—Dharmarāja Aśoka

Aśoka's empire appears to fragment after his death. It is likely that Kashmir, Gandhara, and Vidarbha assert independence and that several of Aśoka's descendents rule simultaneously. The historical record of this period is obscure and chronology is problematic.

230 B.C.E. Sīmuka rises to power in the Deccan and becomes the first ruler of the Sātavāhana Dynasty, a lineage of rulers that continues to the third century C.E. and provides a supportive environment for Buddhism to flourish in South India.

199 B.C.E. Mahinda passes away in the Cetiyapabbata Vihāra in Śrī Laṅkā at the age of sixty years. Sanghamittā passes away in Śrī Laṅkā a year later, at the age of fifty-nine. (MV XX: 32–50)

Reign of Virasena Vigatāśoka's son Virasena, who rules Aśoka's old empire while the Arhat Kāśyapa works for the welfare of humanity in Gandhāra, provides generously for the Sangha. During his reign the Brahmin Yaśasvin builds the Śarāvatī Monastery in Mathurā and supports about a hundred thousand monks.

During Virasena's reign, the monk Mahādeva distorts the meaning of the Sūtras at the Śarāvatī Monastery in Mathurā and elsewhere, causing disturbances in the Sangha. After his death, the monk Bhadra perpetuates Mahādeva's teachings and falsely asserts as the word of the Buddha five principles that evoke controversy and spread confusion as to how to understand the Buddha's teachings. These five points of doctrine lead to a formal division between the Sthaviras and the Mahāsaṁghikas and stimulate the arising of the eighteen schools. Controversies dissipate when the Arhats Mahāloma and Nandin work for the Dharma in Mathurā. (Tār 29–30)

Reign of Nanda Virasena is succeeded by his son Nanda, who rules for twenty-nine years. A monk named Nāga repeats the false teaching of Bhadra, occasioning the division of the Sangha into four parts. During Nanda's reign, the Arhat Dharmaśreṣṭhin departs for the north with his disciples, where, as the Buddha had prophesied, King Agnidatta provides for the maintenance of Dharmaśreṣṭhin and three thousand monks. Inspired by Avalokiteśvara, Pāṇinī, the great grammarian, writes the treatise known as the Pāṇinī-vyākāraṇa, which codifies the Sanskrit language. (Tār 82–83)

Reign of Mahāpadma Tāranātha relates that the Śrāvaka traditions divide into eighteen schools while Mahāpadma, son of Nanda, is king. (Tār 85) The cause for this division is traditionally ascribed to the renewed propagation of the five false doctrines by Sthiramati, disciple of the teacher Nāga.

Growth of the Śrāvaka Schools

As Buddhist activity spreads throughout India and beyond, and monks establish centers far beyond the traditional Buddhist heartland, the Sangha begins to grow more diverse. New schools develop, distinctive in their geographic locations and their emphases on specific doctrines. In his Samayabhedoparacanacakre nikāya-bhedopadeśana-saṁgraha (NE 4140), the eighth-century Mūlasarvāstivādin master Vinītadeva names eighteen early Śrāvaka schools, which he groups under four major traditions: Sarvāstivādin, Mahāsāṁghika, Sthavira, and Saṁmatīya. Bu-ston relates that the Sthaviras continue the lineage of the great Arhat Katyāyana, the Mahāsāṁghikas follow the lineage of Mahākāśyapa, the Saṁmatīyas perpetuate the lineage of Upāli, and the Sarvāstivādins continue the lineage of the Buddha's son Rāhula.

Traditionally, the Śrāvaka schools are considered to number eighteen, in accord with a prophecy made in aeons past. During the time of the Buddha Kāśyapa, King Kṛkin dreamed that eighteen men were pulling on a single robe; although each obtained a piece of the robe, the robe itself remained whole. Kāśyapa reassured King Kṛkin that this dream applied to the time of the Buddha Śākyamuni; although eighteen schools would arise and teach various aspects of the Dharma, all would remain a true expression of the Buddha's teachings. The Dharma, like the robe, would continue whole and undiminished.

Before the fifth century, information on locations and doctrines of the eighteen schools derives from inscriptions recovered from archaeological sites and from Buddhist literary sources: the Mahāvaṁsa, a later Śrī Laṅkan chronicle; the Vibhāṣas written down in Kashmir or northwestern India; and manuscript remains from Central Asia. Inscriptions indicate that by the time of Aśoka the Sarvāstivādins are flourishing in Mathurā and in the Northwest as well as in Vārāṇasī and Sārnāth. The Haimavata, a Sthavira subschool, is known at Sonārī and Sāñcī in the second century B.C.E. A contemporary inscription on a pillar at Bhārhut names the Sutaṁtikas (Sautrāntikas), as do inscriptions referring to Sutātakinī found at Sāñcī.

The Vinaya, Sutta, and Abhidhamma of the Sthavira tradition, preserved in Pāli, are written down in Śrī Laṅkā in the first century B.C.E. under the patronage of King Vaṭṭagāmaṇi. The Vinaya, Sūtra (Āgama), and Abhidharma of the Sarvāstivādins are written down in Sanskrit at various times, almost certainly by the time of King Kaniṣka, and carried to China centuries later, where they are preserved in Chinese translation together with the Vinayas of five other Śrāvaka schools. The Vinaya of the Mūlasarvāstivādins (root Sarvāstivādins) is preserved in Tibetan translation, where it provides the foundation of monastic practice. Two sections, the Vinayavastu and Kṣudrakavastu, incorporate the Āgamas as well. Although the scriptures of other early schools are largely lost, many of their specific doctrines are preserved in the Mahāvibhāṣa, an encyclopedic compendium of Abhidharma written at the time of the Third Council, convened during the reign of King Kaniṣka.

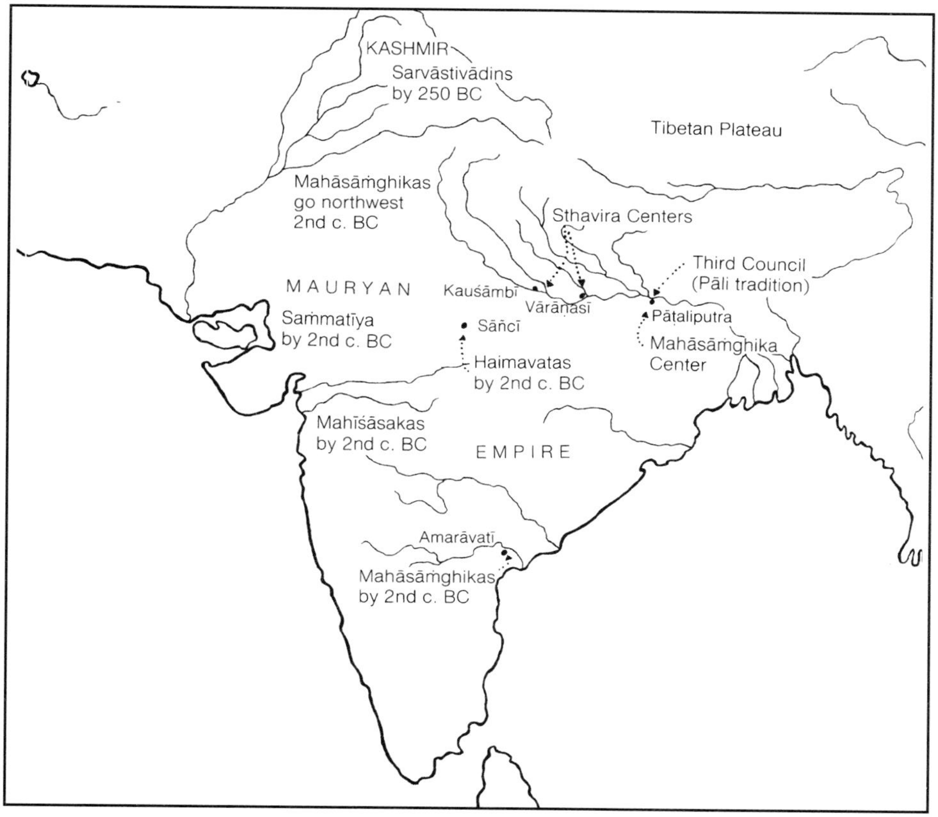

It is possible that Kaniṣka's patronage favored the expansion of the traditions strongest in the northwest—Sarvāstivādins, Mahīśāṣakas, and Dharmaguptakas—into Central Asia in the first or second century C.E. Manuscript remains indicate the early presence of all three traditions, with the Sarvāstivādins predominating. At some point the Mūlasarvāstivādins became the most widely established of the Śrāvaka traditions in Central Asia.

c. 187–151 B.C.E. Puṣyamitra assassinates Bṛhadrātha, the last Mauryan king, around 187 B.C.E, and establishes the Śuṅga Dynasty. He severely persecutes Buddhism in his empire; he destroys numerous monasteries, including Aśoka's monastery in Pātaliputra, the Kukkuṭārāma, and damages the great stūpa and monasteries at Sāñcī. These acts of destruction are remembered as the first hostility to the Dharma. The Greeks, having seized the northwestern portion of the old Mauryan empire, engage Puṣyamitra's army near Jālandhara, preventing the wave of his destruction from sweeping further into the Punjab.

c. 151–75 B.C.E. The city of Vidiśā develops into a thriving center of trade and rivals Pāṭaliputra as a center of political power. Kings and wealthy merchants generously support an unprecedented period of construction, renovation, and ornamentation of Buddhist monasteries and stūpas in ancient Avanti. Their support for the creation of Buddhist art helps shape the development of the Śuṅga artistic school, India's first coherent artistic tradition. The Sthavira and Haimavata traditions continue to flourish strongly in this central location.

Monks and the laity alike work to repair the damage wrought by Puṣyamitra's army. Gauḍavardhana, king of Gauḍa (northern Bengal) rebuilds damaged monasteries. (Tār 121) The Śuṅga kings of central India restore and enlarge the great stūpa of Sāñcī and pave all of Caityagiri (Temple Hill). Prosperous lay communities support the expansion and ornamentation of hundreds of stūpas, monasteries, and shrines at Bhārhut, Sāñcī, and Vidiśā.

Donors from Gandhāra and other distant lands join their resources with those of the local laity to express their devotion to the Dharma in the form of magnificent carvings on railings enclosing the circumambulation paths and on elegant gates facing the four directions of the great stūpas. Artisans inscribe on the gates and railings the names of donors and their occupations, which range from queen to dressmaker and weaver, from governor and merchant to craftsman and scribe.

c. 115–90 B.C.E. Menander, an Indo-Greek king in Gandhāra, establishes his capital in Saketa, where he engages the monk Nāgasena in a famous dialogue recorded in the Milindapañha, Questions of King Milinda. Menander becomes a friend and patron of the Sangha, as do a number of non-Indian rulers on India's northwestern borders.

c. 110 B.C.E. The Jandial Monastery is built at Takṣaśilā and the Dharmarājika Stūpa is renovated and expanded. Takṣaśilā becomes home to the Sarvāstivādin, Kāśyapīya, Mahīṣāsaka, and Bahuśrutīya traditions. Established on the route connecting major trade centers to the north, these monasteries support Dharma transmission into Central Asia and China.

101–77 B.C.E. King Duṭṭhagāmaṇi comes to power in Śrī Laṅkā after a period of political turmoil; he restores order and vigorously supports the Sangha's expansion. In Anurādhapura, he builds the nine-storied Lohapāsāda and has it inlaid with coral and precious stones; he builds the Maricavaṭṭi Vihāra and begins construction on the Great Thūpa, as the Arhat Mahinda requested more than a hundred years before. (MV XXII-XXIX)

100 B.C.E.–200 C.E. The Śrāvaka traditions continue to flourish. Evidence from inscriptions dating from 100 B.C.E. to 200 C.E. indicates that the eighteen schools come to predominate in different regions during this period of rapid expansion, while some monasteries and temples, dedicated to the Sangha of the Four Directions, continue to belong to no specific tradition. The Saṁmatīyas are strong in central India and Gujarāt. Sarvāstivādins travel from central India to Mathurā and then into Kashmir where they survive until the twelfth century C.E. The Mahāsāṁghikas are numerous in Andhra in the south, in the west around Bombay, and in Gandhāra and Takṣaśilā in the northwest. Sthaviras flourish in their centers in Avanti and Magadha in central India and increasingly in Śrī Laṅkā and Burma.

77–70 B.C.E. The Great Thūpa, known today as the Ruvanveli Dāgaba, is completed by Saddhātissa, Duṭṭagāmaṇi's son and successor. Monks from Buddhist Sanghas in India are invited to Anurādhapura to attend the Great Thūpa's consecration: forty thousand come from the Dakṣinagiri Monastery near Ujjain. (MV XXXII)

44 B.C.E. Vaṭṭagāmaṇi becomes king of Śrī Laṅkā, but is driven into exile by the Damiḷas of South India. (MV XXXIII)

29 B.C.E. King Vaṭṭagāmaṇi returns from exile, defeats the Ḍamiḷas (Tamils), and restores Siṁhāli rule to Śrī Laṅkā. During his reign he builds the great stūpa and vihāra of Abhayagiri. (Later rulers enlarged the stūpa to a height of 105 meters, making it the largest stūpa in all of Śrī Laṅkā.) Vaṭṭagāmaṇi donates the Abhayagiri Vihāra to the Arhat Mahātissa. (MV XXXIII) Two Theravādin traditions develop, named after their monasteries: the Mahāvihāravādins and the Abhayagirivādins. During Vaṭṭagāmaṇi's reign, Theravādin elders rehearse the Tripiṭaka (Canon) and write it down in Pāli. The ancient commentaries are written and preserved in Sinhalese.

65–150 C.E. During the reign of King Kaniṣka (exact date problematic), the Kuṣāṇas, a Central Asian people, rule the northwestern provinces and all of central India. Kuṣāṇa influence extends from Pāṭaliputra in the east to the Arabian Sea on the west, and from the Narmadā River on the south to Khotan and Khorāsān in Central Asia. Kaniṣka rules an empire that links India with Central Asia and the trade routes into China; his subjects include Greeks, Indians, Kuṣāṇas, Śakas, and Parthians. Kuṣāṇa rule protects access to the Silk Road, the caravan route that encircles the Taklamakhan Basin of Central Asian and links China with the Middle East. Sarvāstivādin and Mahāyāna monks establish monasteries in the oasis states of Central Asia—Kashgar, Khotan, Kuchā, and Niya.

The Third Council Tradition holds that four hundred years after the Parinirvāṇa, the Kuṣāṇa king Kaniṣka sponsors a Third Council of the Sangha. Hearing that his neighbor Sudarṣana, king of Kashmir, has been ordained into the Sangha and become an Arhat, Kaniṣka travels to Kashmir to hear Sudarṣana teach. He pays homage to all the temples in Kashmir and makes generous offerings to the Sangha. At that time the patron Śūdra is providing for the maintenance of the Vaibhāṣika master Dharmatrāta and the Sautrāntika master Sthavira, together with all their disciples, enabling both masters to propagate extensively the teachings of their traditions.

According to Tāranātha, Kaniṣka observes that in his own realm the Arhat Sañjaya, a popular teacher, has generated enough wealth to support the Sanghas of many different Buddhist communities, and that these communities are coexisting peacefully without arguments or disputes. When the learned Arhat Pārśva arrives from the east and recites a Sūtra describing the Buddha Kāśyapa's prediction concerning the eighteen schools, Kaniṣka determines to convene a council to review all the teachings transmitted within these traditions and clarify which are the true teachings of the Buddha.

Under the patronage of King Kaniṣka, five hundred Arhats, five hundred Bodhisattvas, and four or five hundred paṇḍitas gather together at the Kusumakūṭa Vihāra in Jālandhara, at the Kuvana or Karṇikavana Monastery in Kashmir, or possibly at the Tāmasavana (Dark Forest) Monastery near modern Sultanpur. (Sources vary; the above time, location, and participants are as given by Tāranātha and Bu-ston. Tāranātha also cites a Śrāvaka tradition that the council was attended by five hundred Arhats and five thousand master teachers.)

The Arhat Pārśva, who "had reached the limit of scriptural knowledge," is mentioned as having recited the Suvarṇamālā-avadāna and other rare Sūtras during the council. The Chinese scholar Hsüan-tsang mentions that Vasumitra figured prominently in this council and his name is associated with the Mahāvibhāṣa, the Great Explication of Abhidharma. After reciting the teachings of each tradition, the participants agree that all eighteen schools correctly represent the teachings of the Buddha. At the close of the council, the participants write down the Vinaya texts as well as all parts of the Sūtra and Abhidharma collections that are not yet committed to writing.

Participants in the Third Council summarize the results of their efforts in three massive treatises, one for each of the major classifications of Vinaya, Sūtra, and Abhidharma. Of special importance is the compendium of Abhidharma known as the Mahāvibhāṣa, which tradition associates with the Third

Council. Following the topics of the seven root texts of the Sarvāstivādin Abhidharma, the Mahāvibhāṣa documents the history and doctrines of the eighteen schools, describes their difference in Vinaya observances and Abhidharma tenets, and records in detail the Abhidharma teachings of all the northern schools, giving special prominence to the doctrines of the Sarvāstivādins. The philosophical classifications of the Great Explication provide the foundation for a systematic investigation of all that is knowable. Those who engage in this investigation become known as Vaibhāṣikas.

Simultaneously, a movement develops within the Sarvāstivādin tradition to return to the Sūtras as the central inspiration for study and practice. This movement results in the formation of the Sautrāntika school. While many Sautrāntikas turn away from the analytic approach and focus exclusively on the Āgamas, some masters among the Sautrāntikas engage the Vaibhāṣika position and question its presumptions concerning reality. For these masters, epistemological questions of meaning, being, and the science of knowledge become central issues, and they adopt the Abhidharma method of investigation in pursuing their inquiry.

The Vaibhāṣikas classify all that is knowable into forms, mind and sense consciousness, fifty-one mental events, relational conditions, and uncompounded dharmas. They distinguish between elements that are relatively and ultimately real, and accept that dharmas and actions exist substantially in the three times (past, present, and future). While accepting most of the Vaibhāṣika tenets, the Sautrāntikas question the foundation of the Vaibhāṣika view of reality, that the three times exist substantially. They point to the deceptive nature of appearances and deny the reality of the three uncompounded dharmas, a central tenet of the Vaibhāṣikas.

The master Vasubandhu figures prominently in the dialogues that in the late fourth or early fifth centuries C.E. clarify the distinctions between the Vaibhāṣika and Sautrāntika schools. From the Kashmiri master Saṁghabhadra he learns the Sarvāstivādin Abhidharma and systematizes this great body of teachings in a major treatise, the Abhidharmakoṣa. Later, at Saṁghabhadra's request, he composes a commentary (bhāṣya) on this work. Although Vasubandhu cannot be identified as a Sautrāntika master, his commentary on the Abhidharmakoṣa sets forth Sautrāntika views, stimulating a dialogue between Saṁghabhadra and those who espouse the Sautrāntika view. From this exchange Vaibhāṣika and Sautrāntika emerge as the two major philosophical schools of the Śrāvakayāna.

According to Tāranātha, all eighteen Śrāvaka schools are active in India at the time of the master Vasubandhu. Strong philosophic traditions have developed within two of these schools—the Sarvāstivādins and Sautrāntikas. After the fourth century, they gradually decline—partly as a result of hostilities toward the Dharma, partly because of internal dissensions, and partly because their monks become attracted to the Mahāyāna teachings and gravitate toward the emerging Mahāyāna centers.

By the seventh century only seven early schools remain in India, the most numerous being the Sarvāstivādins, the Saṁmatīyas, and the Sthaviras, who maintain strong centers in Sārnāth, Sāñcī, Malwa, and Valabhī. While some Śrāvaka traditions persist in Central Asia, China, Indonesia, and Southeast Asia, the lineages of only two Śrāvaka schools survive today: the Sthaviras, who develop into the Theravādins of Śrī Laṅkā and Southeast Asia, and the Mūlasarvāstivādins, whose Vinaya lineage continues unbroken in the Buddhist traditions of Tibet.

Speech of the Perfect Buddhas

Homage to the perfect teacher, the Buddha Śākyamuni

Buddhavacana
Word of the Buddha

The Uttaratantra of Maitreya explains the distinguishing qualities of Buddhavacana, the words of a fully enlightened being: Always closely connected with the Dharma, the word of a Buddha inspires beings to reject defilements in the three spheres of existence and demonstrates how to enter the bliss of nirvana. The speech of the Buddha is known as subhāṣita, well-spoken, in at least ten respects: in its attainment, for it comes forth from the omniscience of enlightenment; in its regard for all living beings; in its perseverance; in its completeness; in its manifold dimensions of meaning; and in its foundation. It is well-spoken by the Buddha's voice, which is endowed with the five perfections. It is well-spoken in its efficacy and range of teaching, reaching beings throughout the universe. It is well-spoken in pointing out the path between the extremes of nihilism and eternalism; and it is well-spoken, endowed with sixty unique qualities. (Bu I:25–26)

In the Vyākhyāyukti, Vasubandhu adds that the word of the Buddha is well-spoken in regard to its final result (pointing toward enlightenment); its concern for all living beings; its

དབྱངས་ཀྱི་ཡན་ལག་དྲུག་ཅུའི་མིང་
SIXTY MELODIOUS QUALITIES OF THE BUDDHA'S VOICE

མཉེན་པ་
snigdhā
agreeably smooth

འཇམ་པ་
mṛdukā
mild

ཡིད་དུ་འོང་བ་
manojñā
pleasing the mind

ཡིད་དུ་འཐད་པ་
manoramā
agreeable to the mind

དག་པ་
śuddhā
clear

དྲི་མ་མེད་པ་
vimalā
pure

གསལ་དབྱངས་
prabhāsvarā
clear-sounding

སྙན་ཅིང་འཇེབས་པ་

valgu

agreeable

མཉན་པར་འོས་པ་

śravaṇīya

worthy to be heard

མི་ཚུགས་པ་

anelā

not harsh

སྙན་པ་

kalā

agreeable

དུལ་བ་

vinītā

refined

མི་རྩུབ་པ་

akarkaśā

not disagreeable

མི་བརླང་བ་

aparuṣa

not abusive

རབ་ཏུ་དུལ་བ་

suvinitā

very soft

རྣ་བར་སྙན་པ་

karṇasukhā

pleasing to the ear

ལུས་སིམ་པར་བྱེད་པ་

kāyaprahlādanakarī

refreshing the body

སེམས་སིམ་པར་བྱེད་པ་

cittodvilyakarī

refreshing the mind

སྙིང་དགའ་བར་བྱེད་པ

hṛdayasantuṣṭikarī

gladdening the heart

དགའ་བ་དང་བདེ་བ་བསྐྱེད་པ་

prītisukhajananī

producing joy and happiness

ཡོངས་སུ་གདུང་བ་མེད་པ་

niṣparidāhā

not afflicting

ཀུན་ཏུ་ཤེས་པར་བྱ་བ་

ajñeyā

entirely intelligible

རྣམ་པར་རིག་པར་བྱ་བ་

vijñeyā

fully comprehensible

རྣམ་པར་གསལ་བ་

vispaṣṭā

very intelligible

དགའ་བར་བྱེད་པ་

premaṇīyā

making cheerful

མངོན་པར་དགའ་བར་བྱེད་པ་

abhinandanīyā

causing great delight

ཀུན་ཏུ་ཤེས་པར་བྱེད་པ་

ajñāpanīya

making fully understandable

རྣམ་པར་རིག་པར་བྱེད་པ་

vijñāpanīya

making perceptible

རིགས་པ་

yuktā

joining, connecting

འབྲེལ་པ་

sahitā

consistent

ཚིག་ཟློས་པའི་སྐྱོན་མེད་པ་

punaruktadoṣajahā

free from the fault of frequent repetition

སེང་གེ་ཆེའི་སྒྲའི་ཤུགས་

siṁhasvaravegā

forceful, like the sound of a lion

གླང་པོ་ཆེའི་སྒྲ་སྐད་

nāgesvaraśabdā

words like the trumpeting of an elephant

འབྲུག་གི་སྒྲ་དབྱངས་

meghasvaraghoṣā

voice like the sound of a thundercloud

ཀླུའི་དབང་པོའི་སྒྲ་

nāgendrarutā

sound like that of the nāga king

དྲི་ཟའི་གླུ་དབྱངས་

gandharvasaṅgītighoṣā

voice like the song of gandharvas

ཀ་ལ་པིང་ཀའི་སྐྲ་དབྱངས་

kalaviṅkasvararutā

melodious, like the song of the Kalaviṅka Bird

ཚངས་པའི་སྒྲ་དབྱངས་བསྒྲགས་པ་

brahmasvararutāravitā

uttering a sound like the voice of Brahmā

ཤང་ཤང་ཏེའུསྒྲ་དབྱངས་བསྒྲགས་པ་

jīvañjīvakasvararutāravitā

uttering a sound like the pheasant

ལྷའི་དབང་པོའི་དབྱངས་ལྟར་སྙན་པ་
devendramadhuranirghoṣā
voice pleasing like that of Indra

རྔའི་སྒྲ་
dundubhisvarā
sound of a great drum

མ་ཁེངས་པ་
anunnatā
unassuming

མི་དམའ་བ་
anavanatā
not arrogant

སྒྲ་ཐམས་ཅད་ཀྱི་རྗེས་སུ་ཞུགས་པ་
sarvaśabdānu-praviṣṭā
following every sound

ཚིག་ཟུར་ཆག་པ་མེད་པ་
apaśabdavigatā
free from corrupt words

མཚང་བ་མེད་པ་
avikalā
no defective sound

མ་ཞུམ་པ་
alīnā
not fearful

མི་ཞན་པ་
adīnā
not weak

རབ་ཏུ་དགའ་བ་
pramuditā
joyful

ཁྱབ་པ་
prasṛtā
encompassing

ཆུབ་པ་
sakhilā
perceiving

རྒྱུན་ཆགས་
saritā
continual

འབྲེལ་བ་
lalitā
playful

སྒྲ་ཐམས་ཅད་རྫོགས་པར་བྱེད་པ་
sarvasvarapurāṇī
accomplishment of all sounds

དབང་པོ་ཐམས་ཅད་ཚིམ་པར་བྱེད་པ་
sarvendriyasantoṣaṇī
satisfying every sensory organ

མ་སྨད་པ་
aninditā
not distressed

མི་འཁྲུར་བ་

acañcalā
invincible

མ་བརྫགས་པ་

acapalā
immovable

འཁོར་ཀུན་ཏུ་གྲགས་

sarvapariṣad-ānuravitā
resounding in every company

རྣམ་པ་ཐམས་ཅད་ཀྱི་མཆོག་དང་ལྡན་པ་

sarvākāra-vāropetā
chief among all voices

perseverance, completeness, and manifold dimensions; its foundation; its way of making itself understood; its character of teaching; its time; and its exclusive qualities.

Above is a traditional list of sixty features of perfect speech as given in the Mahāvyutpatti, a dictionary of Sanskrit terms and their Tibetan equivalents compiled in Tibet in the ninth century as a guide to future translators of Buddhist texts. In his Yogācārabhūmi, Asaṅga gives a slightly different list of the qualities of enlightened speech that convey the teachings of liberation: The Buddha's speech is soft, supporting the roots of virtue; mild, for it causes delight even in those involved in worldly life; pleasing by its meaning; agreeable, exquisite in sound; pure, obtained after the highest samādhi; immaculate, free from the influence of the passions; brilliant in its clarity; charming, winning the mind from false teachings; worthy of being studied, as it leads to nirvana; without defect; sweet, giving pleasure to all; cultured; not harsh; not unkind; highly cultured, able to convey the discipline of the three vehicles to enlightenment; agreeable to hear, preventing distraction; producing ease in the body; and satisfying the mind. Clearing away all doubt, the speech of the Buddha gladdens the heart; removing all that is wrong or uncertain, it brings satisfaction and happiness, and does not cause pain.

The word of the Buddha must be known thoroughly—one attains this knowledge by study. It must be known in detail—knowledge that results from investigation. The word of the Buddha is perfectly clear, showing the Dharma as it is, not as shaped by the interpretation of a teacher. It is to be welcomed by those who are realized and to be greeted with rejoicing by those who thirst for realization. It gives thorough knowledge that teaches correctly, and it gives this knowledge in detail.

The word of the Buddha is correct, not contrary to reason; it is connected with its subject and with its purpose. It is powerful, like the roar of the lion; it exudes dignity, like the cry of an elephant; it penetrates deeply, like the roll of thunder. It is worthy of being heard, like the voice of the nāga king. In its sweetness, it is like the music of gandharvas; clear and melodious, it is like the song of the kalavinka. It reaches far, like the sound of Brahmā, lord of the highest heavens; it augurs success, like the melody of the chakora-bird.

The word of the Buddha is delightful, like the voice of Indra; resonant like a drum; free from arrogance and the humiliation of censure; adaptable to various forms of expression; free from corrupt ungrammatical language; not incomplete; independent, not influenced by profit and honor. Free from fear, the word of the Buddha is not timid; liberated from sorrow, it is always joyful. It is comprehensive, perfect in fulfilling the aims of living beings, fluent, and elegant in its variety. The word of the Buddha communicates meaning in diverse languages simultaneously; conveying many ideas in one, it satisfies all human faculties. It is irreproachable, reliable, and not rash. Heard equally well near or far, it reaches beings in all realms of existence. Teaching through parable that uses all worldly experience and objects, it is possessed of the best of forms. (Bu 26–29).

The Teaching of Vimalakīrti extolls the unique quality of the Buddha's voice that communicates meaning to all beings according to their capacity for understanding. While all are uplifted and made happy upon hearing the teachings, some develop merely a sense of the meaning, some realize the meaning, and some are freed from all doubts.

Similar praise for the melodious voice of the Buddha and its capacity to communicate meaning directly are expressed in the Lalitavistara Sūtra:

"Your words are full of love and compassion,
and your speech is soft; your voice rings out with
the sweet accents of Brahmā, going straight to the heart. . . .

"All the sounds and voices of the entire world—
sweet delights for gods and men—
disappear at the sound of your soft voice.

"Your voice calms desire, hatred, and ignorance;
it calms the fettering passions;
it produces pure and heavenly pleasure.
Those assembled will hear the Dharma
with an untroubled mind
and obtain the highest deliverance.

—*Voice of the Buddha II:551*

གསུང་རབ་ཡན་ལག་བཅུ་གཉིས

TWELVE FORMS OF THE BUDDHA'S TEACHINGS

མདོའི་སྡེ་

sūtra

general teachings

དབྱངས་ཀྱིས་བསྙད་པའི་སྡེ་

geya

discourses in verse

ལུང་དུ་བསྟན་པའི་སྡེ་

vyākaraṇa

prophecies

ཚིགས་སུ་བཅད་པའི་སྡེ་

gāthā

verse summaries

ཆེད་དུ་བརྗོད་པའི་སྡེ་

udāna

aphorisms

གླེང་གཞིའི་སྡེ་

nidāna

explanations

རྟོགས་པ་བརྗོད་པའི་སྡེ་

avadāna

biographical narratives

དེ་ལྟ་བུ་བྱུང་བའི་སྡེ་
itivṛttaka
historical accounts

སྐྱེས་པའི་རབས་ཀྱི་སྡེ་
jātaka
narratives of former lives

ཤིན་ཏུ་རྒྱས་པའི་སྡེ་
vaipulya
extensive teachings

རྨད་དུ་བྱུང་བའི་ཆོས་ཀྱི་སྡེ་
adbhutadharma
narratives of wondrous events

གཏན་ལ་ཕབ་པར་བསྟན་པའི་སྡེ་
upadeśa
instructions in profound doctrines

FORMS OF THE BUDDHA'S TEACHINGS At the time of the Parinirvāṇa, the Buddha explained the forms of his teaching, each a means of evoking a different response and realization:

Sūtra Discourses on a single topic. Sūtras are uplifting and inspirational. They readily evoke the listener's response; they increase respect for the Dharma, supporting the rapid application of the teachings; they enable the teachings to penetrate deeply; they inspire serene joy based on faith in the Buddha, faith in the Dharma, and faith in the Sangha; they support supreme happiness even in this lifetime; they please the minds of the wise through exegesis; and they are recognized as communicating enlightened knowledge.

Geya Discourses in verse. Geya are the stanzas often found at the end or beginning of a Sūtra. Often an aspect of the teaching not explained in the Sūtra will be explicated in Geya.

Vyākaraṇa Prophecies stated in the course of discussions of past lives and future actions of individuals within the Sangha. Vyākaraṇa often serve to clarify points presented in a Sūtra.

Gāthā Verse summaries. Expressed in metrical verse within Sūtras, Gāthās recapitulate the main themes. Easily memorized, they fix essential teachings in mind as inspiration and support for the path.

Udāna Words spoken not to instruct individuals but to maintain the Dharma. These teachings are said to have been spoken by the Buddha with a joyful heart.

Nidāna Explanations following a specific incident, often given as a means of clarifying the relationship of cause and effect, as in the Vinaya-vibhaṅga. In Nidāna, the Buddha gives a principle or guideline and explains the reason for it.

Avadāna Instructive accounts of the lives of Buddhas, Bodhisattvas, disciples, and various other individuals.

Itivṛttaka Historical accounts, such as geneologies or the history of the Sangha incorporated into the Vinayavastu.

Jātaka Accounts of the Buddha's previous lives, given for instruction on karma, compassion, and the virtues by which one progresses on the path to enlightenment.

Vaipulya Extensive Sūtras that have a complex organization, including the Mahāyāna Sūtras, which express subtle teachings of profound and vast meaning.

Adbhutadharma Accounts of wondrous accomplishments of the Buddha, the disciples, and the Bodhisattvas.

Upadeśa Topics of specific knowledge, such as the listings meant to be memorized and developed by study and practice.

THREE COLLECTIONS OF BUDDHAVACANA (TRIPIṬAKA)

འདུལ་བའི་སྡེ་སྣོད།

Vinaya

མདོའི་སྡེ་སྣོད།

Sūtra

ཆོས་མངོན་པའི་སྡེ་སྣོད།

Abhidharma

THE THREE COLLECTIONS (TRIPIṬAKA) During the First Council of the Sangha held soon after the Buddha's Parinirvāṇa, five hundred great Arhats arranged the whole of the Buddha's teachings into three major categories: Vinaya, which develops śīla (morality); Sūtra, which extends the power of samādhi (meditation); and Abhidharma, which supports the growth of prajñā (wisdom). (Śīla, samādhi, and prajñā are known as the three trainings.) This threefold compilation of teachings is known as the Tripiṭaka, the three great collections of teachings communicated through the Buddha's speech (Buddhavacana).

Vinaya An expression of the Buddha's perfect conduct, Vinaya supports the embodiment of enlightenment. Associated with training in moral discipline and concentration, the Vinaya teachings point out how to identify wrong action and the causes of wrong action, the way to correct wrong action, and how to overcome tendencies to repeat it. (MSA XI:1–3)

In his interactions with the Sangha, the Buddha reviewed with the assembly of monks each difficulty that arose, analyzed the events that produced it, and traced its cause. Only when the Sangha understood how each action led to the next did the Buddha pronounce the guidelines for conduct. Collected into two texts, a Prātimokṣa for monks and another for nuns, these guidelines became a code of ethical law for the Sangha, an antidote for extremes of behavior and an essential support for mindfulness in every thought, word, and action.

The Vinaya texts of seven traditions have come down to the modern day: Theravādin, preserved in Pāli, Mūlasarvāstivādin, partially extant in Sanskrit and fully preserved in Tibetan and Chinese translation; and the Dharmaguptaka, Sarvāstivādin, Mahāsaṁghika, Mahīśāsaka, and Kāśyapīya, all in Chinese. (Some of the Chinese Vinaya collections are incomplete.)

As preserved within the Tibetan Canon, the Mūlasarvāstivādin Vinaya contains eight texts and incorporates three aṅgas: Nidāna, Itivṛttaka, and Jātaka. (AS, in Bu) The first text is the Vinayavastu, which sets forth the rules pertaining to the general life of the order, the daily needs of bhikṣus, and the functioning of the community. This extensive compilation includes the life of the Buddha, numerous accounts of his teachings (Āgamas), and the early history of the Sangha, together with accounts of past lives of the Buddha and his disciples. Then follow the two Prātimokṣa texts (rules of monastic order), one for monks and another for nuns, each with its accompanying Vibhaṅga, texts containing more detailed explanations of the Prātimokṣa rules and their history.

The final three Vinaya texts are the Kṣudrakavastu, the Vinaya-uttaragrantha, and the Upali-paripṛcchā. The Kṣudrakavastu, a continuation of the Vinayavastu, contains miscellaneous rules and supplements the historical accounts of the Vinayavastu with a history of the Sangha from the final years of the Buddha's life until the time of the Second Council about a hundred years after the Parinirvāṇa. Presented in the form of a dialogue, the Uttaragrantha is a collection of twelve treatises. The Upāli-paripṛcchā, in which the disciple Upāli questions the Buddha on a number of fine points concerning Vinaya observance, ends with the statement "All the questions of Upāli are finished." With this, the Vinaya taught by the Buddha is complete. Teaching in manifold ways, by example and by clear connection of cause and result, these accounts of enlightened action point the way to liberation and inspire emulation.

Sūtra Spoken from the depths of enlightened understanding, Sūtras transmit awakened knowledge directly and represent the very heart of the Buddha. Tradition recognizes three types of Sūtras: teachings spoken directly by the Buddha, teachings inspired by the blessing of the Buddha, and teachings given by mandate of the Buddha. The Sūtras of the first Turning incorporate the aṅgas of Sūtra, Geya, Vyākaraṇa, Gāthā, and Udāna, while the Sūtras of the Second and Third Turnings also include the aṅgas of Vaipulya and Adbhutadharma, which express the deep insight and extensive vision of the Buddhas and great Bodhisattvas.

The Mahāyāna-sūtrālaṁkāra describes Sūtras as antidotes for doubt, because they communicate precise solutions and meanings. While they support training in moral discipline and wisdom, they are especially associated with training in meditative concentration. (MSA XI:1–3)

Sūtras usually include the five excellences, namely, the presenter of the teachings, the location, the audience, the circumstances of the teaching, and the names of those requesting the teaching. The central teaching is usually given in response to a question or an event, or else unfolds in the course of a dialogue among the Buddha and members of the assemblies. Within the Buddha's responses, even everyday occurences become catalysts of universal truths that transcend boundaries of place and time. For an overview of Sūtras preserved in the bKa'-'gyur, see Settings of the Sūtras, beginning on page 183.

Abhidharma To promote analysis and insight into the nature of mind and experience, the Buddha gave upadeśa, or instructions, in the form of lists of essential topics meant to be developed through study and practice. Embedded in Sūtras as seeds (mātṛkā) for realization, arranged in numerical categories of study topics, or condensed and defined in the Arthaviniścāya and similar compendiums, these teachings form the foundation of the Abhidharma.

The Abhidharma reflects the Buddha's quality of speech, communicating the workings of samsara and nirvana and promoting a clear understanding of the nature of existence. Associated with the training in wisdom, the Abhidharma trains the mind in analytical thinking and empowers direct insight, giving access to the meaning of the Sūtras.

Abhidharma can mean the higher, the most distinguished Dharma, the Dharma that gives access to the higher subtleties of Sūtra and Vinaya. (Bu I:37) The Abhidharmakoṣa defines abhi as highest: the Abhidharma is the highest Dharma, revealing all that is knowable and pointing the way to enlightenment, the supreme realization. The Mahāyāna-sūtrālaṁkāra explains the Abhidharma as the Dharma that directs one toward nirvana; offering repeated and varied instruction on each element of the teaching, it clarifies the true nature of the Dharma and provides a remedy for wrong views:

"The Abhidharma (is called so) because it makes manifest,
(teaches) repeatedly, (is a cause of) predominance,
and gives full comprehension."

—Mahāyāna-sūtrālaṁkāra XI:1–3

According to accounts of the Buddha's life preserved in the Vinaya, the Buddha discovered the Abhidharma in the unfolding of enlightenment, while seated on the Vajrāsana at Bodh Gayā. He taught the Abhidharma first to his mother in the Trāyastriṁśa Heaven, then to Śāriputra, his disciple foremost in intellectual understanding. The Abhidharma of the Buddha has come down to the present day through two major traditions, each of which shaped the essential teachings into seven basic texts: the Theravādins of Śrī Laṅkā and the Sarvāstivādins of northern India. Although the Sarvāstivādin school itself has not continued, all but one of the texts transmitted through this tradition survive complete in Chinese translation.

Although the seventh, the Prajñaptiśāstra, is incomplete in the Chinese Tripiṭaka, it is preserved in its entirety in the Tibetan bsTan-'gyur.

In the Theravādin tradition, the Abhidhamma was transmitted in an oral lineage from master to disciple from Śāriputra until the time of Aśoka, when Revata recited it at the Council of Pāṭaliputra. With this recitation, the Abhidhamma in seven texts formally became part of the Sthavira Tipiṭaka, which was written down in the Pāli language in Śrī Laṅkā in the first century B.C.E. These seven texts are: Dhammasaṅgani (Enumeration of the Dhammas), Vibhaṅga (The Book of Analysis), Kathāvatthu (Points of Controversy), the Puggalapaññatti (Designation of Human Types), Dhātukathā (Discourse on Elements), Yamaka (The Book of Pairs), and Paṭṭhāna (Conditional Relations).

The Sarvāstivādins appear to have considered their seven primary Abhidharma texts to be extended versions of the very concise mātṛkā, in full accord with the Buddha's teachings. All of the Abhidharma teachings delineated by the Buddha are included in these seven texts. The Jñānaprasthāna, compiled by Kātyāyanīputra in the second or first century B.C.E., was considered the body or the main exposition of Abhidharma, while the remaining six Abhidharma texts became known as the pada or feet.

According to the Abhidharmakoṣa-bhāṣya, the six pada texts and their authors are the Dharmaskandha, by Śāriputra; the Prajñaptiśāstra, by Maudgalyāyana; the Dhātukāya, by Pūrṇa; the Vijñānakāya, by Devaśarman; the Prakaraṇapada, by Vasumitra; and the Saṁgītiparyāya, by Mahākausthila. The Chinese translations of five of these texts name different authors: the Dharmaskandha, by Maudgalāyana; the Dhātukāya, by Vasumitra; the Vijñānakāya, by Devakṣema; and the Saṁgītiparyāya, by Śāriputra. All seven texts were included as supplementary works in the *Nyingma Edition of the Tibetan Canon* (Berkeley: Dharma Publishing, 1981).

Dharmaskandha The Dharmaskandha (Components of the Dharma) explicates in twenty-one chapters the monk's path to moral and spiritual progress. Beginning with the five sets of precepts to be learned and the stages of the path, it culminates in an analysis of the twenty-two indriyas, twelve ayatānas, five skandhas, eighteen dhātus, and the twelve nidānas that form the chain of pratītyasamutpada (interdependent cooperation).

Prajñaptiśāstra The Prajñaptiśāstra (Treatise on Description) has three major parts: Lokaprajñapti, which deals with defilements and problems related to the world; Kāraṇaprajñapti, concerned with the characteristics of a Bodhisattva; and Karmaprajñapti, which treats the manner of actions.

Saṁgītiparyāya The Samgītiparyāya (Enumeration of Classifications) describes the controversy that gave rise to the Second Council. To clarify the essential structure of the teachings, it compiles the numerical lists given by the Buddha (the four mindfulnesses, etc.) in numerical order, from ekadharmas (one element) to daśadharmas (ten elements). This work concludes with the Buddha's admonition to read and recite the categories of dharmas systematized and explicated in this text.

Vijñānakāya Compiled by Devaśarman about a hundred years after the Parinirvāṇa, the Vijñānakāya (Body of Consciousness) sets forth Maudgalyāyana's view of Abhidharma classifications, including pudgala, indriyas, cittas, kleśas, vijñānas, and bodhyaṅgas; it reviews the theory of pudgala, ways of analyzing mental events, and compares the mental processes of the trainee with those of the Arhat.

Dhātukāya The Dhātukāya (Body of Elements) has two parts. The first explicates topics set forth in the fourth section of the Prakaraṇapāda, including kleśas, skandhas, āyatānas, and dhātus; the second part focuses on the five vedanās, six vijñānas, and two akuśalabhūmis, and progresses to a discussion of eighty-eight categories.

Prakaraṇapāda The eight chapters of the Prakaraṇapāda (Verses of Explication) clarify the nature of the five dharmas, ten kinds of knowledge, and the acquisition of knowledge; the seven categories beginning with dhātus, āyatanas, and skandhas; and ninety-eight minor passions, what can be inferred, and miscellaneous questions on various technical categories. It ends with a summary of the entire text. According to the Mahāprajñāpāramitā-śāstra, half of this text was compiled by Vasumitra and the other half by Kashmiri Arhats. The Prakaraṇapāda was held in high regard by later masters concerned with systematizing the Abhidharma into a basis for study and practice. In the late fourth or early fifth century C.E., Vasubandhu drew upon this work as well as the Jñānaprasthāna in formulating his Abhidharma classifications.

Jñānaprasthāna The Jñānaprasthāna, the "head" of the seven early Abhidharma texts, sets forth the Abhidharma in eight sections (aṣṭagrantha) and forty-four chapters. The first defines and explicates miscellaneous topics such as the means of attaining transcendental knowledge, the origin and types of knowledge, interdependent cooperation, faith, shamelessness, the three marks of existence, the ineffectiveness of ascetic practices, and mind and mental events. The following seven specific sections analyze knowledge, karma, the four great elements that give rise to all forms, sensory organs and their functions, the stages of meditation, and correct and incorrect views. There are two versions of this work in Chinese translation, which may represent two different traditions: the Aṣṭagrantha (T 1544) and the Abhidharma-śāstra (T 1543).

Sūtras of the Second and Third Turning Bhāvaviveka writes in his Tarkajvāla that while the Arhats recited the scriptures as heard by the Śrāvakas, a million Bodhisattvas assembled on Mt. Vimalasvabhāva, south of Rājagṛha, to rehearse the teachings of the Second and Third Turnings. Mañjuśrī recited the Abhidharma, Maitreya the Vinaya, and Vajrapāṇi the Sūtras. Vajrapāṇi preserved the Mahāyāna Sūtras in the realm of the nāgas and in other places, where they were readily available to humans who attained the profound samādhis. The Tantras remained in the Dharmakāya and Sambhogakāya realms inaccessible to human beings, until the appropriate time for their transmission.

Tantras Often considered as a fourth collection, and sometimes as part of the Sūtra or Abhidharma collections, the Tantras encompass the teachings and qualities of all three collections, supporting the trainings of śīla, samādhi, and prajñā simultaneously. The most extensive collection of Tantras is preserved in Tibetan translation, compiled into such major collections of sacred texts as the bKa'-'gyur, the rNying-ma-rgyud-'bum, and the bKa'-ma.

THREE VEHICLES TO ENLIGHTENMENT As an expression of universal truth, the Dharma revealed by the Buddha manifests within a wide range of forms and responds to changing circumstances and historical developments. Three major expressions of the Buddha's view and path have emerged to date, providing distinct approaches to enlightenment: the way of the Śrāvaka, or listener, and the Mahāyāna, the way of the Bodhisattva, which in turn embraces the paths known as Sūtrayāna and Mantrayāna.

The Śrāvakayāna, with its emphasis on embodiment as the foundation for personal salvation, is closely allied to the monastic Sangha. The Mahāyāna, or Great Vehicle, great in its scope and profundity, great in its aspiration and goal, calls forth selfless compassion and illuminates the potential for enlightenment inherent within all sentient beings.

Settings of The Sūtras

The Buddha taught the Dharma from the time of his enlightenment at the age of thirty-five until he entered nirvāṇa at the age of eighty. The knowledge of the Enlightened One manifested in all actions of body, speech, and mind, from the slightest gesture to the most intricate spoken teachings. The written texts that preserve the Buddha's teachings represent the nucleus of the full transmission of the Dharma as conveyed directly from the Buddha to his disciples.

Perpetuated by unbroken lineages of masters and disciples, the living transmission of the Buddha's Dharma continues in our time. The enlightened knowledge the Blessed One brought into the world shines through the actions of living exemplars of the Buddha's way and through the writings of the great masters of later centuries. Whether one follows the guidance of a specific lineage or seeks to learn independently, reading the Sūtras and reflecting on their manifold levels of meaning help us bridge the centuries between the Buddha's time and our own, and open the mind to the all-encompassing wisdom expressed in his teachings.

The Sūtras generally begin by describing the five precious elements—the central speakers, the place where the teaching was given, the composition of the assembly, the person who requested the Buddha's instruction, and the circumstances leading up to the teaching. Here information concerning these elements has been drawn from the opening passages of each Sūtra preserved in the Tibetan Canon. It is hoped that continuing research projects will include a complete and thorough examination of this vast body of teachings, enabling a more comprehensive and even presentation of the five precious elements. The preliminary information given here is offered to encourage Western students of the Dharma to read and translate more of the Buddha's teachings.

The Sūtras are listed by location, beginning with the teachings given at the Vajrāsana, site of the enlightenment at Bodh Gayā, and from there to Vārāṇasī (Sārnāth), Mount Gayā, Rājagṛha (Vulture Peak Mountain, the city and its environs, the Courtyard of the Tathāgatas), Magadha (General), Śrāvastī, Kapilavastu, Vaiśālī, Vṛji (General), Banks of the Ganges, Campā, Kauśāmbī, Ujjayinī, Saketa, Mountains and Forests, the Trāyastriṁśa and Akaniṣṭha Heavens, other Celestial Realms, the Great Ocean, Bodhigarbha, and unnamed or unknown places. The descriptions end with the teachings immediately preceding the Buddha's Parinirvāṇa in a grove of Sāla trees near Kuśinagara.

The Sūtras described below all appear in the Nyingma Edition (NE) of the Tibetan Buddhist Canon. The NE numbers denote the position of the Sūtra in this edition, and the letters S, T, C, E, F, G indicate that the Sūtra exists in its Sanskrit original or in Tibetan, Chinese, English, French, or German translation. (A list of Sūtras translated into English, French, or German as of 1982 appears in *Crystal Mirror VII,* pp. 289–369.)

बुद्धावतंसको नाम महावैपुल्यसूत्रम्

།སངས་རྒྱས་ཕལ་པོ་ཆེ་ཞེས་བྱ་བ་ཤིན་ཏུ་རྒྱས་པ་ཆེན་པོའི་མདོ།

TCE

Buddha-avataṁsaka-nāma-mahāvaipūlya-sūtra At the time of the Buddha's enlightenment, the ground surrounding the Vajrāsana, the diamond seat of the Fully Awakened Ones, was adorned with brilliant jewels. Banners of precious gems and garlands of fragrant flowers manifested all around. Jewels spontaneously took form in the air and fell on the earth like rain. Through the power of the realized Buddha, the site of the enlightenment was ablaze with light magnified by infinite reflections in rows of trees made of jewels.

The Bodhi Tree, its trunk transformed into diamond and its branches into lapis lazuli, spread its leaves in all directions like clouds. From the Tree of Enlightenment emanated radiant light and sublimely beautiful sounds directly communicating truth. In this place an immeasurably great host of enlightened beings, numerous as the atoms in ten Buddhafields, gathered around the Buddha, whose body extended throughout the ten directions and whose light illuminated the world.

To this host of enlightened beings, born from the Buddha's ocean of virtue, seated on jeweled thrones, adorned with variegated flowers, and illuminated by the brilliant light of jewels in their crowns, the Buddha expounded all truths. (NE 44: 116 bampo)

दममूको नाम सूत्रम्

།མཛངས་བླུན་ཞེས་བྱ་བའི་མདོ།

T C E F G

Damamūka-nāma-sūtra Soon after the Buddha's enlightenment, Brahmā, having beheld this wondrous event, descended from the heavens, bowed to the feet of the Buddha, and entreated the Holy One to turn the Wheel of the Dharma. Here follow fifty-one Jātakas that trace the cause of present situations in human lives to events in former lifetimes. (NE 341: 338 folios, 12 bampo)

आर्यबुद्धबलवर्धनप्रातिहार्यविकुर्वाणनिर्देशो नाम महायानसूत्रम्

།འཕགས་པ་སངས་རྒྱས་ཀྱི་སྟོབས་སྐྱེད་པའི་ཆོ་འཕྲུལ་རྣམ་པར་འཕྲུལ་བ་བསྟན་པ་ཞེས་བྱ་བ་ཐེག་པ་ཆེན་པོའི་མདོ།

T C

Ārya-buddhabalavardhana-prātihāryavikurvāṇa-nirdeśa-nāma-mahāyāna-sūtra The Buddha was residing on the banks of the Nairañjana River, together with Avalokiteśvara, Vajrapāṇi, Maitreya, Mañjuśrī, and seven thousand other Great Bodhisattvas; Śāriputra and Maudgalyāyana, with numerous Śrāvakas; the gods Indra and Brahmā, and the Four World Protectors. After delighting the assembly with miraculous displays, the Blessed One entered samādhi and spoke to Avalokiteśvara and Vajrapāṇi of the unfortunate beings in the world. (NE 186: 30 folios, 1 bampo)

धर्मचक्रप्रवर्तनसूत्रम्

།ཆོས་ཀྱི་འཁོར་ལོ་རབ་ཏུ་བསྐོར་བའི་མདོ།

STCEF

Dharmacakra-pravartana-sūtra Soon after his enlightenment, the Buddha came to the Deer Park at Sārnāth, where he gave the Sūtra known as Turning the Wheel of the Dharma, a teaching on the Four Noble Truths, to his five former companions in ascetic practices. Upon hearing this teaching, the five became Arhats, bringing into being the Sangha of the Buddha Śākyamuni. (NE 31: 6 folios; NE 337: 5 folios)

आर्याध्याशयसंचोदनं नाम महायानसूत्रम्

།འཕགས་པ་ལྷག་པའི་བསམ་པ་བསྐུལ་བ་ཞེས་བྱ་བ་ཐེག་པ་ཆེན་པོའི་མདོ།

TCE

Ārya-adhyāśayasaṁcodana-nāma-mahāyāna-sūtra The Great Bodhisattva Maitreya asked the Buddha to speak of the ripening of karma and the consequences of nonvirtuous actions for the benefit of sixty Bodhisattvas whose minds were distracted by worldly pleasures. In response the Buddha gave this teaching known as Exhortation to Intense Insight to the whole assembly, including one thousand bhikṣus and five hundred fully accomplished Bodhisattvas. Spoken in Vārāṇasī, in the Deer Park of Sārnāth. (NE 69: 45 folios, 2 bampo, 600 śloka)

आर्यमायोपमासमाधिर्नाम महायानसूत्रम्

།འཕགས་པ་སྒྱུ་མ་ལྟ་བུའི་ཏིང་ངེ་འཛིན་ཞེས་བྱ་བ་ཐེག་པ་ཆེན་པོའི་མདོ།

T C

Ārya-māyopamā-samādhi-nāma-mahāyāna-sūtra The Great Bodhisattva Padmaśrīgarbha requested the Blessed One to describe the qualities of the Bodhisattva and the attainment of Buddhahood. In response, the Buddha gave the Sūtra known as The Samādhi Resembling an Illusion to an assembly of twenty thousand bhikṣus and twelve thousand Bodhisattvas, together with Mati and others who abided in the Mahāyāna. Spoken in Vārāṇasī, in the Deer Park of Sārnāth. (NE 130: 50 folios, 1.5 bampo)

आर्यश्रीवसुपरिपृच्छा नाम महायानसूत्रम्

།འཕགས་པ་དཔལ་དབྱིག་གིས་ཞུས་པ་ཞེས་བྱ་བ་ཐེག་པ་ཆེན་པོའི་མདོ།

T

Ārya-śrīvasu-paripṛcchā-nāma-mahāyāna-sūtra For the benefit of the merchant Śrīvasu and a host of bhikṣus, the Buddha gave the Sūtra known as The Questions of Śrīvasu. Spoken in Vārāṇasī, in the Deer Park of Sārnāth. (NE 162: 9 folios, 115 śloka)

आर्यश्रीमतीब्राह्मणीपरिपृच्छा नाम महायानसूत्रम्

།འཕགས་པ་བྲམ་ཟེ་མོ་དཔལ་ལྡན་མས་ཞུས་པ་ཞེས་བྱ་བ་ཐེག་པ་ཆེན་པོའི་མདོ།

T C

Ārya-śrīmatībrāhmaṇī-paripṛcchā-nāma-mahāyāna-sūtra For the benefit of Śrīmatī, a Brahmin lady, and the assembly of seven hundred bhikṣus and many Great Bodhisattvas, the Buddha gave the Sūtra known as The Questions of the Brahmin Woman Śrīmatī, a teaching on the nature of existence. Spoken at Vārāṇasī, in the Ṛṣipaṭana. (NE 170, 5 folios, 90 śloka)

बुद्धपिटकदुःशीलनिग्रहो नाम महायानसूत्रम्

།སངས་རྒྱས་ཀྱི་སྡེ་སྣོད་ཚུལ་ཁྲིམས་འཆལ་བ་ཚར་གཅོད་པ་
ཞེས་བྱ་བ་ཐེག་པ་ཆེན་པོའི་མདོ།

T C

Buddhapiṭaka-duḥśīlanigraha-nāma-mahāyāna-sūtra At the request of Śāriputra, the Buddha gave this Sūtra on the future degeneration of the morality of the bhikṣus and the unhappy consequences of unsound principles or theories. This teaching was heard by an assembly of five hundred bhikṣus, including Ānanda, Śāriputra, Maudgalyāyana, and Kāśyapa. Spoken in the Deer Park of Sārnāth. (NE 220: 153 folios, 7 bampo)

कर्मशतकम्

།ལས་བརྒྱ་ཐམ་པ།

T F

Karmaśataka One hundred stories illustrating the operation of karma, told by the Buddha for the purpose of clearing away the darkness of ignorance and error. Most of these stories take place in Vārāṇasī, Rājagṛha, Śrāvastī, Vaiśālī, and Kapilavastu. (NE 340: 870 folios, 37 bampo, 11,100 śloka)

आर्यगयाशीर्षं नाम महायानसूत्रम्

།འཕགས་པ་ག་ཡཱ་མགོའི་རི་ཞེས་བྱ་བ་ཐེག་པ་ཆེན་པོའི་མདོ།

T C

Ārya-gayāśīrṣa-nāma-mahāyāna-sūtra Sometime after the enlightenment, in the shrine on the summit of Mount Gayā, the Bhagavan went into retreat to examine from within the essence of the Dharmadhātu. Having investigated various aspects of knowledge and the path to enlightenment, the Buddha engaged the Bodhisattva Mañjuśrī in a dialogue on the nature of the Bodhisattva. This teaching, known as The Sūtra of Gayā Hill, was spoken on Mount Gayā (Gayāśīrṣa) for the benefit of Mañjuśrī and the assembly of one thousand bhikṣus and many Great Bodhisattvas. (NE 109: 15 folios, 188 śloka)

आर्यरत्नमेघो नाम महायानसूत्रम्

།འཕགས་པ་དཀོན་མཆོག་སྤྲིན་ཞེས་བྱ་བ་ཐེག་པ་ཆེན་པོའི་མདོ།

T C

Ārya-ratnamegha-nāma-mahāyāna-sūtra At the request of the Bodhisattva Śaranivaraṇaviṣkambhin, the Buddha gave the Sūtra known as The Cloud of Jewels, an extensive teaching on the great virtues and how they may be practiced, to an assembly composed of seventy-two thousand bhikṣus including Ānanda, a large number of great upāsakas, eighty-four thousand Bodhisattvas, and many other beings. Spoken on the summit of Mount Gayā (Gayāśīrṣa). (NE 231: 223 folios, 7 bampo)

आर्यपरमार्थधर्मविजयो नाम महायानसूत्रम्

།འཕགས་པ་དོན་དམ་པའི་ཆོས་ཀྱིས་རྣམ་པར་རྒྱལ་བ་ཞེས་བྱ་བ་ཐེག་པ་ཆེན་པོའི་མདོ།

T C

Ārya-paramārtha-dharmavijaya-nāma-mahāyāna-sūtra On Mt. Gayā, the Bodhisattva Jinarāśi requested the Buddha to quickly teach all that had not yet been taught, as there were demons all around. The ascetics, great ṛṣis led by Jvālapradīpa, questioned the Buddha on birth and death and numerous other topics. Then the Enlightened One gave the Sūtra known as The Victory of the Dharma of Highest Truth to the assembly composed of a great number of bhikṣus, ninety-nine times ten million Bodhisattvas, eighty-six thousand bhikṣuṇīs, upāsakas, numerous gods, and many naked ascetics. Spoken on the summit of Mount Gayā (Gayāśīrṣa). (NE 246: 20 folios, 280 śloka)

शतसाहस्रिकाप्रज्ञापारमिता

།ཤེས་རབ་ཀྱི་ཕ་རོལ་ཏུ་ཕྱིན་པ་སྟོང་ཕྲག་བརྒྱ་པ།

T C

Śatasāhasrikā-prajñāpāramitā On the Vulture Peak near Rājagṛha, the Buddha gave this most extensive Prajñāpāramitā teaching in one hundred thousand śloka to five thousand members of the Sangha including Ānanda, a multitude of bhikṣus and bhikṣuṇīs, and millions of other Bodhisattvas, gods, and other beings. (NE 8: 9,416 folios, 301 bampo, 100,000 śloka)

पञ्चविंशतिसाहस्रिका प्रज्ञापारमिता

།ཤེས་རབ་ཀྱི་ཕ་རོལ་ཏུ་ཕྱིན་པ་སྟོང་ཕྲག་ཉི་ཤུ་ལྔ་པ།

T C E

Pañcaviṁśatisāhasrikā-prajñāpāramitā On the Vulture Peak near Rājagṛha, the Buddha gave this extensive Prajñāpāramitā teaching in twenty-five thousand śloka to five thousand bhikṣus including Ānanda, hundreds of thousands of nyutis of koṭis of Bodhisattvas with Maitreya at their head, gods, nāgas, many devout householders, and numerous other beings. (NE 9: 2,306 folios, 78 bampo, 25,000 śloka)

आर्याष्टादशसाहस्रिका प्रज्ञापारमिता नाम महायानसूत्रम्

།འཕགས་པ་ཤེས་རབ་ཀྱི་ཕ་རོལ་ཏུ་ཕྱིན་པ་ཁྲི་བརྒྱད་སྟོང་པ་ཞེས་བྱ་བ་ཐེག་པ་ཆེན་པོའི་མདོ།

T C

Ārya-aṣṭādaśasāhasrikā-prajñāpāramitā-nāma-mahāyāna-sūtra On the Vulture Peak near Rājagṛha, the Buddha gave this large Prajñāpāramitā teaching in eighteen thousand śloka to five thousand bhikṣus including Ānanda, countless Bodhisattvas including Mañjuśrī and Bhadrapāla, and many gods and other forms of beings. (NE 10: 1,613 folios, 60 bampo, 18,000 śloka)

आर्यदशसाहस्रिका प्रज्ञापारमिता नाम महायानसूत्रम्

།འཕགས་པ་ཤེས་རབ་ཀྱི་ཕ་རོལ་ཏུ་ཕྱིན་པ་ཁྲི་པ་ཞེས་བྱ་བ་ཐེག་པ་ཆེན་པོའི་མདོ།

T

Ārya-daśasāhasrikā-prajñāpāramitā-nāma-mahāyāna-sūtra On the Vulture Peak near Rājagṛha, the Buddha gave this teaching on the Perfection of Wisdom in ten thousand śloka to many thousands of bhikṣus including Ānanda, hundreds of thousands of Bodhisattvas, and a great number of gods, kinnaras, mahorāgas, nāgas, and other beings. (NE 11: 791 folios, 34 bampo, 10,000 śloka)

आर्याष्टसाहस्रिका प्रज्ञापारमिता

།འཕགས་པ་ཤེས་རབ་ཀྱི་ཕ་རོལ་ཏུ་ཕྱིན་པ་བརྒྱད་སྟོང་པ།

STCE

Ārya-aṣṭasāhasrikā-prajñāpāramitā By inspiring the dialogues of the disciples Subhūti, Śāriputra, Ānanda, and Pūrṇa, and the Great Bodhisattva Maitreya, the Buddha revealed the profound Prajñāpāramitā teaching in eight thousand śloka on the Vulture Peak near Rājagṛha. This teaching was heard by 1,250 bhikṣus, all of them Arhats, excepting only Ānanda; by hosts of Bodhisattvas, with Maitreya at their head; and by Śakra, chief of the Trāyastriṁśa gods. (NE 12: 570 folios, 24 bampo, 8,000 śloka)

आर्यप्रज्ञापारमिता सञ्चयगाथा

།འཕགས་པ་ཤེས་རབ་ཀྱི་ཕ་རོལ་ཏུ་ཕྱིན་པ་སྡུད་པ་ཚིགས་སུ་བཅད་པ།

STCE

Ārya-prajñāpāramitā-sañcayagāthā "Call forth as much as you can of love, of respect, and of faith. Remove the obstructing defilements, and clear away all your impurities. Listen to the Perfect Wisdom of the gentle Buddhas, taught for the welfare of the world, for the benefit of the heroic." With these words begins this verse summary of the Prajñāpāramitā teaching in eight thousand śloka. Spoken on the Vulture Peak near Rājagṛha. (NE 13: 37 folios, 1.5 bampo, 300 śloka)

आर्यपञ्चशतिका प्रज्ञापारमिता

།འཕགས་པ་ཤེས་རབ་ཀྱི་ཕ་རོལ་ཏུ་ཕྱིན་པ་ལྔ་བརྒྱ་པ།

TCE

Ārya-pañcaśatikā-prajñāpāramitā To his disciple Subhūti, a large assembly of bhikṣus, and a great number of Bodhisattvas, the Buddha gave this teaching on the emptiness of form and the rest of the skandhas and the implications of this knowledge to the Bodhisattva's practice. This teaching, known as The Perfection of Wisdom in Five Hundred Verses, delighted the venerable disciple Subhūti and the assemblies of bhikṣus and bhikṣuṇīs, laymen and laywomen, filling with joy the world with its gods, men, asuras, and gandharvas. Spoken on the Vulture Peak near Rājagṛha. (NE 15: 34 folios, 1 bampo)

आर्यप्रज्ञापारमितानयशतपञ्चशतिका

།འཕགས་པ་ཤེས་རབ་ཀྱི་ཕ་རོལ་ཏུ་ཕྱིན་པའི་ཚུལ་བརྒྱ་ལྔ་བཅུ་པ།

STC

Ārya-prajñāpāramitā-naya-śatapañcāśatikā The Perfection of Wisdom in One Hundred and Fifty Verses, spoken to one hundred times ten million Great Bodhisattvas, including Vajrapāṇi, Avalokiteśvara, and Akāśagarbha. Spoken on the Vulture Peak near Rājagṛha. (NE 17: 14 folios, 150 śloka)

आर्यभगवतीप्रज्ञापारमितापञ्चशतिका

།འཕགས་པ་བཅོམ་ལྡན་འདས་མ་ཤེས་རབ་ཀྱི་ཕ་རོལ་ཏུ་ཕྱིན་པ་ལྔ་བཅུ་པ།

T C E

Ārya-bhagavatī-prajñāpāramitā-pañcāśatikā The Perfection of Wisdom in Fifty Verses, a teaching enumerating the dharmas leading to enlightenment, given by the Buddha to the disciple Subhūti, a large assembly of Arhats, bhikṣus, bhikṣuṇīs, laymen and laywomen, and a vast host of Bodhisattvas, together with Indra, Brahmā, the four world protectors, gods, nāgas, asuras, and numerous other beings. Spoken on the Vulture Peak near Rājagṛha. (NE 18: 6 folios, 50 śloka)

आर्यकौशिकप्रज्ञापारमिता नाम

།འཕགས་པ་ཤེས་རབ་ཀྱི་ཕ་རོལ་ཏུ་ཕྱིན་པ་ཀཽ་ཤི་ཀ་ཞེས་བྱ་བ།

S T C E

Ārya-kauśika-prajñāpāramitā-nāma A teaching on the meaning of perfect wisdom known as The Perfection of Wisdom for Kauśika, given for the benefit of Kauśika (Indra), lord of the gods, to a large assembly of bhikṣus and many hundreds of thousands of Bodhisattvas who had attained the stage of Crown Prince. Spoken on the Vulture Peak near Rājagṛha. (NE 19: 4 folios, 31 śloka)

भगवतीप्रज्ञापारमिताहृदयः

།བཅོམ་ལྡན་འདས་མ་ཤེས་རབ་ཀྱི་ཕ་རོལ་ཏུ་ཕྱིན་པའི་སྙིང་པོ།

STCEFG

Bhagavatī-prajñāpāramitā-hṛdaya When the Buddha entered the samādhi known as Profound Illumination, the Bodhisattva Avalokiteśvara perceived the five skandhas and their natural emptiness. Inspired by the Buddha, Śāriputra said to Avalokiteśvara, "How should those noble ones learn, who wish to follow the profound practice of transcendent knowledge?" In answer, Avalokiteśvara related the Sūtra known as The Heart of the Perfection of Wisdom, bringing joy to Śāriputra and the great assemblies of bhikṣus, Bodhisattvas, gods, asuras, and gandharvas. Spoken on the Vulture Peak near Rājagṛha. (NE 21: 4 folios, 25 śloka)

आर्यस्वल्पाक्षरा प्रज्ञापारमिता नाम महायानसूत्रम्

།འཕགས་པ་ཤེས་རབ་ཀྱི་ཕ་རོལ་ཏུ་ཕྱིན་པ་ཡི་གེ་ཉུང་ངུ་ཞེས་བྱ་བ་ཐེག་པ་ཆེན་པོའི་མདོ།

STCE

Ārya-svalpākṣara-prajñāpāramitā-nāma-mahāyāna-sūtra At the request of the Great Bodhisattva Avalokiteśvara, the Buddha taught the mantra known as The Perfection of Wisdom in a Few Words to an assembly of twelve thousand five hundred bhikṣus and many hundreds of thousands of billions of Bodhisattvas, as well as Indra, Brahmā, the world protectors, and many gods. Spoken on the Vulture Peak near Rājagṛha. (NE 22: 4 folios, 30 śloka)

एकाक्षरीमाता नाम सर्वतथागती प्रज्ञापारमिता

།དེ་བཞིན་གཤེགས་པ་ཐམས་ཅད་ཀྱི་ཡུམ་ཤེས་རབ་ཀྱི་ཕ་རོལ་ཏུ་ཕྱིན་མ་ཡི་གེ་གཅིག་མ་ཞེས་བྱ་བ།

T E

Ekākṣarīmātā-nāma-sarvatathāgata-prajñāpāramitā The Perfection of Wisdom of All the Tathāgatas in One Letter, expressed by the Buddha as the letter A, given to Ānanda, many bhikṣus, and ten million times one hundred billion Bodhisattvas for the sake of the welfare and happiness of all beings. Spoken on the Vulture Peak near Rājagṛha. (NE 23: 1 folio)

आर्यप्रज्ञापारमिता नाम अष्टशतकम्

།འཕགས་པ་ཤེས་རབ་ཀྱི་ཕ་རོལ་ཏུ་ཕྱིན་པའི་མཚན་བརྒྱ་རྩ་བརྒྱད་པ་ཞེས་བྱ་བ།

T C E

Ārya-prajñāpāramitā-nāmāṣṭaśataka The 108 Names of the Perfection of Wisdom, mother of all the Buddhas, beginning with Omniscience, Knowledge of the Modes of the Path, and Knowledge of All Modes. One who bears in mind the names of Prajñāpāramitā will become free from all karmic obscurations; in the next life he will bear in mind the teachings of all the Tathāgatas of the three times and will become mindful, self-controlled, and most excellently wise. Spoken by the Buddha. (no place or assembly named) (NE 25: 4 folios, 30 śloka)

आर्यचन्द्रगर्भप्रज्ञापारमिता महायानसूत्रम्

།འཕགས་པ་ཟླ་བའི་སྙིང་པོ་ཤེས་རབ་ཀྱི་ཕ་རོལ་ཏུ་ཕྱིན་པ་ཐེག་པ་ཆེན་པོའི་མདོ།

T E

Ārya-candragarbha-prajñāpāramitā-mahāyāna-sūtra At the request of the Bodhisattva Candragarbha, the Buddha gave the teaching on the Bodhisattva's perfection of wisdom known as The Perfection of Wisdom for Candragarbha to an assembly of innumerable bhikṣus and a great number of Bodhisattvas. Spoken on the Vulture Peak near Rājagṛha. (NE 27: 3 folios)

आर्यप्रज्ञापारमिता वज्रपाणिमहायानसूत्रम्

།འཕགས་པ་ཤེས་རབ་ཀྱི་ཕ་རོལ་ཏུ་ཕྱིན་པ་ལག་ན་རྡོ་རྗེའི་མདོ་ཐེག་པ་ཆེན་པོ།

T E

Ārya-prajñāpāramitā-vajrapāṇi-mahāyāna-sūtra While the Buddha was dwelling at Rājagṛha, surrounded by a great assembly of bhikṣus and bhikṣuṇīs, laymen and laywomen, and numerous Bodhisattvas, the Bodhisattva Vajrapāṇi rose from his seat and asked the Blessed One, "How should a Bodhisattva train in the perfection of wisdom?" In response to this question, the Buddha gave the teaching known as The Perfection of Wisdom for Vajrapāṇi, advising the Great Bodhisattva concerning the non-production of all dharmas. (NE 29: 2 folios)

आर्यप्रज्ञापारमिता वज्रकेतुमहायानसूत्रम्

།འཕགས་པ་ཤེས་རབ་ཀྱི་ཕ་རོལ་ཏུ་ཕྱིན་པ་རྡོ་རྗེ་རྒྱལ་མཚན་གྱི་མདོ་ཐེག་པ་ཆེན་པོ།

T E

Ārya-prajñāpāramitā-vajraketu-mahāyāna-sūtra While the Buddha was dwelling at Rājagṛha together with a great assembly of bhikṣus and bhikṣuṇīs, laymen and laywomen, and innumerable Bodhisattvas, the Bodhisattva Vajraketu asked, "With which dharmas is the perfection of wisdom endowed?" In reply, the Buddha gave a teaching on the four kinds of dharmas associated with the production of wisdom. This teaching is known as The Perfection of Wisdom for Vajraketu. (NE 30: 2 folios)

आटानाटीयसूत्रम्

།ལྕང་ལོ་ཅན་གྱི་ཕོ་བྲང་གི་མདོ།

T C E

Āṭānāṭīya-sūtra At the request of Vaiśravaṇa, Lord of the Yakṣas, the Buddha gave this teaching on moral conduct and the consequences of actions to an assembly of the four great kings, many clans of yakṣas, gandharvas, kumbhāṇḍas, nāgas, and other beings who guard the four directions. Spoken on the Vulture Peak near Rājagṛha. (NE 33: 20 folios)

आर्यसर्वधर्मस्वभावसमताविपञ्चितसमाधिराजो नाम महायानसूत्रम्

།འཕགས་པ་ཆོས་ཐམས་ཅད་ཀྱི་རང་བཞིན་མཉམ་པ་ཉིད་རྣམ་པར་སྤྲོས་པ་
ཏིང་ངེ་འཛིན་གྱི་རྒྱལ་པོ་ཞེས་བྱ་བ་ཐེག་པ་ཆེན་པོའི་མདོ།

S T C

Ārya-sarvadharma-svabhāva-samatāvipañcita-samādhirāja-nāma-mahāyāna-sūtra At the request of Candrakumāra, the Buddha described the various forms of meditation, especially the Samādhirāja, the King of Samādhis, which gives rise to the highest realization. This teaching was heard by one hundred thousand bhikṣus, one hundred billion Bodhisattvas led by Maitreya, and sixty Bodhisattvas with Mañjuśrī at their head. Also present were the sixteen devout householders led by Bhadrapāla, the Four Great Kings, and many devaputras and nāgas. Spoken on the Vulture Peak near Rājagṛha. (NE 127: 338 folios, 15 bampo, 4,500 śloka)

आर्यप्रशान्तविनिश्चयप्रातिहार्यसमाधिर्नाम महायानसूत्रम्

།འཕགས་པ་རབ་ཏུ་ཞི་བ་རྣམ་པར་ངེས་པའི་ཆོ་འཕྲུལ་གྱི་ཏིང་ངེ་འཛིན་
ཞེས་བྱ་བ་ཐེག་པ་ཆེན་པོའི་མདོ།

T C

Ārya-praśānta-viniścaya-prātihārya-samādhi-nāma-mahāyāna-sūtra The Buddha imparted the Sūtra known as The Samādhi of the Definite Manifestation of True Peace, a teaching on the nature of existence, to an assembly of 1,250 bhikṣus, Mañjuśrī, Avalokiteśvara, and a great number of Bodhisattvas, nāgas, and innumerable other beings. Spoken on the Vulture Peak near Rājagṛha. (NE 129: 72 folios, 3 bampo)

आर्यशूरंगमसमाधिर्नाम महायानसूत्रम्

།འཕགས་པ་དཔའ་བར་འགྲོ་བའི་ཏིང་ངེ་འཛིན་ཞེས་བྱ་བ་ཐེག་པ་ཆེན་པོའི་མདོ།

TCEF

Ārya-śūraṁgamasamādhi-nāma-mahāyāna-sūtra At the request of the Bodhisattva Sthiramati, the Buddha taught the profound meditation known as The Samādhi That Proceeds Strongly to Realization to an assembly of thirty-two thousand bhikṣus, one hundred and four thousand Bodhisattvas, Indra, Brahmā, the world-protectors, gods, nāgas, and a vast multitude of other beings. Spoken on the Vulture Peak near Rājagṛha. (NE 132: 125 folios, 5 bampo)

आर्यमहायानप्रसादप्रभावनं नाम महायानसूत्रम्

།འཕགས་པ་ཐེག་པ་ཆེན་པོ་ལ་དད་པ་རབ་ཏུ་སྒོམ་པ་ཞེས་བྱ་བ་ཐེག་པ་ཆེན་པོའི་མདོ།

T

Ārya-mahāyāna-prasāda-prabhāvana-nāma-mahāyāna-sūtra At the request of the Bodhisattva Upāyaprasāda, the Buddha explained the degrees of accomplishment of the Bodhisattvas. This teaching, known as Revealing the Truth of the Great Vehicle, was heard by five thousand Bodhisattvas from many different Buddha-realms, 1,250 bhikṣus led by Kāśyapa, and a vast assembly of gods, nāgas, and numerous other beings. Spoken on the Vulture Peak near Rājagṛha. (NE 144: 36 folios, 2 bampo)

आर्यरत्नोल्का नाम धारणी महायानसूत्रम्

།འཕགས་པ་དཀོན་མཆོག་ཏ་ལ་ལའི་གཟུངས་ཞེས་བྱ་བ་ཐེག་པ་ཆེན་པོའི་མདོ།

T C

Ārya-ratnolkā-nāma-dhāraṇī-mahāyāna-sūtra At the request of the Bodhisattva Samantabhadra, the Buddha taught this invocation of the Dharmadhātu and the Mahāyāna to an assembly of one thousand bhikṣus and many Great Bodhisattvas. Spoken on the Vulture Peak near Rājagṛha. (NE 145: 127 folios, 4 bampo)

आर्यतथागतमहाकरुणानिर्देशो नाम महायानसूत्रम्

།འཕགས་པ་དེ་བཞིན་གཤེགས་པའི་སྙིང་རྗེ་ཆེན་པོ་ངེས་པར་བསྟན་པ་
ཞེས་བྱ་བ་ཐེག་པ་ཆེན་པོའི་མདོ།

T C

Ārya-tathāgata-mahākaruṇā-nirdeśa-nāma-mahāyāna-sūtra Near a great stūpa built to commemorate the former Buddhas, the Buddha gave a teaching known as The Great Compassion of the Tathāgatas, giving numerous accounts of different beings and their actions. Spoken on the Vulture Peak for the benefit of the assembly of six thousand bhikṣus and innumerable Bodhisattvas. (NE 147: 202 folios, 7 bampo)

आर्यमैत्रेयपरिपृच्छा नाम महायानसूत्रम्

།འཕགས་པ་བྱམས་པས་ཞུས་པ་ཞེས་བྱ་བ་ཐེག་པ་ཆེན་པོའི་མདོ།

T C

Ārya-maitreya-paripṛcchā-nāma-mahāyāna-sūtra In response to the Bodhisattva Maitreya, who inquired concerning the merit arising from instructing beings in the Dharma, the Buddha taught that the Dharma was the most valuable of all gifts, and that the merit of giving the Dharma was beyond compare. This teaching, known as The Questions of Maitreya, was spoken on the Vulture Peak near Rājagṛha to a large assembly of bhikṣus and Bodhisattvas. (NE 149: 2 folios, 70 śloka)

आर्यावलोकितेश्वरपरिपृच्छा सप्तधर्मकं नाम महायानसूत्रम्

།འཕགས་པ་སྤྱན་རས་གཟིགས་དབང་ཕྱུག་གིས་ཞུས་པ་ཆོས་བདུན་པ་ཞེས་བྱ་བ་ཐེག་པ་ཆེན་པོའི་མདོ།

T

Ārya-avalokiteśvara-paripṛcchā-saptadharmaka-nāma-mahāyāna-sūtra At the request of the Bodhisattva Avalokiteśvara, the Buddha explained the seven dharmas necessary for a Bodhisattva to comprehend. This teaching, known as The Question of Avalokiteśvara on the Seven Dharmas, was spoken on the Vulture Peak near Rājagṛha to an assembly of 1,250 bhikṣus and innumerable Great Bodhisattvas. (NE 150: 2 folios)

आर्यसागरनागराजपरिपृच्छा नाम महायानसूत्रम्

།འཕགས་པ་ཀླུའི་རྒྱལ་པོ་རྒྱ་མཚོས་ཞུས་པ་ཞེས་བྱ་བ་ཐེག་པ་ཆེན་པོའི་མདོ།

T C

Ārya-sāgaranāgarāja-paripṛcchā-nāma-mahāyāna-sūtra At the request of Sāgara, king of the nāgas, the Buddha gave the Sūtra known as The Questions of the Nāga King Sāgara for the benefit of Sāgara and his eight hundred and forty million attendants, and for the nāga princesses and their seven hundred and twenty million attendants. Present in the Buddha's assembly were eight thousand bhikṣus, Great Bodhisattvas who gathered there from the ten directions, Bhadrapāla, the Four Great Kings, and a multitude of gods and other beings. Spoken on the Vulture Peak near Rājagṛha. (NE 153: 165 folios, 7 bampo)

आर्यद्रुमकिन्नरराजपरिपृच्छा नाम महायानसूत्रम्

།འཕགས་པ་མི་འམ་ཅིའི་རྒྱལ་པོ་སྡོང་པོས་ཞུས་པ་ཞེས་བྱ་བ་ཐེག་པ་ཆེན་པོའི་མདོ།

T C E

Ārya-drumakinnararāja-paripṛcchā-nāma-mahāyāna-sūtra At the request of the Great Bodhisattva Mukuṭadeva, who asked about the self-reliance of the Bodhisattva and skillful means, the Buddha gave the teaching known as The Questions of Druma, king of the Kinnaras, to the assembly of sixty-two thousand bhikṣus, seventy-two thousand Bodhisattvas of the highest attainments, and many other beings. Spoken on the Vulture Peak near Rājagṛha. (NE 157: 131 folios, 5 bampo)

आर्यराष्ट्रपालपरिपृच्छा नाम महायानसूत्रम्

།འཕགས་པ་ཡུལ་འཁོར་སྐྱོང་གིས་ཞུས་པ་ཞེས་བྱ་བ་ཐེག་པ་ཆེན་པོའི་མདོ།

T E

Ārya-rāṣṭrapāla-paripṛcchā-nāma-mahāyāna-sūtra For the benefit of the Bodhisattva Rāṣṭrapāla, the Buddha gave this Sūtra known as The Questions of Rāṣṭrapāla, a teaching on the means of insuring the longevity of the Dharma and the great importance of moral conduct for those who wish to transcend suffering. Spoken on the Vulture Peak near Rājagṛha to the assembly of 1,250 bhikṣus and numerous other beings. (NE 166: 8 folios, 73 śloka)

विमलप्रभपरिपृच्छा

།དྲི་མ་མེད་པའི་འོད་ཀྱིས་ཞུས་པ།

T

Vimalaprabha-paripṛcchā While the Buddha was explaining the Candragarbha-sūtra on the Vulture Peak, the time came to entrust the world to the great guardians. Assembling the gods and Vaiśravaṇa, master of the yakṣas, the Buddha gave the teaching known as The Questions of Vimalaprabha, in which he prophesied that one hundred years after his Parinirvāṇa the Dharma would enter the country named Li-yul (Khotan). The Tathāgata then entrusted this country to Vaiśravaṇa's protection. Spoken on the Vulture Peak. (NE 168: 98 folios, 4 bampo)

आर्यबोधिपक्षनिर्देशो नाम महायानसूत्रम्

།འཕགས་པ་བྱང་ཆུབ་ཀྱི་ཕྱོགས་བསྟན་པ་ཞེས་བྱ་བ་ཐེག་པ་ཆེན་པོའི་མདོ།

T C

Ārya-bodhipakṣanirdeśa-nāma-mahāyāna-sūtra In response to a request by the Great Bodhisattva Mañjuśrī, the Buddha gave the Sūtra known as Instruction on the Wings of Enlightenment to the assembly of five hundred bhikṣus, Mañjuśrī, Maitreya, and a multitude of Bodhisattvas. Spoken on the Vulture Peak near Rājagṛha. (NE 178: 8 folios, 92 śloka)

आर्यसंवृतिपरमार्थसत्यनिर्देशो नाम महायानसूत्रम्

།འཕགས་པ་ཀུན་རྫོབ་དང་དོན་དམ་པའི་བདེན་པ་བསྟན་པ་
ཞེས་བྱ་བ་ཐེག་པ་ཆེན་པོའི་མདོ།

T C

Ārya-samvṛtiparamārthasatya-nirdeśa-nāma-mahāyāna-sūtra At the request of a devaputra, the Buddha called Mañjuśrī from the Buddhafield of the Tathāgata Ratnaketu to give the Sūtra known as the Instruction on Relative and Absolute Truth. This Sūtra was heard by the assembly of eight thousand bhikṣus and seventy-two thousand Bodhisattvas as well as by numerous gods, devaputras, and other beings. Spoken on the Vulture Peak near Rājagṛha. (NE 179: 45 folios, 2 bampo)

आर्यसर्वधर्मप्रवृत्तिनिर्देशो नाम महायानसूत्रम्

།འཕགས་པ་ཆོས་ཐམས་ཅད་འབྱུང་བ་མེད་པར་བསྟན་པ
ཞེས་བྱ་བ་ཐེག་པ་ཆེན་པོའི་མདོ།

T C

Ārya-sarvadharmapravṛttinirdeśa-nāma-mahāyāna-sūtra The Bodhisattva Siṁhavikrama asked questions concerning the selfless nature of the elements of existence and the attainment of tranquility. In response, the Buddha gave the Sūtra known as The Instruction on the Arising of All Dharmas to the assembly of five hundred bhikṣus and twelve thousand Bodhisattvas. Spoken on the Vulture Peak near Rājagṛha. (NE 180: 59 folios, 3 bampo)

आर्यस्त्रीविवर्तव्याकरणं नाम महायानसूत्रम्

།འཕགས་པ་བུད་མེད་འགྱུར་བ་ལུང་བསྟན་པ་ཞེས་བྱ་བ་ཐེག་པ་ཆེན་པོའི་མདོ།

T C

Ārya-strīvivarta-vyākaraṇa-nāma-mahāyāna-sūtra The Bodhisattva Subhūti, inspired by the Buddha, gave a discourse on doctrine to a Bodhisattva who had taken the form of a woman and predicted the woman's attainment to Buddhahood. Known as The Prediction to the Transformed Woman, this teaching was heard by five thousand bhikṣus and eight thousand Bodhisattvas including Maitreya and all the Bodhisattvas of the Golden Aeon, as well as the king, princes, merchants, householders, and other residents of Rājagṛha. Spoken on the Vulture Peak near Rājagṛha. (NE 190: 48 folios, 2 bampo)

आर्यावलोकनं नाम महायानसूत्रम्

།འཕགས་པ་སྤྱན་རས་གཟིགས་ཞེས་བྱ་བ་ཐེག་པ་ཆེན་པོའི་མདོ།

T

Ārya-avalokana-nāma-mahāyāna-sūtra At the request of the Bodhisattva Viśuddhamati, the Buddha spoke on the benefits arising from the practice of moral purity. This teaching, given on the Vulture Peak near Rājagṛha, was heard by an assembly of bhikṣus and numerous Great Bodhisattvas. (NE 195: 31 folios, 1 bampo)

आर्यमञ्जुश्रीविहारो नाम महायानसूत्रम्

།འཕགས་པ་འཇམ་དཔལ་གནས་པ་ཞེས་བྱ་བ་ཐེག་པ་ཆེན་པོའི་མདོ།

T C

Ārya-mañjuśrīvihāra-nāma-mahāyāna-sūtra Once Mañjuśrī, inspired by the Buddha, discoursed with Śāriputra on the nature of worldly existence and other profound insights. This teaching, known as The Dwelling-Place of Mañjuśrī, was heard by an assembly of five hundred bhikṣus and a multitude of Great Bodhisattvas. Spoken on the Vulture Peak near Rājagṛha. (NE 196: 11 folios, 140 śloka)

आर्यनियतानियतगतिमुद्रावतारो नाम महायानसूत्रम्

།འཕགས་པ་ངེས་པ་དང་མ་ངེས་པར་འགྲོ་བའི་ཕྱག་རྒྱ་ལ་འཇུག་པ་ཞེས་བྱ་བ་ཐེག་པ་ཆེན་པོའི་མདོ།

T C

Ārya-niyatāniyatagatimudrāvatāra-nāma-mahāyāna-sūtra At the request of Mañjuśrī, the Buddha gave this Sūtra, a teaching on certain and uncertain means of advancing to enlightened perfection, to an assembly of 1,250 bhikṣus and millions of Bodhisattvas including Mañjuśrī and Avalokiteśvara. Spoken on the Vulture Peak near Rājagṛha. (NE 202: 31 folios, 1 bampo)

हस्तिकक्ष्यं नाम महायानसूत्रम्

།གླང་པོའི་རྩལ་ཞེས་བྱ་བ་ཐེག་པ་ཆེན་པོའི་མདོ།

T C

Hastikakṣya-nāma-mahāyāna-sūtra The Buddha gave this Sūtra known as Managing the Elephant, a teaching on managing one's body and mind and subduing the passions, for the benefit of Śāriputra and an assembly of five hundred bhikṣus and sixty thousand Bodhisattvas. Spoken on the Vulture Peak. (NE 207: 29 folios, 1 bampo)

आर्याजातशत्रुकौकृत्यविनोदनं नाम महायानसूत्रम्

།འཕགས་པ་མ་སྐྱེས་དགྲའི་འགྱོད་པ་བསལ་བ་ཞེས་བྱ་བ་ཐེག་པ་ཆེན་པོའི་མདོ།

T C

Ārya-ajātaśatru-kaukṛttyavinodana-nāma-mahāyāna-sūtra Deep in despair after causing the death of his father, Ajātaśatru, king of Magadha, climbed the Vulture Peak to hear the Buddha's advice. On this occasion the Buddha comforted the repentant king with the teaching known as Dispelling the Doing of Evil. This teaching was heard by the assembly of 1,250 bhikṣus, eighty-four thousand Bodhisattvas from various Buddhafields, gods, nāgas, devaputras, and many thousands of other beings. Spoken on the Vulture Peak near Rājagṛha. (NE 216: 115 folios, 5 bampo)

आर्यश्रीगुप्तो नाम सूत्रम्

།འཕགས་པ་དཔལ་སྦས་ཞེས་བྱ་བའི་མདོ།

T C

Ārya-śrīgupta-nāma-sūtra The Buddha related the story of the misguided householder Śrīgupta, who first attempted to destroy the Blessed One, then repented and took refuge in the Buddha. This teaching was heard by the assembly of 1,250 bhikṣus, kings, ministers, householders, and many others, including adherents of non-Buddhist views. Spoken on the Vulture Peak near Rājagṛha. (NE 217: 31 folios, 1 bampo)

आर्यस्थिराध्याशयपरिवर्तो नाम महायानसूत्रम्

།འཕགས་པ་ལྷག་པའི་བསམ་པ་བརྟན་པའི་ལེའུ་ཞེས་བྱ་བ་ཐེག་པ་ཆེན་པོའི་མདོ།

T

Ārya-sthirādhyāśaya-parivarta-nāma-mahāyāna-sūtra To benefit the Bodhisattva Sthirādhyāśaya and the assembly of 1,250 bhikṣus and five hundred Bodhisattvas, the Buddha gave this teaching on freeing the mind from lustful desires. Spoken on the Vulture Peak near Rājagṛha. (NE 224: 20 folios, 1 bampo)

आर्यसर्ववैदल्यसंग्रहो नाम महायानसूत्रम्

།འཕགས་པ་རྣམ་པར་འཐག་པ་ཐམས་ཅད་བསྡུས་པ་ཞེས་བྱ་བ་ཐེག་པ་ཆེན་པོའི་མདོ།

T C

Ārya-sarvavaidalya-saṁgraha-nāma-mahāyāna-sūtra At the request of the Great Bodhisattva Maitreya, the Buddha gave a collection of teachings for attaining enlightenment. This teaching, given in the last few years of the Buddha's life, was heard by sixty-two thousand bhikṣus and eighty times ten million Bodhisattvas. Spoken on the summit of the Vulture Peak near Rājagṛha. (NE 227: 24 folios, 1 bampo)

आर्यमहामेघो नाम महायानसूत्रम्
།འཕགས་པ་སྤྲིན་ཆེན་པོ་ཞེས་བྱ་བ་ཐེག་པ་ཆེན་པོའི་མདོ།

T C

Ārya-mahāmegha-nāma-mahāyāna-sūtra At the request of the Bodhisattva Mahāmeghagarbha, the Buddha gave The Sūtra for Mahāmegha, a teaching on the perfections of the Buddha's qualities, the excellence of the doctrine, and other Dharma topics, to an assembly of nine million eight hundred thousand great bhikṣus including Kāśyapa, and six million five hundred thousand bhikṣuṇīs including Gautamī, together with Bodhisattvas, gods, and other beings. Spoken on the Vulture Peak near Rājagṛha. (NE 232: 204 folios, 10 bampo, 3,000 śloka)

आर्यमहामेघसूत्राद् दशदिग्बोधिसत्त्वसमुद्रसन्निपाति महोत्सवविक्रीडितं नाम परिवर्तः
།འཕགས་པ་སྤྲིན་ཆེན་པོའི་མདོ་ལས་ཕྱོགས་བཅུའི་བྱང་ཆུབ་སེམས་དཔའ་རྒྱ་མཚོ་འདུས་པའི་དགའ་སྟོན་ཆེན་པོ་ལ་རྩེ་བ་ཞེས་བྱ་བའི་ལེའུ།

T

Ārya-mahāmegha-sūtrād daśadig-bodhisattvasamudrasannipāti-mahotsava-vikrīḍita-nāma-parivarta At the request of the Bodhisattva Samantabhadra, the Buddha gave the Dharma teaching known as The Amusements of an Ocean of Bodhisattvas Assembled from the Ten Directions to an assembly of eighty million bhikṣus, six million five hundred thousand bhikṣuṇīs, six million eight hundred thousand Bodhisattvas, and five million eight hundred thousand Licchavi youths including Siṁha. Spoken on the Vulture Peak near Rājagṛha. (NE 233: 62 folios, 3 bampo)

आर्यसमाधिचक्रं नाम महायानसूत्रम्

།འཕགས་པ་ཏིང་ངེ་འཛིན་གྱི་འཁོར་ལོ་ཞེས་བྱ་བ་ཐེག་པ་ཆེན་པོའི་མདོ།

T

Ārya-samādhicakra-nāma-mahāyāna-sūtra At the request of the Great Bodhisattva Mañjuśrī, the Buddha gave the Sūtra known as The Wheel of Samādhi, a teaching on the nature of existence and samādhi, to the assembly of 1,250 bhikṣus, innumerable Bodhisattvas, and a multitude of gods, nāgas, yakṣas, and other beings. Spoken on the Vulture Peak near Rājagṛha. (NE 241: 3 folios)

बोधिसत्त्वप्रातिमोक्षचतुष्कनिर्हारो नाम महायानसूत्रम्

།བྱང་ཆུབ་སེམས་དཔའི་སོ་སོར་ཐར་པ་ཆོས་བཞི་སྒྲུབ་པ་ ཞེས་བྱ་བ་ཐེག་པ་ཆེན་པོའི་མདོ།

T

Bodhisattva-prātimokṣa-catuṣkanirhara-nāma-mahāyāna-sūtra At the request of Śāriputra, the Buddha gave this teaching on the four virtues through which a Bodhisattva arrives at the highest perfection. Spoken on the Vulture Peak near Rājagṛha. (NE 248: 26 folios, 1 bampo)

आर्यानक्षरकरण्डकवैरोचनगर्भो नाम महायानसूत्रम्

།འཕགས་པ་ཡི་གེ་མེད་པའི་ཟ་མ་ཏོག་རྣམ་པར་སྣང་མཛད་ཀྱི་སྙིང་པོ་ཞེས་བྱ་བ་ཐེག་པ་ཆེན་པོའི་མདོ།

T C

Ārya-anakṣarakaraṇḍaka-vairocanagarbha-nāma-mahāyāna-sūtra At the request of the Bodhisattva Viśeṣacinti, the Buddha gave this teaching on the nature of the Tathāgata, clarifying things to be avoided by the Bodhisattva and virtues to be practiced. Present in the assembly were many bhikṣus including Śāriputra, Maudgalyāyana, and Kāśyapa, and hundreds of thousands of billions of Bodhisattvas including Mañjuśrī and Maitreya. Spoken on the Vulture Peak near Rājagṛha. (NE 259: 10 folios, 100 śloka)

आर्यकुसुमसञ्चयो नाम महायानसूत्रम्

།འཕགས་པ་མེ་ཏོག་གི་ཚོགས་ཞེས་བྱ་བ་ཐེག་པ་ཆེན་པོའི་མདོ།

T C

Ārya-kusumasañcaya-nāma-mahāyāna-sūtra At the request of Śāriputra, the Buddha gave to an assembly of 1,250 bhikṣus the Sūtra known as The Multitude of Blossoms, enumerating some of the Buddhas who dwell in the ten directions and describing the benefits to be gained by reciting their names. Spoken on the Vulture Peak near Rājagṛha. (NE 266: 63 folios, 3 bampo)

दशबुद्धकं नाम महायानसूत्रम्

།སངས་རྒྱས་བཅུ་པ་ཞེས་བྱ་བ་ཐེག་པ་ཆེན་པོའི་མདོ།

T C

Daśabuddhaka-nāma-mahāyāna-sūtra At the request of the Bodhisattva Guṇaratnaśaṅku, the Buddha gave the Sūtra on the Ten Buddhas, describing the Buddhas of the ten directions and the benefits of reciting their names. This teaching was heard by the assembly of 1,250 bhikṣus and many thousands of Bodhisattvas. Spoken on the Vulture Peak near Rājagṛha. (NE 272: 10 folios, 140 śloka)

आर्यद्वादशबुद्धकं नाम महायानसूत्रम्

།འཕགས་པ་སངས་རྒྱས་བཅུ་གཉིས་པ་ཞེས་བྱ་བ་ཐེག་པ་ཆེན་པོའི་མདོ།

T C

Ārya-dvādaśabuddhaka-nāma-mahāyāna-sūtra Śākyamuni Buddha gave The Sūtra of the Twelve Buddhas, a teaching describing twelve Buddhas in various realms and the benefits of reciting their names, to the assembly of 1,250 bhikṣus and twelve thousand Bodhisattvas led by Maitreya. Spoken on the Vulture Peak near Rājagṛha. (NE 273: 8 folios, 77 śloka)

आर्यबुद्धमुकुटो नाम महायानसूत्रमहाधर्मपर्यायः

།འཕགས་པ་སངས་རྒྱས་ཀྱི་དབུ་རྒྱན་ཞེས་བྱ་བ་ཐེག་པ་ཆེན་པོའི་མདོ་ཆོས་ཀྱི་རྣམ་གྲངས་ཆེན་པོ།

T C

Ārya-buddhamukuṭa-nāma-mahāyāna-sūtra-mahā-dharma-paryāya In this Sūtra known as The Diadem of Buddhas, the Enlightened One described Tathāgatas of Buddha-realms in the far distant east and the benefits of reciting their names. This teaching was offered for the benefit of Kāśyapa and the assembly of 1,250 bhikṣus, the Bodhisattvas Maitreya and Mañjuśrī, and a host of gods, nāgas, and gandharvas. Spoken on the Vulture Peak near Rājagṛha. (NE 274: 13 folios, 200 śloka)

आर्यबुद्धाक्षेपणं नाम महायानसूत्रम्

།འཕགས་པ་སངས་རྒྱས་མི་སྤྱང་པ་ཞེས་བྱ་བ་ཐེག་པ་ཆེན་པོའི་མདོ།

T C

Ārya-buddhākṣepaṇa-nāma-mahāyāna-sūtra At the request of the Bodhisattva Acchambhin, Śākyamuni Buddha gave the Buddhākṣepaṇa Sūtra, a teaching on the virtues that empower perfection, for the benefit of Aśokadatta and ten other Bodhisattvas, and the assembly composed of 1,250 bhikṣus and eighty thousand Bodhisattvas. Spoken on the Vulture Peak near Rājagṛha. (NE 276: 11 folios, 120 śloka)

आर्यत्रिकायो नाम महायानसूत्रम्

།འཕགས་པ་སྐུ་གསུམ་ཞེས་བྱ་བ་ཐེག་པ་ཆེན་པོའི་མདོ།

T E

Ārya-trikāya-nāma-mahāyāna-sūtra At the request of the Bodhisattva Kṣitigarbha, the Buddha gave this teaching on the three forms of the Tathāgata—Nirmāṇakāya, Sambhogakāya, and Dharmakāya—to the assembly of innumerable Bodhisattvas, gods, and nāgas. Spoken on the Vulture Peak near Rājagṛha. (NE 283: 3 folios)

आर्यनन्दिकसूत्रम्

།འཕགས་པ་དགའ་བ་ཅན་གྱི་མདོ།

T F

Ārya-nandika-sūtra At the request of the disciple Nandika, Śākyamuni Buddha gave this instruction on the consequences of the ten nonvirtuous actions to the assembly of 1,250 bhikṣus. Spoken on the Vulture Peak near Rājagṛha. (NE 334: 7 folios, 200 śloka)

दीर्घनखपरिव्राजकपरिपृच्छा नाम सूत्रम्

། ཀུན་ཏུ་རྒྱུ་པ་སེན་རིངས་ཀྱིས་ཞུས་པ་ཞེས་བྱ་བའི་མདོ།

T C

Dīrghanakha-parivrājaka-paripṛcchā-nāma-sūtra In response to Dīrghanakha, the ascetic with extremely long fingernails, the Buddha gave the Sūtra known as The Questions of the Mendicant Dīrghanakha, in which he described the Buddha's former deeds and the merit that supported his progress toward complete, perfect enlightenment. Spoken on the Vulture Peak near Rājagṛha. (NE 342: 4 folios, 37 śloka)

महोपायकौशल्यबुद्धप्रत्युपकारकसूत्रम्

།ཐབས་ལ་མཁས་པ་ཆེན་པོ་སངས་རྒྱས་དྲིན་ལན་བསབ་པའི་མདོ།

T C E

Mahopāya-kauśalyabuddha-pratyupakāraka-sūtra On the Vulture Peak near Rājagṛha, the Buddha gave this teaching on the proper way of expressing gratitude and returning kindness to Ānanda and the assembly of twenty-eight thousand bhikṣus led by Kāśyapa, Śāriputra, Ānanda, Rāhula, and many others, including thirty-eight thousand Bodhisattvas and many gods of the desire realm. (NE 353: 223 folios, 7.5 bampo)

आर्यसुविक्रान्तविक्रामिपरिपृच्छा प्रज्ञापारमिता निर्देशः

།འཕགས་པ་རབ་ཀྱི་རྩལ་གྱིས་རྣམ་པར་གནོན་པས་ཞུས་པ་
ཤེས་རབ་ཀྱི་ཕ་རོལ་ཏུ་ཕྱིན་པ་བསྟན་པ།

TCE

Ārya-suvikrāntavikrāmi-paripṛcchā-prajñāpāramitā-nirdeśa For the benefit of the Bodhisattva Suvikrāntavikrāmin, the Buddha gave the teaching known as The Perfection of Wisdom Occasioned by the Questions of Suvikrāntavikrāmin, concerning the nature of the Bodhisattva's intention, perfection, and the manner of practice that matures and fulfills intention. Through this teaching, heard by 1,250 bhikṣus and a host of Bodhisattvas ready to enter their final birth, countless Bodhisattvas perfected their understanding, while innumerable other beings generated the thought of enlightenment and received their prediction to Buddhahood. Spoken in Rājagṛha, in the Bamboo Grove. (NE 14: 168 folios, 7 bampo)

आर्यवर्मव्यूहनिर्देशो नाम महायानसूत्रम्

།འཕགས་པ་གོ་ཆའི་བཀོད་པ་བསྟན་པ་ཞེས་བྱ་བ་ཐེག་པ་ཆེན་པོའི་མདོ།

TC

Ārya-varmavyūha-nirdeśa-nāma-mahāyāna-sūtra For the benefit of the Bodhisattva Anantamati, who requested that the Blessed One free him from all doubts and hesitations, the Buddha gave the teaching known as The Instruction on the Array of Protective Armor. This Dharma teaching was heard by countless hundreds of thousands of bhikṣus, Bodhisattvas, and other beings. Spoken in Rājagṛha, in the Bamboo Grove. (NE 51: 140 folios, 6 bampo)

आर्यानन्तमुखपरिशोधननिर्देशपरिवर्तो नाम महायानसूत्रम्

།འཕགས་པ་སྒོ་མཐའ་ཡས་པ་རྣམ་པར་སྦྱོང་བ་བསྟན་པའི་ལེའུ་ཞེས་བྱ་བ་ཐེག་པ་ཆེན་པོའི་མདོ།

T C

Ārya-anantamukha-pariśodhana-nirdeśa-parivarta-nāma-mahā-yāna-sūtra At the request of the Bodhisattva Anantavyūha, the Buddha gave this Sūtra known as The Instruction on the Purification of the Door to Infinity, explaining the qualities of the Bodhisattva and the Bodhisattva's skillful means to an assembly of many hundreds of thousands, including bhikṣus and countless Bodhisattvas who had assembled from the various Buddhafields. Spoken in Rājagṛha, in the Bamboo Grove. (NE 46: 89 folios, 4 bampo)

आर्यपूर्णपरिपृच्छा नाम महायानसूत्रम्

།འཕགས་པ་གང་པོས་ཞུས་པ་ཞེས་བྱ་བ་ཐེག་པ་ཆེན་པོའི་མདོ།

T C

Ārya-pūrṇaparipṛcchā-nāma-mahāyāna-sūtra The devoted disciple Pūrṇa asked the Blessed One, "How does one learn to make the mind pure, how does one learn to give greatly, how does one free living beings and meditate with a joyful mind?" In response, the Buddha gave the Sūtra known as The Questions of Pūrṇa, in which he explained the practices of Bodhisattvas to a vast assembly of bhikṣus and innumerable Great Bodhisattvas. Spoken in Rājagṛha, in the Bamboo Grove. (NE 61: 118 folios, 6 bampo)

आर्यसुबाहुपरिपृच्छा नाम महायानसूत्रम्

།འཕགས་པ་ལག་བཟངས་ཀྱིས་ཞུས་པ་ཞེས་བྱ་བ་ཐེག་པ་ཆེན་པོའི་མདོ།

T C

Ārya-subāhu-paripṛcchā-nāma-mahāyāna-sūtra In response to a question asked by the Bodhisattva Subāhu, the Buddha gave this discourse on the six pāramitās to Subāhu and the assembly of bhikṣus, clarifying how the Great Bodhisattvas practice the perfections. Spoken in Rājagṛha, in the Bamboo Grove. (NE 70: 54 folios, 2 bampo)

आर्यभद्रपालश्रेष्ठिपरिपृच्छा नाम महायानसूत्रम्

།འཕགས་པ་ཚོང་དཔོན་བཟང་སྐྱོང་གིས་ཞུས་པ་ ཞེས་བྱ་བ་ཐེག་པ་ཆེན་པོའི་མདོ།

T C E

Ārya-bhadrapālaśreṣṭhi-paripṛcchā-nāma-mahāyāna-sūtra Accompanied by a vast retinue, the merchant Bhadrapāla visited the Buddha and asked, among other questions, "What form does consciousness assume? Where does it go after it leaves the body? How can a future body reap the merit of deeds performed in this life?" For the benefit of Bhadrapāla, his retinue, the assembly of 1,250 bhikṣus led by Śāriputra, and innumerable Bodhisattvas, the Buddha gave this teaching on the nature of consciousness known as The Questions of Śreṣṭhin Bhadrapāla. Spoken in Rājagṛha, in the Bamboo Grove. (NE 83: 48 folios, 2 bampo, 600 śloka)

आर्यकुशलमूलसम्परिग्रहो नाम महायानसूत्रम्

།འཕགས་པ་དགེ་བའི་རྩ་བ་ཡོངས་སུ་འཛིན་པ་ཞེས་བྱ་བ་ཐེག་པ་ཆེན་པོའི་མདོ།

T C

Ārya-kuśalamūla-saṁparigraha-nāma-mahāyāna-sūtra The Buddha gave the Sūtra known as Grasping the Root of Happiness, an extensive teaching on moral and metaphysical doctrine, to the assembly of one hundred thousand bhikṣus including Śāriputra and Maudgalyāyana, five hundred other bhikṣus, and a thousand Bodhisattvas from different regions. Spoken in Rājagṛha, in the Bamboo Grove. (NE 101: 450 folios, 18 bampo, 5,400 śloka)

आर्यसर्वधर्मगुणव्यूहराजो नाम महायानसूत्रम्

།འཕགས་པ་ཆོས་ཐམས་ཅད་ཀྱི་ཡོན་ཏན་བཀོད་པའི་རྒྱལ་པོ་
ཞེས་བྱ་བ་ཐེག་པ་ཆེན་པོའི་མདོ།

T C

Ārya-sarvadharmaguṇavyūharāja-nāma-mahāyāna-sūtra At the request of the Bodhisattvas Vajrapāṇi and Avalokiteśvara, the Buddha gave a discourse on the qualities of all dharmas that developed from the Bodhisattva Guṇavyūha's description of what he saw around him. Present in this vast assembly were five hundred bhikṣus and numerous Bodhisattvas including Maitreya and Avalokiteśvara; Indra, Brahmā, and the Four World Guardians as well as many nāga kings and yakṣas; and six thousand ascetics and other adherents of non-Buddhist doctrines. Spoken in Rājagṛha, in the Bamboo Grove. (NE 114: 30 folios, 6 bampo)

आर्यतथागतज्ञानमुद्रासमाधिर्नाम महायानसूत्रम्

།འཕགས་པ་དེ་བཞིན་གཤེགས་པའི་ཡེ་ཤེས་ཀྱི་ཕྱག་རྒྱའི་ཏིང་ངེ་འཛིན་ཞེས་བྱ་བ་ཐེག་པ་ཆེན་པོའི་མདོ།

T C

Ārya-tathāgata-jñānamudrā-samādhi-nāma-mahāyāna-sūtra When the Buddha entered the samādhi known as the Gesture of the Tathāgata's Pristine Awareness, light filled the great trichiliocosm, illuminating Mt. Meru and all surroundings so brightly that even the blind could see them. At the Vulture Peak, lotus petals filled the air; beings of all kinds gathered to hear the Buddha, although none could see him. Abiding in this deep samādhi, the Buddha imparted the fruit of its wisdom to a vast assembly composed of 1,250 bhikṣus and three hundred million Bodhisattvas. Spoken in Rājagṛha, in the Bamboo Grove. (NE 131: 46 folios, 2 bampo)

आर्यप्रत्युत्पन्ने बुद्धसंमुखावस्थितसमाधिर्नाम महायानसूत्रम्

།འཕགས་པ་ད་ལྟར་གྱི་སངས་རྒྱས་མངོན་སུམ་དུ་བཞུགས་པའི་ཏིང་ངེ་འཛིན་ཞེས་བྱ་བ་ཐེག་པ་ཆེན་པོའི་མདོ།

T C E

Ārya-pratyutpanne buddha-saṁmukhāvasthita-samādhi-nāma-mahāyāna-sūtra At the request of the Bodhisattva Bhadrapāla, the Buddha related the teaching known as The Samādhi of the Arising of Enlightenment in the Present Moment to an assembly of five hundred bhikṣus, five hundred Bodhisattvas, and many others. Spoken in Rājagṛha, in the Bamboo Grove. (NE 133: 139 folios, 7 bampo)

आर्यराष्ट्रपालपरिपृच्छा नाम महायानसूत्रम्

།འཕགས་པ་ཡུལ་འཁོར་སྐྱོང་གིས་ཞུས་པ་ཞེས་བྱ་བ་ཐེག་པ་ཆེན་པོའི་མདོ།

STCE

Ārya-rāṣṭrapāla-paripṛcchā-nāma-mahāyāna-sūtra Rāṣṭrapāla asked the Blessed One, "Who are the ones who will bring the doctrine to ruin?" For the benefit of Rāṣṭrapāla and the entire assembly, the Buddha gave the Sūtra known as The Question of Rāṣṭrapāla, telling of those who adopted the spiritual life only in outward appearance and praising the true followers of the Dharma. Present were 1,250 bhikṣus, five thousand Bodhisattvas led by Samantabhadra, sixteen Great Bodhisattvas led by Mañjuśrī, together with Bhadrapāla and sixty other devout beings, Indra, Brahmā, the Four World Guardians, gods, nāgas, and hundreds of thousands of ḍākas and ḍākinīs. Spoken at Rājagṛha (Vulture Peak). (NE 62: 61 folios, 3 bampo)

बुद्धधर्मकोषकारः नाम महायानसूत्रम्

།སངས་རྒྱས་ཀྱི་མཛོད་ཀྱི་ཆོས་ཀྱི་ཡི་གེ།

TC

Buddhadharmakoṣakāra-nāma-mahāyāna-sūtra While abiding on Mt. Khumatha near Rājagṛha, at the request of the great elder Śāriputra, the Buddha explained the nature of conditioned existence in the Sūtra known as The Teaching of the Treasury of Buddhadharma. This Sūtra was heard by an assembly of many bhikṣus and an immeasurable number of Bodhisattvas. (NE 123: 119 folios, 4 bampo, 1,200 śloka)

आर्यसमाध्यग्रोत्तम

།འཕགས་པ་ཏིང་ངེ་འཛིན་མཆོག་དམ་པ།

T

Ārya-samādhyagrottama At the request of the bhikṣu Nanda, the Buddha gave this instruction known as The Highest Peak of Samādhi, a teaching on the accumulation of merit and the practice of moral conduct, to an assembly of thirty thousand bhikṣus, five thousand Bodhisattvas, many gods and nāgas, the four world-protectors, and a gathering of cannibals and hungry ghosts. Spoken in Rājagṛha. (NE 137: 18 folios, 1 bampo)

आर्याविकल्पप्रवेशा नाम धारणी

།འཕགས་པ་རྣམ་པར་མི་རྟོག་པར་འཇུག་པ་ཞེས་བྱ་བའི་གཟུངས།

T C

Ārya-avikalpapraveśa-nāma-dhāraṇī At the request of the Bodhisattva Avikalpāloka, the Buddha explained The Dhāraṇī of Nonconceptuality to many bhikṣus and Great Bodhisattvas led by Avalokiteśvara. Spoken in Rājagṛha. (NE 142: 11 folios, 120 śloka)

आर्यरत्नचन्द्रपरिपृच्छा नाम महायानसूत्रम्

།འཕགས་པ་རིན་ཆེན་ཟླ་བས་ཞུས་པ་ཞེས་བྱ་བ་ཐེག་པ་ཆེན་པོའི་མདོ།

T C

Ārya-ratnacandra-paripṛcchā-nāma-mahāyāna-sūtra Observing the Buddha approaching the city on his alms-rounds, King Bimbisāra's son Ratnacandra, filled with faith, came up to the Buddha, bowed, and asked the Bhagavan to explain the attainment of Buddhahood. For his benefit, the Buddha gave the Sūtra known as The Questions of Ratnacandra to the assembly of seven million two hundred thousand bhikṣus, ninety thousand Great Bodhisattvas including Mañjuśrī and Maitreya, and many hundreds of thousands of gods, nāga kings, and other beings. Spoken in Rājagṛha. (NE 164: 16 folios, 227 śloka)

आर्यतथागतगुणज्ञानाचिन्त्यविषयावतारनिर्देशो नाम महायानसूत्रम्

།འཕགས་པ་དེ་བཞིན་གཤེགས་པའི་ཡོན་ཏན་དང་ཡེ་ཤེས་བསམ་གྱིས་མི་ཁྱབ་པའི་ཡུལ་ལ་འཇུག་པ་བསྟན་པ་ཞེས་བྱ་བ་ཐེག་པ་ཆེན་པོའི་མདོ།

T C

Ārya-tathāgataguṇa-jñānācintya-viṣayāvatāra-nirdeśa-nāma-mahāyāna-sūtra In Magadha, the Buddha gave this teaching on the perfections of the Tathāgata to Mañjuśrī and an assembly of sixty-two times one hundred thousand bhikṣus including Śāriputra, Maudgalyāyana, and Kāśyapa, many Bodhisattvas, gods, yakṣas, and numerous other beings. Spoken in Rājagṛha. (NE 185: 76 folios, 3 bampo)

आर्यशालिस्तम्भो नाम महायानसूत्रम्

།འཕགས་པ་སཱ་ལུའི་ལྗང་པ་ཞེས་བྱ་བ་ཐེག་པ་ཆེན་པོའི་མདོ།

S T C F

Ārya-śālistambha-nāma-mahāyāna-sūtra While walking near fields of green rice, the Buddha gave to Śāriputra a teaching on pratītyasamutpāda using the rice field as an example of causal connection, beginning with the seed as the cause of the sprout. This teaching, known as The Sūtra of the Green Rice Stalks, was heard by the assembly of 1,250 bhikṣus and many Great Bodhisattvas. Spoken in Rājagṛha. (NE 210: 16 folios, 226 śloka)

आर्यबुद्धसंगीतिर्नाम महायानसूत्रम्

།འཕགས་པ་སངས་རྒྱས་བགྲོ་བ་ཞེས་བྱ་བ་ཐེག་པ་ཆེན་པོའི་མདོ།

T C

Ārya-buddhasaṁgīti-nāma-mahāyāna-sūtra Once, when the Buddha was dwelling in Magadha in a large cavern in the Mango Grove, four groups of beings concerned with the turbulence in the world came to hear the Buddha teach the Dharma. But after hearing the Blessed One, these beings did not always agree with or honor the Tathāgata. Knowing these unhappy beings did not understand the Dharma, the Buddha gave the teaching known as Song of the Enlightened One to the assembly of five thousand bhikṣus, twenty-five thousand Bodhisattvas including Maitreya and Mañjuśrī, and eighty-four thousand devaputras who followed the Mahāyāna. (NE 228: 75 folios, 3 bampo)

राजदेशो नाम महायानसूत्रम्

།རྒྱལ་པོ་ལ་གདམས་པ་ཞེས་བྱ་བ་ཐེག་པ་ཆེན་པོའི་མདོ།

T C

Rājadeśa-nāma-mahāyāna-sūtra For the benefit of Bimbisāra, king of Magadha, and the assembly of many bhikṣus and Great Bodhisattvas, the Buddha gave this Sūtra called Precepts for Kings, an instruction on ruling wisely. Spoken in Rājagṛha. (NE 214: 7 folios)

आर्यतथागतगर्भो नाम महायानसूत्रम्

།འཕགས་པ་དེ་བཞིན་གཤེགས་པའི་སྙིང་པོ་ཞེས་བྱ་བ་ཐེག་པ་ཆེན་པོའི་མདོ།

T C

Ārya-tathāgatagarbha-nāma-mahāyāna-sūtra Ten years after attaining enlightenment, when the Buddha was residing on a mountain near Rājagṛha, he gave the Sūtra known as The Heart of the Tathāgata, explaining the excellent qualities of the Tathāgata and some of the shortcomings of humans and animal beings. This teaching, requested by the Bodhisattva Vajrabodhi, was given to an assembly of hundreds of thousands of bhikṣus including the Arhats Subhūti, Śāriputra, and Maudgalyāyana, together with Maitreya and a vast multitude of other Great Bodhisattvas as numerous as the sands of the Ganges. (NE 258: 29 folios, 1 bampo)

आर्यघनजामहाभ्रिचफुलकर्म अविर्नशोधय भूधरकुसुमसञ्चयो नाम महायानसूत्रम्

།འཕགས་པ་ཐར་པ་ཆེན་པོ་ཕྱོགས་སུ་རྒྱས་པ་འགྱོད་ཚངས་ཀྱིས་སྡིག་སྦྱངས་ཏེ་ སངས་རྒྱས་སུ་གྲུབ་པར་རྣམ་པར་བཀོད་པ་ཞེས་བྱ་བ་ཐེག་པ་ཆེན་པོའི་མདོ།

T

Ārya-ghanajā-mahābhricaphula-karma-avirnaśodhaya-bhū-dhara-kusuma-sañcaya-nāma-mahāyāna-sūtra To a vast convocation of eighty thousand bhikṣus and thirty-six thousand Bodhisattvas, Śākyamuni Buddha gave this teaching on how to absolve transgressions through sincere repentance and by invoking the Buddhas and Great Bodhisattvas. Spoken in Rājagṛha. (NE 264: 9 folios, 2 bampo)

आर्यसद्धर्मस्मृत्युपस्थानम्

།འཕགས་པ་དམ་པའི་ཆོས་དྲན་པ་ཉེ་བར་གཞག་པ།

T C

Ārya-saddharmasmṛtyupasthāna As the Blessed One and his disciples were traveling to Rājagṛha, the Buddha gave in the Brahmin village of Nayati the Sūtra known as Abiding in Remembrance of the True Dharma, an extensive teaching on moral responsibilities and duties to be remembered and practiced. This teaching was heard by a large assembly of bhikṣus and a group of wandering ascetics interested in discussing the Dharma. (NE 287: 2162 folios, 120 bampo)

बिम्बिसारप्रत्युद्गमनं नाम महासूत्रम्

།མདོ་ཆེན་པོ་གཟུགས་ཅན་སྙིང་པོས་བསུ་བ་ཞེས་བྱ་བ།

T C

Bimbisāra-pratyudgamana-nāma-mahāsūtra In a grove near Rājagṛha, the capital of Magadha, King Bimbisāra came to visit the Blessed One accompanied by many hundreds of thousands of the people of Magadha, who also wished to behold the Buddha and pay their respects. For the benefit of the king and his people, the Buddha gave an instruction on the nature of compounded things and interdependent cooperation. This teaching became known as The Approach of Bimbisāra. (NE 289: 11 folios, .5 bampo)

आर्यचतुःसत्यसूत्रम्

།འཕགས་པ་བདེན་པ་བཞིའི་མདོ།

T C

Ārya-catuḥsatya-sūtra In a grove on the way from Rājagṛha to Lohita-Gaṅga, the Buddha gave to the assembly of bhikṣus this explanation of his teaching on the Four Noble Truths. (NE 316: 2 folios)

ब्रह्मजालसूत्रम्

།ཚངས་པའི་དྲ་བའི་མདོ།

T C E F G

Brahmajāla-sūtra In Magadha, on the way from Rājagṛha to Pāṭaliputra, the Buddha and his disciples rested in a royal grove where the ascetic Pramudita and his young disciple Brahmadatta were also staying. While the ascetic Pramudita spoke against the Buddha and the Sangha, the disciple Brahmadatta praised them. The following day the Buddha gave the Sūtra known as The Net of Brahmā, a teaching on the diversity of opinions concerning the origin and duration of the world, cautioning the assembly of 1,250 bhikṣus, one thousand upāsakas, and five hundred mendicant monks to keep their minds free from harmful thoughts and views. (NE 352: 32 folios, 2 bampo)

आर्यगोशृङ्गव्याकरणं नाम महायानसूत्रम्

།འཕགས་པ་གླང་རུ་ལུང་བསྟན་པ་ཞེས་བྱ་བ་ཐེག་པ་ཆེན་པོའི་མདོ།

T E

Ārya-gośṛṅgavyākaraṇa-nāma-mahāyāna-sūtra In the Sūtra known as The Prophecy of the Oxhorn Mountain, the Buddha described the future arising of the kingdom of Li-yul (Khotan) to the assembly of 1,250 bhikṣus, a vast multitude of Great Bodhisattvas with Maitreya at their head, Brahmā, Indra, a host of other gods, and Bimbisāra and other kings. Spoken in Rājagṛha. (NE 357: 23 folios, 1 bampo)

आर्याचिन्त्यराजसूत्रं नाम महायानसूत्रम्

།འཕགས་པ་བསམ་གྱིས་མི་ཁྱབ་པའི་རྒྱལ་པོའི་མདོ་ཞེས་བྱ་བའི་ཐེག་པ་ཆེན་པོའི་མདོ།

T

Ārya-acintyarājasūtra-nāma-mahāyāna-sūtra Once, when the Buddha was residing in Magadha, seated in deep samādhi in the heart of a lotus on the lion throne, the Bodhisattva Acintyarāja said to the assemby of Great Bodhisattvas, "O sons of the Conqueror, one kalpa of this Sahalokadhātu, realm of the world of endurance, this Buddhafield of Śākyamuni, is one day in the realm of Sukhāvatī." (NE 268: 4 folios, 75 śloka)

आर्यवज्रच्छेदिका नाम प्रज्ञापारमिता महायानसूत्रम्

།འཕགས་པ་ཤེས་རབ་ཀྱི་ཕ་རོལ་ཏུ་ཕྱིན་པ་རྡོ་རྗེ་གཅོད་པ་

ཞེས་བྱ་བ་ཐེག་པ་ཆེན་པོའི་མདོ།

S T C E F G

Ārya-vajracchedikā-nāma-prajñāpāramitā-mahāyāna-sūtra The Buddha, surrounded by a large assembly of 1,250 bhikṣus and many Bodhisattvas, responded to the question of his disciple Subhūti. This teaching on the Bodhisattva's vow, practice, Buddhahood, and the profound Prajñāpāramitā became known as The Perfection of Wisdom that Cuts Like a Diamond. Spoken in Śrāvastī, in the ārāma of Jeta's Grove built by the great patron Anāthapiṇḍada. (NE 16: 24 folios, 1 bampo)

आर्यसप्तशतिका प्रज्ञापारमिता नाम महायानसूत्रम्

། འཕགས་པ་ཤེས་རབ་ཀྱི་ཕ་རོལ་ཏུ་ཕྱིན་པ་བདུན་བརྒྱ་པ་ ཞེས་བྱ་བ་ཐེག་པ་ཆེན་པོའི་མདོ།

STCE

Ārya-saptaśatikā-nāma-prajñāpāramitā-nāma-mahāyāna-sūtra In Jeta's Grove, in the ārāma of Anāthapiṇḍada, a large Sangha of bhikṣus led by a thousand Arhats and a million Bodhisattvas who had reached the stage of irreversibility gathered to hear the teaching of the Blessed One. Among the Bodhisattvas who honored the Buddha were Mañjuśrī, Maitreya, Asaṅgapratibhāna, and Anikṣiptadura, and among the Arhats were Śāriputra, Pūrṇa, Maudgalyāyana, Mahākāśyapa, Mahākātyāyana, and Mahākauṣṭhila. In a dialogue with Śāriputra and Mañjuśrī, the Buddha gave the teaching on the nature of dharmas known as The Perfection of Wisdom in Seven Hundred Verses. Spoken in Śrāvastī. (NE 24: 53 folios, 2 bampo)

जातकनिदानम्

། སྐྱེས་པ་རབས་ཀྱི་གླེང་གཞི།

TEF

Jātaka-nidāna At the request of the great elder Arthadṛṣṭi, the Buddha described three ways of presenting the Blessed One's past lives and gave many accounts of his previous births. Spoken in Śrāvastī, in Jeta's Grove, to a large assembly of bhikṣus, bhikṣuṇīs, laymen and laywomen, and other beings. (NE 32: 135 folios)

मैत्रीभावनासूत्रम्

།བྱམས་པ་བསྒོམ་པའི་མདོ།

TCEF

Maitrī-bhāvanā-sūtra To the assembly of bhikṣus gathered in Jeta's Grove, the Enlightened One gave this Sūtra known as Generating Friendship, a teaching on the importance of meditating on loving-kindness. (NE 36: 2 folios)

गिरि-आनन्दसूत्रम्

།རིའི་ཀུན་དགའ་བོའི་མདོ།

TEF

Giri-ānanda-sūtra Once, when Giri Ānanda suffered a painful illness, the Buddha sent the disciple Ānanda to convey to him the meaning and nature of the ten perceptions. This teaching, inspired by the Buddha and given by Ānanda, completely relieved Giri Ānanda's illness. Spoken in Śrāvastī, in Jeta's Grove. (NE 38: 7 folios)

नन्दोपनन्दनागराजदमनसूत्रम्

།ཀླུའི་རྒྱལ་པོ་དགའ་བོ་ཉེར་དགའ་འདུལ་བའི་མདོ།

TCEF

Nandopananda-nāgarājadamana-sūtra In this teaching, given to the assembly of five hundred bhikṣus, the Buddha describes how Maudgalyāyana converted the Nāga king Nanda to the Dharma. Spoken in Śrāvastī, in Jeta's Grove. (NE 39: 6 folios)

आर्यधर्मधातुप्रकृति-असंभेदनिर्देशो नाम महायानसूत्रम्

།འཕགས་པ་ཆོས་ཀྱི་དབྱིངས་ཀྱི་རང་བཞིན་དབྱེར་མེད་པ་བསྟན་པ་ཞེས་བྱ་བ་ཐེག་པ་ཆེན་པོའི་མདོ།

TC

Ārya-dharmadhātu-prakṛti-asaṁbheda-nāma-nirdeśa The Bodhisattva Mañjuśrī, at the Buddha's request, gave the Sūtra known as The Undivided Nature of the Dharmadhātu to the assembly of eight thousand bhikṣus, twelve thousand Bodhisattvas, and thirty-two thousand perfected Bodhisattvas and devaputras. Spoken in Śrāvastī, in Jeta's Grove. (NE 52: 48 folios, 2 bampo)

चन्द्रसूत्रम्

།ཟླ་བའི་མདོ།

TCEF

Candra-sūtra The devaputra Candra, the Moon, frees himself from the grasp of the asura Rāhula by taking refuge in the Buddha. Spoken in Śrāvastī, in Jeta's Grove. (NE 42: 2 folios)

महामङ्गलसूत्रम्
།བཀྲ་ཤིས་ཆེན་པོའི་མདོ།

T E F

Mahāmaṅgala-sūtra At the request of numerous gods, the Buddha gave the Sūtra known as The Great Benediction, verses for blessings and prosperity. Spoken in Śrāvastī, in Jeta's Grove. (NE 43: 3 folios)

आर्यायुष्मन्नन्दगर्भावक्रान्तिनिर्देशः नाम महायानसूत्रम्
།འཕགས་པ་ཚེ་དང་ལྡན་པ་དགའ་བོ་ལ་མངལ་དུ་འཇུག་པ་བསྟན་པ་ཞེས་བྱ་བ་ཐེག་པ་ཆེན་པོའི་མདོ།

T C

Āryāyuṣman-nanda-garbhāvakrānti-nirdeśa-nāma-mahāyāna-sūtra Once the Buddha gave the teaching known as Entering the Womb, a Sūtra on rebirth and the miseries that proceed from rebirth, for the benefit of the Āyuṣman Nanda and five hundred other great Arhats. Spoken in Śrāvastī, in Jeta's Grove. (NE 58: 23 folios, 1 bampo, 300 śloka)

सूर्यसूत्रम्
།ཉི་མའི་མདོ།

T C E F

Sūrya-sūtra This teaching relates how the devaputra Sūrya, the Sun, frees himself from the grasp of the asura Rāhula by taking refuge in the Buddha. Spoken in Śrāvastī, in Jeta's Grove. (NE 41: 2 folios)

आर्यगृहपति-उग्रपरिपृच्छा नाम महायानसूत्रम्

།འཕགས་པ་ཁྱིམ་བདག་དྲག་ཤུལ་ཅན་གྱིས་ཞུས་པ་ཞེས་བྱ་བ་ཐེག་པ་ཆེན་པོའི་མདོ།

T C E

Ārya-gṛhapati-ugraparipṛcchā-nāma-mahāyāna-sūtra While the Buddha resided in Jeta's Grove, five hundred householders (gṛhapati) came to honor the Buddha and listen to his teaching. The householder Ugra, inspired by the Blessed One and seeking to generate the mind of enlightenment, asked how, as a layman, he might perform the activities of the Bodhisattvas and the renunciates. Before the assembly of 1,250 bhikṣus and five thousand Great Bodhisattvas led by Mañjuśrī, Maitreya, and Avalokiteśvara, the Buddha gave the teaching known as the Question of the Householder Ugra, explaining the meaning of refuge in the Buddha, Dharma, and Sangha, the importance of mindfulness, and the duty owed to one's family. Spoken in Śrāvastī, in Jeta's Grove. (NE 63: 63 folios, 3 bampo)

आर्यमहाप्रातिहार्यनिर्देशो नाम महायानसूत्रम्

།འཕགས་པ་ཆོ་འཕྲུལ་ཆེན་པོ་བསྟན་པ་ཞེས་བྱ་བ་ཐེག་པ་ཆེན་པོའི་མདོ།

T C

Ārya-mahāprātihārya-nirdeśa-nāma-mahāyāna-sūtra Once the great devaputra Sārthavāha asked the Buddha: "By what miraculous feats does the Tathāgata cultivate sentient beings?" In this teaching known as The Instruction On the Great Miracle, the Buddha explained the meaning of three great accomplishments—demonstrating omniscience, teaching the Dharma, and showing manifestations—to the assembly of 1,250 bhikṣus and eight thousand Bodhisattvas, including Mañjuśrī. Spoken in Śrāvastī, in Jeta's Grove. (NE 66: 64 folios, 3 bampo)

आर्यमैत्रेयमहासिंहनादो नाम महायानसूत्रम्

།འཕགས་པ་བྱམས་པའི་སེང་གེའི་སྒྲ་ཆེན་པོ་ཞེས་བྱ་བ་ཐེག་པ་ཆེན་པོའི་མདོ།

T C

Ārya-maitreya-mahāsiṁhanāda-nāma-mahāyāna-sūtra Once, when the Buddha was teaching the Dharma to a great assembly of five thousand bhikṣus and many Great Bodhisattvas including Mañjuśrī, Maitreya, and Avalokiteśvara, the disciple Kāśyapa asked, "In seeking to pass beyond sorrow, having renounced the world, how does one practice? How does one act?" In response, the Buddha gave the teaching known as The Great Lion's Roar of Maitreya, advising the practice of the moral precepts and explaining the vehicles of Śrāvakas, Pratyekabuddhas, and Bodhisattvas. Spoken in Śrāvastī, in Jeta's Grove. (NE 67: 94 folios, 4 bampo, 1,200 śloka)

आर्यविनयविनिश्चये उपालिपरिपृच्छा नाम महायानसूत्रम्

།འཕགས་པ་འདུལ་བ་རྣམ་པར་གཏན་ལ་དབབ་པ་ཉེ་བར་འཁོར་གྱིས་ཞུས་པ་ཞེས་བྱ་བ་ཐེག་པ་ཆེན་པོའི་མདོ།

T C

Ārya-vinayaviniścaya-upāliparipṛcchā-nāma-mahāyāna-sūtra At the request of the Arhat Upāli, the Buddha explained how the Tathāgatas practice, always mindful of ways to mature sentient beings. This teaching, known as the Questions of Upāli Concerning the Practice of Vinaya, was heard by the assembly of five hundred bhikṣus and one thousand Bodhisattvas, including Maitreya, Siṁha, and Vajrapāṇi. Spoken in Śrāvastī, in Jeta's Grove. (NE 68: 33 folios, 2 bampo, 600 śloka)

आर्यसुरतपरिपृच्छा नाम महायानसूत्रम्

།འཕགས་པ་དེས་པས་ཞུས་པ་ཞེས་བྱ་བ་ཐེག་པ་ཆེན་པོའི་མདོ།

T C

Ārya-surata-paripṛcchā-nāma-mahāyāna-sūtra This Sūtra, known as The Question of Surata, describes how the god Indra tested the virtues of the Bodhisattva Surata, a poor man completely devoted to the Buddha, Dharma, and Sangha. This instruction in the power of virtue and the wisdom of practicing virtue was given in the hearing of 1,250 bhikṣus and thirty-two thousand Bodhisattvas. Spoken in Śrāvastī, in Jeta's Grove. (NE 71: 26 folios, 1 bampo, 300 śloka)

आर्यवीरदत्तगृहपतिपरिपृच्छा नाम महायानसूत्रम्

།འཕགས་པ་ཁྱིམ་བདག་དཔའ་བྱིན་གྱིས་ཞུས་པ་ཞེས་བྱ་བ་ཐེག་པ་ཆེན་པོའི་མདོ།

T C

Ārya-vīradatta-gṛhapati-paripṛcchā-nāma-mahāyāna-sūtra Once the wealthy householder Vīradatta and five hundred other laymen, aware of the difficulties of attaining liberation, expressed their desire to learn how to become a Buddha. In response, the Buddha gave the Sūtra known as The Question of the Householder Vīradatta, explaining the Bodhisattva's qualities and path. Spoken in Śrāvastī, in Jeta's Grove. (NE 72: 22 folios, 1 bampo, 300 śloka)

आर्यगङ्गोत्तरापरिपृच्छा नाम महायानसूत्रम्

།འཕགས་པ་གང་གཱའི་མཆོག་གིས་ཞུས་པ་ཞེས་བྱ་བ་ཐེག་པ་ཆེན་པོའི་མདོ།

TCE

Ārya-gaṅgottarā-paripṛcchā-nāma-mahāyāna-sūtra Entering into a dialogue with the laywoman Gaṅgottarā, the Buddha explained through questions and answers the illusory nature of all existence and the means of stopping the endless rounds of samsara. This teaching, given for the benefit of the entire assembly, became known as The Questions of Gaṅgottarā. Spoken in Śrāvastī, in Jeta's Grove. (NE 75: 8 folios, 110 śloka)

आर्यविमलदत्तापरिपृच्छा नाम महायानसूत्रम्

།འཕགས་པ་དྲི་མ་མེད་ཀྱིས་བྱིན་པས་ཞུས་པ་ཞེས་བྱ་བ་ཐེག་པ་ཆེན་པོའི་མདོ།

TCE

Ārya-vimaladattā-paripṛcchā-nāma-mahāyāna-sūtra Seeing eight disciples and eight Great Bodhisattvas, Vimaladattā, King Prasenajit's young daughter, became filled with faith. Honoring them, she questioned each in turn, astounding them with her knowledge. Then, before an assembly of more than a thousand Arhats including the eight great disciples, twelve thousand Bodhisattvas, King Prasenajit, Brahmā and the eight classes of gods, and a large gathering of humans and non-humans, the Buddha gave this teaching on Bodhisattvas known as the Questions of Vimaladattā, explaining how, as a result of honoring Buddhas in previous lives, Vimaladattā had attained the superknowledges of a Bodhisattva. Spoken in Śrāvastī, in Jeta's Grove. (NE 77: 12 folios, 2 bampo)

आर्याचिन्त्यबुद्धविषयनिर्देशो नाम महायानसूत्रम्

།འཕགས་པ་སངས་རྒྱས་ཀྱི་ཡུལ་བསམ་གྱིས་མི་ཁྱབ་པ་བསྟན་པ་
ཞེས་བྱ་བ་ཐེག་པ་ཆེན་པོའི་མདོ།

T C E

Ārya-acintya-buddha-viśaya-nirdeśa-nāma-mahāyāna-sūtra The Great Bodhisattva Mañjuśrī, inspired by the Blessed One and upon his request, gave this teaching on the inconceivable nature of the Buddha to an assembly of hundreds of thousands, including one thousand bhikṣus, ten thousand Bodhisattvas, and the devaputra Suguṇa, together with many gods. Manifesting wondrous acts, the Bhagavan inspired even Pāpīyān (Māra) to vow to refrain from hindering the Dharma. Spoken in Śrāvastī, in Jeta's Grove. (NE 79: 2 bampo, 36 folios, 600 śloka)

आर्यसर्वबुद्धमहारहस्योपायकौशल्यज्ञानोत्तर बोधिसत्त्वपरिपृच्छा परिवर्तो नाम महायानसूत्रम्

།འཕགས་པ་སངས་རྒྱས་ཐམས་ཅད་ཀྱི་གསང་ཆེན་ཐབས་ལ་མཁས་པ་
བྱང་ཆུབ་སེམས་དཔའ་ཡེ་ཤེས་དམ་པས་ཞུས་པའི་ལེའུ་
ཞེས་བྱ་བ་ཐེག་པ་ཆེན་པོའི་མདོ།

T C E

Ārya-sarvabuddha-mahārahasyopāya-kauśalya-jñānottara-bodhisattva-paripṛcchā-parivarta-nāma-mahāyāna-sūtra Responding to the Bodhisattva Jñānottara's inquiry as to the nature of skillful means, the Buddha described how Bodhisattvas foster enlightenment in those who follow the Mahāyāna path and the teachings conveyed through the acts of a Buddha. Spoken in Śrāvastī, in Jeta's Grove, to an assembly of eight thousand bhikṣus, twelve thousand Bodhisattvas, and innumerable other beings. (NE 82: 82 folios, 4 bampo, 1,230 śloka)

आर्यदारिकाविमलश्रद्धापरिपृच्छा नाम महायानसूत्रम्

།འཕགས་པ་བུ་མོ་རྣམ་དག་དད་པས་ཞུས་པ་ཞེས་བྱ་བ་ཐེག་པ་ཆེན་པོའི་མདོ།

T C

Ārya-dārikā-vimalaśraddhā-paripṛcchā-nāma-mahāyāna-sūtra The beautiful and virtuous Princess Vimalaśraddhā, daughter of King Prasenajit, requested that the Buddha grant teachings on the path to perfection. Assenting, the Buddha gave the teaching known as The Question of the Maiden Vimalaśraddhā to the assembly of five hundred bhikṣus, eight thousand Great Bodhisattvas, including the Bodhisattvas of the Golden Aeon led by Maitreya, the sixty supreme Bodhisattvas with Mañjuśrī at their head, the sixteen Bodhisattvas led by Bhadrapāla, and twenty thousand Tuṣita gods. Spoken in Śrāvastī, in Jeta's Grove. (NE 84: 20 folios, 1 bampo, 150 śloka)

आर्यसप्तशतिका नाम प्रज्ञापारमिता महायानसूत्रम्

།འཕགས་པ་ཤེས་རབ་ཀྱི་ཕ་རོལ་ཏུ་ཕྱིན་པ་བདུན་བརྒྱ་པ་
ཞེས་བྱ་བ་ཐེག་པ་ཆེན་པོའི་མདོ།

S T C E

Ārya-saptaśatikā-nāma-prajñāpāramitā-mahāyāna-sūtra The Bodhisattvas Mañjuśrī and Maitreya, together with the Arhats Śāriputra, Maudgalyāyana, Kāśyapa, and others, came to pay homage to the Buddha. Inspired by the Enlightened One, Mañjuśrī gave this Sūtra On Perfect Wisdom in Seventy Ślokas to the congregation of one thousand bhikṣus and Bodhisattvas. Delighted with this teaching, Śakra and the gods of the Trāyastriṁśa realm caused wondrous flowers to fall from the heavens, descending through air filled with the sound of celestial music and the scent of exquisite incense. Spoken in Śrāvastī, in Jeta's Grove. (NE 90: 55 folios, 2 bampo)

आर्यश्रीमालादेवीसिंहनादो नाम महायानसूत्रम्

།འཕགས་པ་ལྷ་མོ་དཔལ་ཕྲེང་གི་སེང་གེའི་སྒྲ་ཞེས་བྱ་བ་ཐེག་པ་ཆེན་པོའི་མདོ།

T C E

Ārya-śrīmālādevī-siṁhanāda-nāma-mahāyāna-sūtra Hearing of the Buddha from her parents, King Prasenajit and Queen Mallikā, Śrīmālā, Queen of Ayodhyā, became filled with faith and wished to see him. Immediately the Blessed One appeared before her, bathed in radiant light. Awakening Bodhicitta, the queen received from the Blessed One the prediction that she would in time attain the realization of a Buddha, and she made the ten inconceivably great vows of a Bodhisattva. Then, inspired by the Enlightened One, she gave the teaching known as The Lion's Roar of Queen Śrīmālā, delighting the great assembly of gods, humans, asuras, gandharvas, and others. Spoken in Śrāvastī, in Jeta's Grove. (NE 92: 46 folios, 2 bampo, 600 śloka)

आर्यललितविस्तरो नाम महायानसूत्रम्

།འཕགས་པ་རྒྱ་ཆེར་རོལ་པ་ཞེས་བྱ་བ་ཐེག་པ་ཆེན་པོའི་མདོ།

S T C E F

Ārya-lalitavistara-nāma-mahāyāna-sūtra At the request of the gods of the Tuṣita heaven, the Buddha taught the Lalitavistara Sūtra, the great instruction on his life and early teachings, to an assembly of twelve thousand bhikṣus and thirty-two thousand Bodhisattvas, the king of Śrāvastī and his son, ministers, and attendants, and to the merchants and townspeople of Śrāvastī. (NE 95: 431 folios, 18 bampo)

आर्यमञ्जुश्रीविकुर्वाणपरिवर्तो नाम महायानसूत्रम्

།འཕགས་པ་འཇམ་དཔལ་རྣམ་པར་འཕྲུལ་པའི་ལེའུ་
ཞེས་བྱ་བ་ཐེག་པ་ཆེན་པོའི་མདོ།

T C

Ārya-mañjuśrī-vikurvāṇa-parivarta-nāma-mahāyāna-sūtra At the request of the devaputra Prabhabhuta, the Great Bodhisattva Mañjuśrī, inspired by the Buddha, gave the teaching known as The Manifestations of Mañjuśrī to an assembly of 1,250 bhikṣus, a vast host of Bodhisattvas, and a multitude of gods from the heaven realms. Spoken in Śrāvastī, in Jeta's Grove. (NE 97: 32 folios, 1 bampo)

आर्यनिष्ठागतभगवज्ज्ञानवैपुल्यसूत्ररत्नानन्तं नाम महायानसूत्रम्

།འཕགས་པ་བཅོམ་ལྡན་འདས་ཀྱི་ཡེ་ཤེས་རྒྱས་པའི་མདོ་སྡེ་རིན་པོ་ཆེ་
མཐའ་ཡས་པ་མཐར་ཕྱིན་པ་ཞེས་བྱ་བ་ཐེག་པ་ཆེན་པོའི་མདོ།

T

Ārya-niṣṭhāgatabhagavajjñāna-vaipūlya-sūtra-ratnānta-nāma mahāyāna-sūtra When a magician presented the Sangha with the gift of a sandalwood palace, the Buddha gave this teaching, The Extensive Sūtra on the Boundless Wisdom of the Bhagavan Known as the Infinite Jewel, to the assembly of 1,250 bhikṣus. Spoken in Śrāvastī, in Jeta's Grove. (NE 99: 550 folios, 25 bampo, 7,500 śloka)

आर्याचिन्त्यप्रभासनिर्देशो नाम धर्मपर्यायः

།འཕགས་པ་ཁྱེའུ་སྣང་བ་བསམ་གྱིས་མི་ཁྱབ་པས་བསྟན་པ་
ཞེས་བྱ་བའི་ཆོས་ཀྱི་རྣམ་གྲངས།

T C

Ārya-acintyaprabhāsa-nirdeśa-nāma-dharmaparyāya As the Buddha entered the gates of Śrāvastī, wondrous emanations appeared: the blind saw, the deaf heard, and the naked were clothed. All who dwelled in that city awakened faith in the Dharma and paid homage to the Buddha. The disciple Ānanda then spoke of a child found alone in an empty house. Engaging in a dialogue with this child, the Buddha gave this teaching known as The Instruction on Inconceivable Splendor to the assembly of 1,250 bhikṣus, five hundred Bodhisattvas, great kings, Brahmins, and householders. (NE 103: 21 folios, 270 śloka)

आर्यमण्डलाष्टकं नाम महायानसूत्रम्

།འཕགས་པ་དཀྱིལ་འཁོར་བརྒྱད་ཅེས་བྱ་བའི་ཆོས་ཀྱི་རྣམ་གྲངས་ཐེག་པ་ཆེན་པོའི་མདོ།

T C

Ārya-maṇḍalāṣṭaka-nāma-mahāyāna-sūtra In Śrāvastī, in Jeta's Grove, the Buddha gave this teaching known as The Mahāyāna Sūtra Concerning the Eight Mandalas. (NE 105: 3 folios)

आर्यसुखावतीव्यूहो नाम महायानसूत्रम्

།འཕགས་པ་བདེ་བ་ཅན་གྱི་བཀོད་པ་ཞེས་བྱ་བ་ཐེག་པ་ཆེན་པོའི་མདོ།

S T C E F

Ārya-sukhāvatī-vyūha-nāma-mahāyāna-sūtra In this teaching the Buddha describes Sukhāvatī, the paradise of Amitābha Buddha where beings free from suffering live in perpetual bliss, to the assembly of 1,250 bhikṣus; sixteen elders, including Śāriputra, Maudgalyāyana, and Kāśyapa; Mañjuśrī and a multitude of other Great Bodhisattvas, together with Indra and many hundreds of billions of gods. Spoken in Jeta's Grove, near Śrāvastī, King Prasenajit's royal city. (NE 115: 9 folios, 30 śloka)

आर्यकरण्डव्यूहो नाम महायानसूत्रम्

།འཕགས་པ་ཟ་མ་ཏོག་བཀོད་པ་ཞེས་བྱ་བ་ཐེག་པ་ཆེན་པོའི་མདོ།

S T C

Ārya-karaṇḍavyūha-nāma-mahāyāna-sūtra When great rays of light emanating from Avalokiteśvara shone forth from the hell-realms, many wonders emanating from that light were clearly seen by the Sangha assembled in Jeta's Grove. In this Sūtra known as The Array of Receptacles, the Buddha describes Avalokiteśvara's tireless efforts to liberate the beings in the hells. This teaching was heard by 1,250 bhikṣus and a host of Great Bodhisattvas led by the Bodhisattva Vajramati and the future Buddha Maitreya, together with many gods, nāgas, gandharvas, and innumerable other beings. (NE 116: 125 folios, 4.5 bampo)

आर्यरत्नकरण्डो नाम महायानसूत्रम्

།འཕགས་པ་དཀོན་མཆོག་གི་ཟ་མ་ཏོག་ཅེས་བྱ་བ་ཐེག་པ་ཆེན་པོའི་མདོ།

T C

Ārya-ratnakaraṇḍa-nāma-mahāyāna-sūtra Having come to Jeta's Grove, Mañjuśrī asked the Buddha for permission to hold a discussion on the Dharma. Then, through the inspiration of the Buddha, Subhūti discussed with Mañjuśrī the meaning of being a fit vessel for the teachings. The Buddha then gave a teaching on the moral and metaphysical aspects of the Dharma, and Mañjuśrī emphasized that earnest application and purity of life are the most certain means of attaining perfection. This discussion, known as The Vessel of Jewels, was heard by five thousand Bodhisattvas, Indra, Brahmā, and the world-protectors. (NE 117: 84 folios, 4 bampo)

आर्यसुवर्णसूत्रं नाम महायानसूत्रम्

།འཕགས་པ་གསེར་གྱི་མདོ་ཞེས་བྱ་བ་ཐེག་པ་ཆེན་པོའི་མདོ།

T

Ārya-suvarṇasūtra-nāma-mahāyāna-sūtra When Ānanda asked the Buddha how one should view the mind of the Bodhisattva, the Bhagavan gave the teaching known as The Gold Sūtra, explaining that one should view the mind of the Bodhisattva as if it were of the nature of pure gold. The Blessed One continued this teaching, beginning by describing in detail the mind of the Bodhisattva. Spoken in Śrāvastī, in Jeta's Grove. (NE 125: 1 folio)

आर्यसुवर्णबालुकोपमं नाम महायानसूत्रम्

།འཕགས་པ་གསེར་གྱི་བྱེ་མ་ལྟ་བུ་ཞེས་བྱ་བ་ཐེག་པ་ཆེན་པོའི་མདོ།

T

Ārya-suvarṇabālukopamā-nāma-mahāyāna-sūtra At Ānanda's request, the Buddha gave the teaching called The Most Excellent Grains of Gold, describing the infinite perfections of the Tathāgatas to an assembly of 1,250 bhikṣus and many thousands of Bodhisattvas. Spoken in Śrāvastī, in Jeta's Grove. (NE 126: 6 folios, 80 śloka)

आर्यानन्तमुखसाधक नाम धारणी

།འཕགས་པ་སྒོ་མཐར་ཡས་པ་སྒྲུབ་པ་ཞེས་བྱ་བའི་གཟུངས།

T C

Ārya-anantamukha-sādhaka-nāma-dhāraṇī In the terraced palace at Śrāvastī, knowing that the time for his Parinirvāṇa was approaching, the Buddha asked Maudgalyāyana to call all the bhikṣus in the three realms. In an instant, the great disciple went to the peak of Mt. Meru, and called out to the thousands of worlds: "Students of the Tathāgata, listen! Whoever wishes to receive the rain of the Dharma, come to the terraced palace in Śrāvastī!" To the forty thousand bhikṣus who assembled, the Buddha gave the teaching known as The Dhāraṇīs That Facilitate the Entrance into Infinity, four dhāraṇīs that delight body, speech, and mind. (NE 140: 20 folios, 210 śloka)

आर्यप्रतिभानमतिपरिपृच्छा नाम महायानसूत्रम्

།འཕགས་པ་སྤོབས་པའི་བློ་གྲོས་ཀྱིས་ཞུས་པ་ཞེས་བྱ་བ་ཐེག་པ་ཆེན་པོའི་མདོ།

T C

Ārya-pratibhānamati-paripṛcchā-nāma-mahāyāna-sūtra The merchant Pratibhānamati asked the Buddha, "What are the teachings by which one obtains merit and cuts off the forces leading to lower states of being?" In response, the Buddha gave the teaching known as The Question of Pratibhānamati to the assembly of 1,250 bhikṣus, ten thousand Bodhisattvas, and five hundred merchants with their five hundred servants. Spoken in Śrāvastī, in Jeta's Grove. (NE 151: 26 folios, 1 bampo)

आर्यब्रह्मदत्तपरिपृच्छा नाम महायानसूत्रम्

།འཕགས་པ་ཚངས་པས་བྱིན་གྱིས་ཞུས་པ་ཞེས་བྱ་བ་ཐེག་པ་ཆེན་པོའི་མདོ།

T

Ārya-brahmadatta-paripṛcchā-nāma-mahāyāna-sūtra The Bodhisattva Amoghadarśana, having received the blessing of the Buddha, imparted this teaching, beginning with the five royal dharmas, for the benefit of King Brahmadatta, while the Buddha was dwelling in Śrāvastī, in Jeta's Grove. This teaching, known as The Question of Brahmadatta, was actually given in Brahmadatta's kingdom. (NE 159: 25 folios, 1 bampo)

आर्यसुविक्रान्तचिन्तदेवपुत्रपरिपृच्छा नाम महायानसूत्रम्

།འཕགས་པ་ལྷའི་བུ་རབ་རྩལ་སེམས་ཀྱིས་ཞུས་པ་ཞེས་བྱ་བ་ཐེག་པ་ཆེན་པོའི་མདོ།

T C

Ārya-suvikrānta-cintadevaputra-paripṛcchā-nāma-mahāyāna-sūtra At the request of the devaputra Suvikrānta, the Buddha described the efforts and merits of the Bodhisattva in the teaching known as The Question of the Devaputra Suvikrānta. This Sūtra was heard by an assembly of ten thousand bhikṣus and many thousands of Bodhisattvas including Mañjuśrī. Spoken in Śrāvastī, in Jeta's Grove. (NE 161: 78 folios, 3 bampo)

आर्यविकुर्वाणराजपरिपृच्छा नाम महायानसूत्रम्

།འཕགས་པ་རྣམ་པར་འཕྲུལ་བའི་རྒྱལ་པོས་ཞུས་པ་ཞེས་བྱ་བ་ཐེག་པ་ཆེན་པོའི་མདོ།

T C

Ārya-vikurvāṇarāja-paripṛcchā-nāma-mahāyāna-sūtra Requested by Vikurvāṇarāja, the Buddha gave the Sūtra known as The Question of Vikurvāṇarāja, a teaching on the practice of the Mahāyāna, to the assembly of twenty thousand bhikṣus and a host of Great Bodhisattvas including Avalokiteśvara and the future Buddha Maitreya. Spoken in Śrāvastī, in Jeta's Grove. (NE 167: 71 folios, 3 bampo)

आर्यमञ्जुश्रीपरिपृच्छा नाम महायानसूत्रम्

།འཕགས་པ་འཇམ་དཔལ་གྱིས་དྲིས་པ་ཞེས་བྱ་བ་ཐེག་པ་ཆེན་པོའི་མདོ།

T C

Ārya-mañjuśrī-paripṛcchā-nāma-mahāyāna-sūtra In a magnificent house in Śrāvastī, at the request of the Great Bodhisattva Mañjuśrī, the Buddha gave a teaching on the merit generated from following the Buddhist path and practicing the ten virtuous actions. This Sūtra, known as The Questions of Mañjuśrī, was heard by the assembly of 1,250 bhikṣus and many hundreds of thousands of Great Bodhisattvas led by the compassionate Avalokiteśvara. (NE 172: 8 folios, 1 bampo)

आर्यमञ्जुश्रीनिर्देशो नाम महायानसूत्रम्

།འཕགས་པ་འཇམ་དཔལ་གྱིས་བསྟན་པ་ཞེས་བྱ་བ་ཐེག་པ་ཆེན་པོའི་མདོ།

T C

Ārya-mañjuśrīnirdeśa-nāma-mahāyāna-sūtra At the request of the devaputra Susīma, the Great Bodhisattva Mañjuśrī taught the correct attitude for making offerings to a large assembly of many hundreds of thousands, including 1,250 bhikṣus and five thousand Bodhisattvas. This Sūtra is known as An Instruction of Mañjuśrī. Spoken in Śrāvastī, in Jeta's Grove. (NE 177: 2 folios, 14.5 śloka)

आर्यपञ्चपारमितानिर्देशो नाम महायानसूत्रम्

།འཕགས་པ་ཕ་རོལ་ཏུ་ཕྱིན་པ་ལྔ་བསྟན་པ་ཞེས་བྱ་བ་ཐེག་པ་ཆེན་པོའི་མདོ།

T C

Ārya-pañcapāramitā-nirdeśa-nāma-mahāyāna-sūtra To the disciple Śāriputra and the assembly of 1,250 bhikṣus, Bodhisattvas, nāgas, gods, and other beings, the Buddha gave the Sūtra known as The Teaching on Five Perfections. Spoken in Śrāvastī, in Jeta's Grove. (NE 181: 151 folios, 6 bampo)

आर्यदानानुशंसानिर्देशः

།འཕགས་པ་སྦྱིན་པའི་ཕན་ཡོན་བསྟན་པ།

S T C E

Ārya-dānānuśaṁsā-nirdeśa For the benefit of the assembly of bhikṣus, the Buddha gave the Sūtra known as The Benefits of Generosity, a teaching on the gifts of a Bodhisattva and the practice of giving. Spoken in Śrāvastī, in Jeta's Grove. (NE 183: 3 folios, 30 śloka)

आर्यबुद्धधर्माचिन्त्यनिर्देशः

།འཕགས་པ་སངས་རྒྱས་ཀྱི་ཆོས་བསམ་གྱིས་མི་ཁྱབ་པ་བསྟན་པ།

T C

Ārya-buddhadharmācintya-nirdeśa For the benefit of the Great Bodhisattvas, the Buddha gave this instruction known as The Inconceivable Dharma of the Buddha. Spoken in Śrāvastī, in Jeta's Grove. (NE 187: 67 folios, 3 bampo)

आर्यदीपंकरव्याकरणं नाम महायानसूत्रम्

།འཕགས་པ་མར་མེ་མཛད་ཀྱིས་ལུང་བསྟན་པ་ཞེས་བྱ་བ་ཐེག་པ་ཆེན་པོའི་མདོ།

T F

Ārya-dīpaṁkara-vyākaraṇa-nāma-mahāyāna-sūtra To the faithful disciple Ānanda, the Buddha described how, in kalpas past, he received his prediction to Buddhahood from the Tathāgata Dīpaṁkara. This teaching, known as The Prophecy of Dīpaṁkara, was heard by the assembly of 1,250 bhikṣus and many hundreds of thousands of Bodhisattvas. Spoken in Śrāvastī, in Jeta's Grove. (NE 188: 17 folios, 210 śloka)

आर्यब्रह्मश्रीव्याकरणं नाम महायानसूत्रम्

འཕགས་པ་ཚངས་པའི་དཔལ་ལུང་བསྟན་པ་ཞེས་བྱ་བ་ཐེག་པ་ཆེན་པོའི་མདོ།

T F

Ārya-brahmaśrī-vyākaraṇa-nāma-mahāyāna-sūtra To the Brahmins and the assembly of bhikṣus, the Buddha gave the teaching known as The Prediction of Brahmaśrī, describing how the young Brahmin Brahmaśrī would attain Buddhahood in a future aeon. Spoken in Śrāvastī, in Jeta's Grove. (NE 189: 4 folios, 40 śloka)

आर्यजयमतिर्नाम महायानसूत्रम्

།འཕགས་པ་རྒྱལ་བའི་བློ་གྲོས་ཞེས་བྱ་བ་ཐེག་པ་ཆེན་པོའི་མདོ།

T

Ārya-jayamati-nāma-mahāyāna-sūtra At the request of the Bodhisattva Jayamati, the Buddha described by what actions one arrives at perfection and happiness, for the benefit of Jayamati and the assembly of many bhikṣus and Bodhisattvas. Spoken in Śrāvastī, in Jeta's Grove. (NE 194: 2 folios, 11 śloka)

आर्यमैत्रेयप्रस्थानं नाम महायानसूत्रम्

།འཕགས་པ་བྱམས་པ་འཇུག་པ་ཞེས་བྱ་བ་ཐེག་པ་ཆེན་པོའི་མདོ།

T

Ārya-maitreyaprasthāna-nāma-mahāyāna-sūtra At the request of a Bodhisattva, the Buddha gave the Sūtra known as The Abiding of Maitreya, a teaching on the conduct of Maitreya and his great merit, to the assembly of five thousand bhikṣus and ten thousand Bodhisattvas led by Mañjuśrī. Spoken in Śrāvastī, in Jeta's Grove. (NE 198: 44 folios, 2 bampo)

आर्यमैत्रेयबोधिसत्त्वस्य तुषितस्वर्गे जन्मग्रहणसूत्रम्

།འཕགས་པ་བྱང་ཆུབ་སེམས་དཔའ་བྱམས་པ་དགའ་ལྡན་གནས་སུ་སྐྱེ་བ་བླངས་པའི་མདོ།

T C

Ārya-maitreya-bodhisattvasya tuṣitasvarge janmagrahaṇa-sūtram At the request of the disciple Upāli, the Buddha gave the teaching known as Maitreya's Taking Birth in the Tuṣita Heaven to a great number of bhikṣus and Bodhisattvas. Spoken in Śrāvastī, in Jeta's Grove. (NE 199: 14 folios)

आर्यधर्ममुद्रा नाम महायानसूत्रम्

།འཕགས་པ་ཆོས་ཀྱི་ཕྱག་རྒྱ་ཞེས་བྱ་བ་ཐེག་པ་ཆེན་པོའི་མདོ།

T

Ārya-dharmamudrā-nāma-mahāyāna-sūtra At the request of Śāriputra, the Buddha gave the Sūtra known as Gesture of Dharma, a teaching on the nature of renunciation and how bhikṣus are to observe the moral code, to the assembly of five thousand bhikṣus and a host of Great Bodhisattvas. Spoken in Śrāvastī, in Jeta's Grove. (NE 203: 8 folios, 80 śloka)

आर्यप्रदीपदानीयं नाम महायानसूत्रम्

།འཕགས་པ་མར་མེ་འབུལ་བ་ཞེས་བྱ་བ་ཐེག་པ་ཆེན་པོའི་མདོ།

T C

Ārya-pradīpadānīya-nāma-mahāyāna-sūtra The Buddha gave the Sūtra known as An Offering of Butterlamps, a teaching on the merit of offering lights to the Buddhas and Bodhisattvas, for the benefit of Śāriputra and the Sangha. Spoken in Śrāvastī, in Jeta's Grove. (NE 204: 22 folios, 1 bampo)

आर्यनागरावलम्बिका नाम महायानसूत्रम्

།འཕགས་པ་གྲོང་ཁྱེར་གྱིས་འཚོ་བ་ཞེས་བྱ་བ་ཐེག་པ་ཆེན་པོ་འི་མདོ།

T

Ārya-nāgarāvalambikā-nāma-mahāyāna-sūtra The Buddha described how Nandakā, a poor woman of Śrāvastī, prepared oil and offered a lamp with such devotion that she received a prediction that in a future life she would become a Buddha. This Sūtra, known as A Woman of the City, was heard by the assembly of bhikṣus, bhikṣuṇīs, and Bodhisattvas, by gods including Indra and Brahmā, by the world-protectors, and by nāgas, yakṣas, kings, and ministers. Spoken in Śrāvastī, in Jeta's Grove. (NE 205: 4 folios, 100 śloka)

आर्यमहारणं नाम महायानसूत्रम्

།འཕགས་པ་སྣྲ་ཆེན་པོ་ཞེས་བྱ་བ་ཐེག་པ་ཆེན་པོ་འི་མདོ།

T

Ārya-mahāraṇa-nāma-mahāyāna-sūtra At the request of Ānanda, the Buddha gave the Sūtra known as Great Joy, a teaching on the benefits of honoring the shrines and relics of the Tathāgatas, to the assembly of many bhikṣus. Spoken in Śrāvastī, in Jeta's Grove. (NE 208: 6 folios, 64 śloka)

प्रतीत्यसमुत्पादादिविभंगनिर्देशो नाम सूत्रम्

།རྟེན་ཅིང་འབྲེལ་བར་འབྱུང་བ་དང་པོ་དང་རྣམ་པར་དབྱེ་བ་བསྟན་པ་ཞེས་བྱ་བའི་མདོ།

S T C G

Pratītyasamutpādādivibhaṅga-nirdeśa-nāma-sūtra For the benefit of the Sangha of bhikṣus, the Buddha gave this teaching on the first of the twelve links in the chain of interdependent cooperation (pratītyasamutpāda). Spoken in Śrāvastī, in Jeta's Grove. (NE 211: 4 folios, 30 śloka)

आर्याङ्गुलिमालीयं नाम महायानसूत्रम्

།འཕགས་པ་སོར་མོའི་ཕྲེང་བ་ལ་ཕན་པ་ཞེས་བྱ་བ་ཐེག་པ་ཆེན་པོའི་མདོ།

T C

Ārya-aṅgulimālīya-nāma-mahāyāna-sūtra On the road to Śrāvastī, the Buddha revealed to the assassin Aṅgulimālīya the grievous immorality of his actions, the virtues of the Bodhisattva, and effective means to final emancipation. This Sūtra, which opened the heart of Aṅgulimālīya and converted him to the Dharma, was heard by the assembly of Bodhisattvas, gods, nāgas, and other beings. (NE 213: 162 folios, 7 bampo)

आर्यकर्मावरणप्रतिप्रश्रब्धिर्नाम महायानसूत्रम्

།འཕགས་པ་ལས་ཀྱི་སྒྲིབ་པ་རྒྱུན་གཅོད་པ་ཞེས་བྱ་བ་ཐེག་པ་ཆེན་པོའི་མདོ།

T C

Ārya-karmāvaraṇa-pratipraśrabdhi-nāma-mahāyāna-sūtra At the request of his disciple Śāriputra, the Buddha gave the Sūtra known as Cutting Off the Stream of the Defilements of Karma, a teaching on setting aside all imperfections and attaining perfection, to the assembly of 1,250 bhikṣus and seventy thousand Bodhisattvas. Spoken in Śrāvastī, in Jeta's Grove. (NE 219: 20 folios, 230 śloka)

आर्यराजाववादकं नाम महायानसूत्रम्

།འཕགས་པ་རྒྱལ་པོ་ལ་གདམས་པ་ཞེས་བྱ་བ་ཐེག་པ་ཆེན་པོའི་མདོ།

T C

Ārya-rājāvavādaka-nāma-mahāyāna-sūtra Prasenajit, king of Kosala, traveled to Jeta's Grove with an entourage of many hundreds of thousands to hear the Dharma. Accompanied by the clashing of cymbals and the sound of drums, the king went to where the Buddha was abiding. After paying homage, the king asked the Buddha for his counsel. For the benefit of Prasenajit and the assembly of 1,250 bhikṣus, the Buddha gave the Sūtra known as Precepts for the King, a teaching on morality and wise government. (NE 221: 14 folios, 160 śloka)

आर्यमहाभेरीहारकपरिवर्तो नाम महायानसूत्रम्

།འཕགས་པ་རྔ་བོ་ཆེ་ཆེན་པོའི་ལེའུ་ཞེས་བྱ་བ་ཐེག་པ་ཆེན་པོའི་མདོ།

T C

Ārya-mahābherīhāraka-parivarta-nāma-mahāyāna-sūtra In this teaching, named for the large drums sounded by King Prasenajit's musicians, the Buddha explained the undependable nature of the world and the bliss of great deliverance for the benefit of King Prasenajit, his attendants, and the assembly of 1,250 bhikṣus, many hundreds of thousands of Bodhisattvas, gods, and nāgas, and hundreds of thousands of bhikṣuṇīs, together with Brahmā, Indra, the Four World Protectors, and a host of other beings. Spoken in Śrāvastī, in Jeta's Grove. (NE 222: 85 folios, 5 bampo)

आर्यत्रिशरणगमनं नाम महायानसूत्रम्

།འཕགས་པ་གསུམ་ལ་སྐྱབས་སུ་འགྲོ་བ་ཞེས་བྱ་བ་ཐེག་པ་ཆེན་པོའི་མདོ།

T

Ārya-triśaraṇagamana-nāma-mahāyāna-sūtra For the benefit of the great disciple Śāriputra and the assembly of 1,250 bhikṣus, the Buddha gave this teaching on the merit of taking refuge in the Three Jewels. Spoken in Śrāvastī, in Jeta's Grove. (NE 225: 3 folios, 30 śloka)

तथागतसंगीतिर्नाम महायानसूत्रम्

།དེ་བཞིན་གཤེགས་པ་བགྲོ་བ་ཞེས་བྱ་བ་ཐེག་པ་ཆེན་པོའི་མདོ།

T

Tathāgatasaṁgīti-nāma-mahāyāna-sūtra At the request of Mañjuśrī, the Buddha recounted the virtues of the Tathāgata in the Sūtra known as The Song of the Tathāgata. This teaching was heard by an assembly of 1,250 bhikṣus including Śāriputra, Maudgalyāyana, Kāśyapa, and many great upāsakas. Spoken in Śrāvastī, in Jeta's Grove. (NE 229: 79 folios, 3 bampo)

आर्यावैवर्तचक्रं नाम महायानसूत्रम्

།འཕགས་པ་ཕྱིར་མི་ལྡོག་པའི་འཁོར་ལོ་ཞེས་བྱ་བ་ཐེག་པ་ཆེན་པོའི་མདོ།

T C

Ārya-avaivartacakra-nāma-mahāyāna-sūtra At Śāriputra's request, the Buddha gave the teaching known as The Irreversible Wheel, an instruction on the Bodhisattva path, to a large assembly of bhikṣus. Spoken in Śrāvastī, in Jeta's Grove. (NE 240: 121 folios, 6 bampo)

आर्यधर्मनयो नाम महायानसूत्रम्

།འཕགས་པ་ཆོས་ཀྱི་ཚུལ་ཞེས་བྱ་བ་ཐེག་པ་ཆེན་པོའི་མདོ།

T

Ārya-dharmanaya-nāma-mahāyāna-sūtra For the benefit of many Bodhisattvas, the Buddha gave the Sūtra known as The Way of the Holy Dharma, a teaching on the duties, practices, and activities of the Bodhisattva. Spoken in Śrāvastī, in Jeta's Grove. (NE 244: 25 folios, 1 bampo)

आर्यधर्मार्थविभंगो नाम महायानसूत्रम्

།འཕགས་པ་ཆོས་དང་དོན་རྣམ་པར་འབྱེད་པ་ཞེས་བྱ་བ་ཐེག་པ་ཆེན་པོའི་མདོ།

T

Ārya-dharmārthavibhaṅga-nāma-mahāyāna-sūtra At the request of the Bodhisattva Jayānanda, the Buddha gave this teaching on various aspects of Dharma to an assembly of many bhikṣus and Bodhisattvas. Spoken in Śrāvastī, in Jeta's Grove. (NE 247: 8 folios, 90 śloka)

चतुर्धर्मकसूत्रम्

།ཆོས་བཞི་པའི་མདོ།

T F

Caturdharmaka-sūtra To an assembly of 1,250 bhikṣus and a great many upāsakas, the Buddha gave the teaching known as The Sūtra on the Four Dharmas, an instruction on the four things to be avoided by the wise. Spoken in Śrāvastī, in Jeta's Grove. (NE 250: 2 folios, 10 śloka)

आर्यचतुर्धर्मकं नाम महायानसूत्रम्

།འཕགས་པ་ཆོས་བཞི་པ་ཞེས་བྱ་བ་ཐེག་པ་ཆེན་པོའི་མདོ།

T C F

Ārya-caturdharmaka-nāma-mahāyāna-sūtra To an assembly of 1,250 bhikṣus, many great upāsakas, and a large number of Bodhisattvas, the Buddha gave a second Sūtra on the Four Dharmas, describing the four things to be observed by the wise. Spoken in Śrāvastī, in Jeta's Grove. (NE 251: 2 folios)

आर्यचतुष्कनिर्हारो नाम महायानसूत्रम्

།འཕགས་པ་བཞི་པ་སྒྲུབ་པ་ཞེས་བྱ་བ་ཐེག་པ་ཆེན་པོའི་མདོ།

T C F

Ārya-catuṣkanirhāra-nāma-mahāyāna-sūtra The Great Bodhisattva Mañjuśrī gave this Sūtra known as The Four Achievements, a teaching on the Bodhisattva's perfection of four essential accomplishments, for the benefit of a devaputra and the assembly of five hundred bhikṣus and hundreds of thousands of Bodhisattvas. Spoken in Śrāvastī, in Jeta's Grove. (NE 252: 18 folios, 260 śloka)

त्रिधर्मकं नाम सूत्रम्

།ཆོས་གསུམ་པ་ཞེས་བྱ་བའི་མདོ།

T F

Tridharmaka-nāma-sūtra For the benefit of a large assembly of bhikṣus, the Buddha gave The Sūtra on Three Dharmas, an instruction on three things to be avoided to ensure future happiness. Spoken in Śrāvastī, in Jeta's Grove. (NE 253: 3 folios)

आर्यधर्मकेतुर् महायानसूत्रम्

།འཕགས་པ་ཆོས་ཀྱི་རྒྱལ་མཚན་གྱི་མདོ་ཐེག་པ་ཆེན་པོ།

T

Ārya-dharmaketu-mahāyāna-sūtra At the request of the Bodhisattva Dharmaketu, the Buddha gave this Sūtra known as the Victory Banner of the Dharma, a teaching on the ten virtues that enable Bodhisattvas to quickly attain the state of a Buddha. Spoken in Śrāvastī, in Jeta's Grove. (NE 254: 2 folios)

आर्य-उपायकौशल्यं नाम महायानसूत्रम्

།འཕགས་པ་ཐབས་མཁས་པ་ཞེས་བྱ་བ་ཐེག་པ་ཆེན་པོའི་མདོ།

T C

Ārya-upāyakauśalya-nāma-mahāyāna-sūtra At the request of the Bodhisattva Jñānottara, the Buddha gave this teaching on the skillful means of the Bodhisattva to an assembly of eight thousand bhikṣus and to sixteen thousand Bodhisattvas who had mastered the dhāraṇīs and whose eloquence was unhindered. In Śrāvastī, in Jeta's Grove. (NE 261: 54 folios, 2 bampo)

आर्याष्टबुद्धकं नाम महायानसूत्रम्

།འཕགས་པ་སངས་རྒྱས་བརྒྱད་པ་ཞེས་བྱ་བ་ཐེག་པ་ཆེན་པོའི་མདོ།

T C

Ārya-aṣṭabuddhaka-nāma-mahāyāna-sūtra At Śāriputra's request, and for the assembly of 1,250 bhikṣus, the Buddha gave The Sūtra of the Eight Buddhas, describing the eight Buddhas who appear in the east and the benefits of reciting their names. Spoken in Śrāvastī, in Jeta's Grove. (NE 271: 8 folios, 90 śloka)

आर्याष्टमण्डलकं नाम महायानसूत्रम्

།འཕགས་པ་དཀྱིལ་འཁོར་བརྒྱད་པ་ཞེས་བྱ་བ་ཐེག་པ་ཆེན་པོའི་མདོ།

T C

Ārya-aṣṭamaṇḍalaka-nāma-mahāyāna-sūtra To Śāriputra, five hundred bhikṣus, Maitreya, and a great many more Bodhisattvas, the Buddha gave The Sūtra of the Eight Mandalas, describing eight Buddhas far to the east and the benefits of reciting their names. Spoken in Śrāvastī, in Jeta's Grove. (NE 277: 7 folios, 70 śloka)

मायाजालं नाम महासूत्रम्

།མདོ་ཆེན་པོ་སྒྱུ་མའི་དྲ་བ་ཞེས་བྱ་བ།

T

Māyājāla-nāma-mahāsūtra For the benefit of the assembly of bhikṣus, the Buddha gave the Sūtra known as The Net of Illusion, a teaching on the nature of reality and the highest knowledge of Śrāvakas. Spoken in Śrāvastī, in Jeta's Grove. (NE 288: 29 folios, 31 bampo)

शून्यता नाम महासूत्रम्

།མདོ་ཆེན་པོ་སྟོང་པ་ཉིད་ཅེས་བྱ་བ།

T C

Śūnyatā-nāma-mahāsūtra At Ānanda's request, the Buddha gave this teaching on śūnyatā to the assembly of bhikṣus. Spoken in Śrāvastī, in Jeta's Grove. (NE 290: 8 folios, 90 śloka)

ध्वजाग्रं नाम महासूत्रम्

།མདོ་ཆེན་པོ་རྒྱལ་མཚན་དམ་པ།

T C

Dhvajāgra-nāma-mahāsūtra The Buddha gave the Sūtra known as The Holy Banner of Victory, a teaching on the importance of taking refuge in the Buddha, Dharma, and Sangha, to a large assembly of bhikṣus. Spoken in Śrāvastī, in Jeta's Grove. (NE 293: 4 folios, 40 śloka)

पञ्चत्रयं नाम महासूत्रम्

།མདོ་ཆེན་པོ་ལྔ་གསུམ་པ་ཞེས་བྱ་བ།

T

Pañcatraya-nāma-mahāsūtra The Buddha gave this teaching on the nature of consciousness for the benefit of the bhikṣus assembled in Jeta's Grove. (NE 294: 17 folios, 220 śloka)

कुमारदृष्टान्तसूत्रम्

།གཞོན་ནུ་དཔེའི་མདོ།

T C F

Kumāradṛṣṭānta-sūtra At the request of King Prasenajit, the Buddha gave the king advice on the Dharma and wise rule in the Sūtra known as The Allegory of the Young Man. This teaching was heard by King Prasenajit and the assembly of bhikṣus. Spoken in Śrāvastī, in Jeta's Grove. (NE 296: 4 folios, 20 śloka)

धातुबहुकसूत्रम्

།ཁམས་མང་པོའི་མདོ།

T C

Dhātubahuka-sūtra At Ānanda's request, the Buddha gave this teaching on the realms of the senses and the knowledge that disperses all forms of fear. Spoken in Śrāvastī, in Jeta's Grove. (NE 297: 10 folios, 200 śloka)

भिक्षुप्रियसूत्रम् नाम

།དགེ་སློང་ལ་རབ་ཏུ་གཅེས་པའི་མདོ་ཞེས་བྱ་བ།

T E

Bhikṣupriya-sūtra-nāma At the request of Upāli, the disciple foremost in Vinaya observance, the Buddha gave this teaching known as The Diligence of Bhikṣus, a Sūtra on upholding the moral qualities of monks, to the 1,250 bhikṣus assembled in the vihāra named Flowering Lotus, near Śrāvastī. (NE 302: 5 folios)

शीलसंयुक्तसूत्रम्

།ཚུལ་ཁྲིམས་ཡང་དག་པར་ལྡན་པའི་མདོ།

T E

Śīlasaṁyukta-sūtra To the assembly of 1,250 bhikṣus, the Buddha gave the teaching known as Completely Merged With Śīla, an instruction in the benefits of moral conduct and ethics. Spoken in Śrāvastī, in Jeta's Grove. (NE 303: 2 folios)

पञ्चापत्तिनिकायशुभाशुभफलपरीक्षासूत्रम्

།ལྟུང་བ་སྡེ་ལྔའི་དགེ་བ་དང་མི་དགེ་བའི་འབྲས་བུ་བརྟག་པའི་མདོ།

T

Pañcāpattinikāya-śubhāśubha-phalaparīkṣa-sūtra To the assembly of bhikṣus, the Buddha gave this instruction on the consequences of good and bad actions. Spoken in Śrāvastī, in Jeta's Grove. (NE 304: 6 folios)

आयुष्पर्यन्तसूत्रम्
།ཚེའི་མཐའི་མདོ།

S T C

Āyuṣparyanta-sūtra For the benefit of the assembly of bhikṣus, the Buddha gave this teaching on the lifespan of beings in the six destinies. Spoken in Śrāvastī, in Jeta's Grove. (NE 307: 14 folios, 205 śloka)

अनित्यतासूत्रम्
།མི་རྟག་པ་ཉིད་ཀྱི་མདོ།

T C

Anityatā-sūtra To the assembly of bhikṣus, the Buddha gave this teaching on the impermanence of such things as health, wealth, and life. Spoken in Śrāvastī, in Jeta's Grove. (NE 309: 2 folios, 15 śloka)

अनित्यतासूत्रम्
།མི་རྟག་པ་ཉིད་ཀྱི་མདོ།

S T C

Anityatā-sūtra To the assembly of bhikṣus, the Buddha gave this teaching on the impermanence of all conditioned things. Spoken in Śrāvastī, in Jeta's Grove. (NE 310: 4 folios)

तमोवनमुखं नाम सूत्रम्

།མུན་གྱི་ནགས་ཚལ་གྱི་སྒོ་ཞེས་བྱ་བའི་མདོ།

T

Tamovanamukha-nāma-sūtra At Śrāvasti, the Buddha gave this teaching known as The Door of the Dark Forest, describing Paradarśin and his entry into the Sangha of bhikṣus. (NE 314: 12 folios)

पितृमातृसूत्रम्

།ཕ་མའི་མདོ།

T

Pitṛmātṛ-sūtra To the assembly of bhikṣus, the Buddha gave the teaching known as The Father and Mother Sūtra, an instruction on the importance of respecting one's parents. Spoken in Śrāvastī, in Jeta's Grove. (NE 315: 2 folios, 1 bampo)

अर्थविनिश्चयो नाम धर्मपर्यायः

།དོན་རྣམ་པར་ངེས་པ་ཞེས་བྱ་བའི་ཆོས་ཀྱི་རྣམ་གྲངས།

S T C E

Arthaviniścaya-nāma-dharmaparyāya In the Pūrvārāma, the hall built in Śrāvastī by Mother Mṛgāra, the Buddha gave this Sūtra known as The Compendium of Categories, explaining the five skandhas, the eighteen dhātus, the twelve āyatānas, the limbs of interdependent cooperation, the four noble truths, the twenty-two faculties, the four meditations, and other essential categories of Dharma teachings to the assembly of 1,250 bhikṣus. (NE 317: 36 folios, 1 bampo)

आर्यजिनपुत्र-अर्थसिद्धिसूत्रम्

།འཕགས་པ་རྒྱལ་བུ་དོན་གྲུབ་ཀྱི་མདོ།

T C

Ārya-jinaputra-arthasiddhi-sūtra Ānanda asked the Buddha the significance of his smile. In the teaching known as The Accomplishment of the Purpose of the Conqueror's Son, the Buddha related the story of Prince Sudana, illustrating the wondrous results of the perfection of giving for the benefit of the assembly of innumerable bhikṣus and bhikṣuṇīs. Spoken in Śrāvastī, in Jeta's Grove. (NE 351: 31 folios, 1 bampo)

कनकवर्णपूर्वयोगो नाम

།གསེར་མདོག་གི་སྔོན་གྱི་སྦྱོར་བ་ཞེས་བྱ་བ།

S T C

Kanakavarṇa-pūrvayoga-nāma In relating the story of King Kanaka, the Buddha illustrated the results of generosity for the benefit of the assembly of 1,250 bhikṣus, bhikṣuṇīs, gods, nāgas, and numerous other beings. Spoken in Śrāvastī, in Jeta's Grove. (NE 350: 13 folios, 17 śloka)

श्रीसेनावदानम्

།དཔལ་གྱི་སྡེའི་རྟོགས་པ་བརྗོད་པ།

T

Śrīsenāvadāna The Buddha related this account of Śrīsena, a king celebrated for his generosity and self-sacrifice, as a teaching in the results of meritorious actions for the benefit of the bhikṣus assembled in Jeta's Grove. (NE 349: 37 folios)

आर्यशुभाशुभकार्यकारणभावनिर्देशो नाम महायानसूत्रम्

།འཕགས་པ་ལེགས་ཉེས་ཀྱི་རྒྱུ་དང་འབྲས་བུ་བསྟན་པ་ཞེས་བྱ་བ་ཐེག་པ་ཆེན་པོའི་མདོ།

T C E F

Ārya-śubhāśubhakāryakāraṇabhāva-nirdeśa-nāma-mahāyāna-sūtra At Ānanda's request, the Buddha gave this Sūtra known as The Cause and Effect of Good and Evil, a teaching on the connection between one's present condition and actions performed in the past. Spoken in Śrāvastī, in Jeta's Grove. (NE 354: 23 folios)

शुभाशुभकर्मविपाकनिर्देशसूत्रम्

།དགེ་བ་དང་མི་དགེ་བའི་ལས་ཀྱི་རྣམ་པར་སྨིན་པ་བསྟན་པའི་མདོ།

T

Śubhāśubhakarmavipāka-nirdeśa-sūtra At the request of his disciple Nanda, the Buddha gave the Sūtra known as The Ripening of Virtuous and Non-virtuous Karma, a teaching on the consequences of good and bad actions, to the assembly of innumerable Great Bodhisattvas, humans, and gods. Spoken in Śrāvastī, in Jeta's Grove. (NE 355: 15 folios, 1 bampo)

शार्दूलकर्णावदानम्

།སྟག་རྣའི་རྟོགས་པ་བརྗོད་པ།

S T C

Śārdūlakarṇāvadāna The Buddha illustrated the value of the lack of class distinctions in the Sangha by recounting the life of Śārdūlakarṇa, a bhikṣu who had been raised as the pampered son of a wealthy family. Although his body had become unusually vulnerable to the pains of a mendicant's life, Śārdūlakarṇa, sustained by his love for the Dharma, willingly endured the physical hardships of the homeless wandering monk. Spoken in Śrāvastī, in Jeta's Grove. (NE 358: 91 folios, 2 bampo)

महासमयसूत्रम्

།འདུས་པ་ཆེན་པོའི་མདོ།

T C E

Mahāsamaya-sūtra To an assembly of five hundred Arhats and the gods of the ten realms, the Buddha gave the Sūtra known as The Great Convocation, a teaching on the nature of gods and yakṣas and other subjects. Spoken in Kapilavastu, the Buddha's early home. (NE 34: 8 folios)

मैत्रीसूत्रम्

།བྱམས་པའི་མདོ།

T

Maitri-sūtra In the Nyagrodha (Banyan) Grove on the banks of the Rohiṇī River, at the request of the great disciple Śāriputra, the Buddha gave The Sūtra of Loving-Kindness, describing to the assembly of bhikṣus the qualities of the future Buddha Maitreya and the splendor of his realm. Spoken near the city of Kapilavastu. (NE 35: 15 folios)

आर्यनन्दगर्भावक्रान्तिनिर्देशः नाम महायानसूत्रम्

།འཕགས་པ་དགའ་བོ་ལ་མངལ་ན་གནས་པ་བསྟན་པ་ ཞེས་བྱ་བ་ཐེག་པ་ཆེན་པོའི་མདོ།

T C

Ārya-nandagarbhāvakrānti-nirdeśa-nāma-mahāyāna-sūtra At one time, while residing in the Nyagrodha Grove near Kapilavastu together with many bhikṣus, the Buddha revealed the splendor and pleasures of the heaven realms to his cousin Nanda, enabling Nanda to overcome his attachment to worldly life. (NE 57: 63 folios, 3 bampo, 600 śloka)

आर्यपितापुत्रसमागमनो नाम महायानसूत्रम्

།འཕགས་པ་ཡབ་དང་སྲས་མཇལ་བ་ཞེས་བྱ་བ་ཐེག་པ་ཆེན་པོའི་མདོ།

T C

Ārya-pitāputra-samāgamana-nāma-mahāyāna-sūtra Upon meeting his father King Śuddhodana in the Nyagrodha Grove of Kapilavastu, the Buddha gave the Sūtra known as The Reunion of Father and Son, an extensive instruction on the effects of previous actions. This teaching was given to an assembly consisting of those who were free, those who were humble, those who were tranquil, those who had gone beyond, those who had obtained power and conquered their breath, those who had converted the passions, and many others, together with 1,250 bhikṣus, including Kāśyapa, Śāriputra, and Maudgalyāyana. (NE 60: 334 folios, 15 bampo, 4,500 śloka)

आर्यक्षेमङ्करपरिपृच्छा नाम महायानसूत्रम्

།འཕགས་པ་བདེ་བྱེད་ཀྱིས་ཞུས་པ་ཞེས་བྱ་བ་ཐེག་པ་ཆེན་པོའི་མདོ།

T C

Ārya-kṣemaṅkara-paripṛcchā-nāma-mahāyāna-sūtra In the Nyagrodha Grove, at the request of the Śākya Kṣemaṅkara, the Buddha gave the Sūtra known as the Questions of Kṣemaṅkara, a teaching on how Bodhisattvas benefit all living beings, to the assembly of five hundred bhikṣus and numerous other beings. Spoken at Kapilavastu, in the land of the Śākyas. (NE 165: 9 folios, 80 śloka)

आर्यदानपारमिता नाम महायानसूत्रम्

།འཕགས་པ་སྦྱིན་པའི་ཕ་རོལ་ཏུ་ཕྱིན་པ་ཞེས་བྱ་བ་ཐེག་པ་ཆེན་པོའི་མདོ།

T

Ārya-dānapāramitā-nāma-mahāyāna-sūtra The Buddha was residing in the park of King Śuddhodana near Kapilavastu to benefit the king, his relatives, and all the people of that land. Here, in this park filled with all varieties of fruit trees and flowers, vibrant with many kinds of animals and birds, the Buddha gave the Sūtra known as The Perfection of Giving, describing the Bodhisattva's practice of generosity to a vast assembly consisting of seventy-seven thousand bhikṣus including Śāriputra, Maudgalyāyana, and Subhūti, hundreds of thousands of Bodhisattvas skilled in the pāramitās, gods, demi-gods, and numerous other beings. (NE 182: 38 folios, 2 bampo)

आर्यधर्मस्कन्धो नाम महायानसूत्रम्

།འཕགས་པ་ཆོས་ཀྱི་ཕུང་པོ་ཞེས་བྱ་བ་ཐེག་པ་ཆེན་པོའི་མདོ།

T

Ārya-dharmaskandha-nāma-mahāyāna-sūtra In the Nyagrodha Grove near Kapilavastu, the Buddha gave at Śāriputra's request the Sūtra known as Aggregates of the Dharma, a teaching on the eighty-four thousand aggregates, to an assembly of five hundred bhikṣus including Śāriputra, Maudgalyāyana, Kāśyapa, Ānanda, and Rāhula. (NE 245: 10 folios, 150 śloka)

आर्यदशदिगन्धकारविध्वंसनं नाम महायानसूत्रम्

།འཕགས་པ་ཕྱོགས་བཅུའི་མུན་པ་རྣམ་པར་སེལ་བ་ཞེས་བྱ་བ་ཐེག་པ་ཆེན་པོའི་མདོ།

T C

Ārya-daśadigandhakāra-vidhvaṁsana-nāma-mahāyāna-sūtra At the request of a Śākyan youth, the Buddha gave the Sūtra known as Removing the Darkness of the Ten Directions, a teaching on dispelling the darkness of the ten directions and removing the bases of fear, to the assembly of 1,250 bhikṣus and a multitude of Great Bodhisattvas led by Maitreya and Mañjuśrī. Spoken at Kapilavastu, in the Nyagrodha Grove. (NE 269: 13 folios, 150 śloka)

महाशून्यतानाम महासूत्रम्

།མདོ་ཆེན་པོ་སྟོང་པ་ཉིད་ཆེན་པོ་ཞེས་བྱ་བ།

T C

Mahāśūnyatā-nāma-mahāsūtra For the benefit of Ānanda and other assembled bhikṣus, the Buddha gave the Sūtra known as The Great Śūnyatā, an instruction on śūnyatā and the sources of misery. Spoken in the Śakyan capital of Kapilavastu. (NE 291: 17 folios, .5 bampo)

आयुष्पत्तियथाकारपरिपृच्छा सूत्रम्

།ཚེ་འཕོ་བ་ཇི་ལྟར་འགྱུར་བ་ཞུས་པའི་མདོ།

T

Āyuṣpattiyathākāra-paripṛcchā-sūtra At the request of King Śuddhodana, the Buddha gave this teaching on what happens after death, occasioned by a funeral accompanied by offerings to the deceased. This teaching was heard by the assembly of five hundred bhikṣus and the householders of Kapilavastu. Spoken in the Buddha's homeland, in the city of Kapilavastu. (NE 308: 20 folios)

नन्दप्रव्रज्यासूत्रम्

།དགའ་བོ་རབ་ཏུ་བྱུང་བའི་མདོ།

T

Nandapravrajyā-sūtra Accompanied by Ānanda, the Buddha gave the Sūtra known as The Home Departure for Nanda, a teaching to his kinsman Nanda on the benefits of a religious life. Spoken in the land of the Śakyas, near the capital city of Kapilavastu. (NE 328: 6 folios, 50 śloka)

आर्यस्थानस्थापकसूत्रं नाम

།འཕགས་པ་གནས་འཇོག་གི་མདོ་ཞེས་བྱ་བ།

T

Ārya-sthānasthāpaka-sūtra-nāma In the Banyan (Nyagrodha) Grove donated to the Ārya Sangha by King Śuddhodana, the Enlightened One gave this Sūtra known as Standing Firmly. This teaching, spoken for the benefit of the great ṛṣi Kapila, inspired the powerful sage to take refuge in the Buddha, Dharma, and Sangha. (NE 333: 10 folios, 20 śloka)

आर्यभद्रकल्पिको नाम महायानसूत्रम्

།འཕགས་པ་བསྐལ་པ་བཟང་པོ་ཞེས་བྱ་བ་ཐེག་པ་ཆེན་པོའི་མདོ།

T C E

Ārya-bhadrakalpika-nāma-mahāyāna-sūtra After the rainy season retreat in Śrāvastī, the Buddha came to the Mahāvana in Vaiśālī accompanied by one hundred thousand bhikṣus and eight hundred million Bodhisattvas. Around the Blessed One gathered bhikṣus and bhikṣuṇīs, laymen and laywomen, and great followings of devas, nāgas, yakṣas, gandharvas, asuras, garuḍas, kinnaras, and mahoragas. Here, at the request of the Bodhisattva Pramodyarāja, the Buddha gave the teaching known as The Fortunate Aeon, describing the nature and powers of the great Buddhas, the Buddhas' perfected qualities, and the thousand Buddhas predicted to appear in our present aeon. (NE 94: 678 folios, 26 bampo, 7,800 śloka)

आर्यसर्वपुण्यसमुच्चयसमाधिर्नाम महायानसूत्रम्

།འཕགས་པ་བསོད་ནམས་ཐམས་ཅད་བསྡུས་པའི་ཏིང་ངེ་འཛིན་ཞེས་བྱ་བ་ཐེག་པ་ཆེན་པོའི་མདོ།

T C

Ārya-sarvapuṇya-samuccaya-samādhi-nāma-mahāyāna-sūtra In the Mango Grove of Vaiśālī, at the request of the Bodhisattva Nārāyaṇa, the Buddha gave the Sūtra known as the Accumulation of Everything Meritorious, explaining the efficacy of samādhi and moral conduct to the assembly of ten thousand Arhats, twenty thousand Bodhisattvas, forty thousand devaputras, Indra, Brahmā, and many world protectors. (NE 134: 102 folios, 4 bampo)

आर्यब्रह्मपरिपृच्छा नाम महायानसूत्रम्

།འཕགས་པ་ཚངས་པས་ཞུས་པ་ཞེས་བྱ་བ་ཐེག་པ་ཆེན་པོའི་མདོ།

T

Ārya-brahmā-paripṛcchā-nāma-mahāyāna-sūtra In the garden palace of Vaiśālī, at the request of Brahmā, lord of the gods, the Buddha gave the Sūtra known as The Questions of Brahmā, imparting teachings on the path to Buddhahood to an assembly of twelve thousand bhikṣus and a vast multitude of Bodhisattvas. (NE 158: 19 folios, 200 śloka)

आर्यरत्नजालिपरिपृच्छा नाम महायानसूत्रम्

།འཕགས་པ་རིན་ཆེན་དྲ་བ་ཅན་གྱིས་ཞུས་པ་ཞེས་བྱ་བ་ཐེག་པ་ཆེན་པོའི་མདོ།

T C

Ārya-ratnajāli-paripṛcchā-nāma-mahāyāna-sūtra Having honored many Buddhas in previous lives, Ratnajāli, son of a leader of the Licchavi clan, was blessed with a vision of the Dharma at eight years of age. In a dream he saw the gods of the Tuṣita realm descend from heaven and sing verses in praise of the Enlightened One. After describing this dream to his father, Ratnajāli set forth from the city in search of the Buddha, who was dwelling in a storied house on the banks of the Monkey Pond. In response to Ratnajāli, the Buddha gave the Sūtra known as The Questions of Ratnajāli to Ratnajāli and an assembly of forty-two times ten million Bodhisattvas, sixty times ten million Arhats, and ninety-nine times ten million devas and devaputras. (NE 163: 32 folios, 1 bampo)

आर्यमहाललिकापरिपृच्छा नाम महायानसूत्रम्

།འཕགས་པ་བགྲེས་མོས་ཞུས་པ་ཞེས་བྱ་བ་ཐེག་པ་ཆེན་པོའི་མདོ།

T C E F

Ārya-mahālalikā-paripṛcchā-nāma-mahāyāna-sūtra Mahālalikā, an aged woman of Vaiśālī, became filled with faith upon seeing the Buddha and asked the Bhagavan to teach her about birth, old age, and death. In response, the Buddha gave the Sūtra known as The Questions of Mahālalikā to the old woman, the assembly of 1,250 bhikṣus, and many Bodhisattvas. Spoken in the land of the Vṛjjis. (NE 171: 8 folios, 110 śloka)

आर्यविमलकीर्तिनिर्देशो नाम महायानसूत्रम्

། འཕགས་པ་དྲི་མ་མེད་པར་གྲགས་པས་བསྟན་པ་ཞེས་བྱ་བ་ཐེག་པ་ཆེན་པོའི་མདོ།

TCEFG

Ārya-vimalakīrtinirdeśa-nāma-mahāyāna-sūtra The Buddha was dwelling in the Mango Grove at Vaiśālī with an assembly of eight thousand great bhikṣus, thirty-two thousand Bodhisattvas, numerous thousands of gods, world-protectors, nāgas, yakṣas, gandharvas, asuras, garuḍas, kinnaras, and mahoragas, and the fourfold assembly of bhikṣus, bhikṣuṇīs, laymen, and laywomen. At that time, the Bodhisattva Vimalakīrti, inspired by the Buddha,engaged Mañjuśrī in a dialogue on the nature of illness, the Bodhisattva path, the inconceivable liberation, and other profound topics, culminating in the vision of the splendors of the universe, the arrays of the Buddhafield of Akṣobhya, and the radiance of its disciples and Bodhisattvas. In response to Ānanda's inquiry, the Buddha named this Sūtra The Teaching of Vimalakīrti. (NE 176: 129 folios, 6 bampo)

आर्यबोधिसत्त्वचर्यानिर्देशो नाम महायानसूत्रम्

། འཕགས་པ་བྱང་ཆུབ་སེམས་དཔའི་སྤྱོད་པ་བསྟན་པ་ཞེས་བྱ་བ་ཐེག་པ་ཆེན་པོའི་མདོ།

TC

Ārya-bodhisattvacarya-nirdeśa-nāma-mahāyāna-sūtra Miracles attended the Tathāgata's entrance into Vaiśālī; the blind saw and the deaf heard. In this city beloved by the Bhagavan, the Buddha gave the Sūtra known as The Teaching on the Acts of the Bodhisattva to two thousand bhikṣus and the townspeople of Vaiśālī. (NE 184: 19 folios, 120 śloka)

आर्यचन्द्रोत्तरादारिकाव्याकरणं नाम महायानसूत्रम्

།འཕགས་པ་བུ་མོ་ཟླ་མཆོག་ལུང་བསྟན་པ་ཞེས་བྱ་བ་ཐེག་པ་ཆེན་པོའི་མདོ།

T C

Ārya-candrottarādārikā-vyākaraṇa-nāma-mahāyāna-sūtra In the garden of the Kūṭāgāra, the Buddha gave the Sūtra known as the Prediction of Candrottarādārikā, proclaiming the future attainment of Buddhahood by Candrottarā, daughter of the Bodhisattva householder Vimalakīrti. This Sūtra was heard by the assembly of five hundred bhikṣus and one hundred thousand Bodhisattvas including Mañjuśrī, Maitreya, and Avalokiteśvara, together with many Brahmins and beings of other realms, numbering eight thousand altogether. Spoken in the city of Vaiśālī. (NE 191: 39 folios, 2 bampo)

आर्यकर्मावरणविशुद्धिर्नाम महायानसूत्रम्

།འཕགས་པ་ལས་ཀྱི་སྒྲིབ་པ་རྣམ་པར་དག་པ་ཞེས་བྱ་བ་ཐེག་པ་ཆེན་པོའི་མདོ།

T C

Ārya-karmāvaraṇa-viśuddhi-nāma-mahāyāna-sūtra In the Mango Grove of Vaiśālī, the Buddha gave the Sūtra known as Cleansing the Obstructions of Karma, a teaching on the purification of karma, for the benefit of the bhikṣu Vimalaprabha and the assembly of five hundred bhikṣus and thirty-two thousand Bodhisattvas. (NE 218: 28 folios, 1 bampo)

आर्यमङ्गलाष्टकं नाम महायानसूत्रम्

།འཕགས་པ་བཀྲ་ཤིས་བརྒྱད་པ་ཞེས་བྱ་བ་ཐེག་པ་ཆེན་པོའི་མདོ།

T C

Ārya-maṅgalāṣṭaka-nāma-mahāyāna-sūtra In the Mango Grove of Vaiśālī, at the request of a member of the Licchavi clan, the Buddha gave the Sūtra known as The Eight Blessings, enumerating Tathāgatas far to the east, their purity and perfection, and the virtues of invoking these great beings through prayer. (NE 278: 5 folios, 51 śloka)

ध्वजाग्रं नाम महासूत्रम्

།མདོ་ཆེན་པོ་རྒྱལ་མཚན་མཆོག་ཅེས་བྱ་བ།

T C

Dhvajāgra-nāma-mahāsūtra In a house on the banks of the Monkey Pond, in the land of the Vṛjjis, the Buddha gave the Sūtra known as The Victory Banner, a teaching on the benefits of honoring the Buddha, Dharma, and Sangha, for the welfare of the merchants of Vaiśālī about to depart on a caravan to Takṣaśilā. (NE 292: 8 folios, 40 śloka)

आर्यवैशालीप्रवेशमहासूत्रम्

།འཕགས་པ་ཡངས་པའི་གྲོང་ཁྱེར་དུ་འཇུག་པའི་མདོ་ཆེན་པོ།

T F

Ārya-vaiśālīpraveśa-mahāsūtra In the Mango Grove of Vaiśālī, the Buddha gave this Sūtra known as Entrance Into Vaiśālī, giving to Ānanda mantras for protection and healing for the people of Vaiśālī, who were at that time afflicted with a great plague. (NE 312: 9 folios, 100 śloka)

शिक्षात्रयं नाम सूत्रम्

།བསླབ་པ་གསུམ་གྱི་མདོ།

T

Śikṣātraya-nāma-sūtra In a small town in the country of Vṛji, in a garden of Sāla trees, the Buddha gave this Sūtra known as The Three Trainings, explaining the trainings of śīla, samādhi, and prajñā (morality, meditation, and wisdom) for the benefit of the assembly of bhikṣus. (NE 282: 2 folios)

आर्य-ऋषिव्यासपरिपृच्छा नाम महायानसूत्रम्

།འཕགས་པ་དྲང་སྲོང་རྒྱས་པས་ཞུས་པ་ཞེས་བྱ་བ་ཐེག་པ་ཆེན་པོའི་མདོ།

T C

Ārya-ṛṣivyāsa-paripṛcchā-nāma-mahāyāna-sūtra The Bhagavan was abiding on the banks of the Ganges, together with a vast congregation of bhikṣus, in an area that teemed with wild birds and flowers. At that time the Bhagavan taught the assembled bhikṣus about giving and morality, to the joy of Ānanda, Kāśyapa, Śāriputra, and the rest of the assembly. Then a great light, shining like the sun, appeared in the west, and Ānanda asked the Buddha the cause of this light. The Buddha replied that it emanated from the great ṛṣi Vyāsa. The ṛṣi, who had mastered the most strenuous ascetic practices, soon arrived with his retinue and, recognizing the Buddha, questioned the Bhagavan concerning the Dharma. In response, the Buddha gave the teaching known as The Questions of the Ṛṣi Vyāsa. (NE 93: 43 folios, 2 bampo, 600 śloka)

चन्द्रसूत्रम्

།ཟླ་བའི་མདོ།

T C F

Candra-sūtra To Candra, the god who lives in the disk of the moon, the Buddha gave this teaching on the occasion of the moon's eclipse by the demon Rāhu. Spoken at Campā, capital of the eastern province of Aṅga, located on the southern bank of the Ganges River. (NE 331: 2 folios, 13 śloka)

आर्य-उदयनवत्सराजपरिपृच्छा नाम परिवर्तः

། འཕགས་པ་བད་སའི་རྒྱལ་པོ་འཆར་བྱེད་ཀྱིས་ཞུས་པ་ཞེས་བྱ་བའི་ལེའུ།

T C

Ārya-udayanavatsarāja-paripṛcchā-nāma-parivarta While the Buddha was residing at Kauśāmbī in the Grove of Melodies, the Princess Syāmā, devoted to the Buddha, was wrongfully accused of harboring lascivious desires for the Blessed One. Believing the lies, Udayana, king of Vatsa, ordered the Princess executed. Princess Syāmā entered into the meditation of love and kindness; through the power of the Buddha, the axe did not fall, and King Udayana perceived a great light. Known as The Question of Udayana, King of Vatsa, this teaching was given for that king and the assembly of five hundred bhikṣus and many Bodhisattvas. (NE 73: 23 folios, 1 bampo, 200 śloka)

आर्यबोधिसत्त्वगोचरोपायविषयविकुर्वाणनिर्देशो नाम महायानसूत्रम्

།འཕགས་པ་བྱང་ཆུབ་སེམས་དཔའི་སྤྱོད་ཡུལ་གྱི་ཐབས་ཀྱི་ཡུལ་ལ་རྣམ་པར་འཕྲུལ་པ་
བསྟན་པ་ཞེས་བྱ་བ་ཐེག་པ་ཆེན་པོའི་མདོ།

T C

Ārya-bodhisattva-gocaropāyaviṣaya-vikurvāṇa-nirdeśa-nāma-mahāyāna-sūtra In the garden of the king (in Āryavarta, =Ujjain?), where trees and fragrant flowers abounded and the air was resonant with the sounds of geese and parrots, the Buddha taught the Sūtra known as Manifestations of Skillful Means in the Bodhisattva's Sphere of Action for the benefit of Mañjuśrī and the assembly of twelve thousand bhikṣus, eight hundred thousand bhikṣuṇīs, many millions of Bodhisattvas, Indra, Brahmā, and many gods and nāgas. (NE 146: 120 folios, 5 bampo)

राजदेशो नाम महायानसूत्रम्

།རྒྱལ་པོ་ལ་གདམས་པ་ཞེས་བྱ་བ་ཐེག་པ་ཆེན་པོའི་མདོ།

T

Rājadeśa-nāma-mahāyāna-sūtra While traveling southwest on the road from Kauśāmbī to Ujjayinī, the Buddha came upon Udayana, king of Vatsa, making preparations to conquer the neighboring province of Avanti. For Udayana's benefit, the Buddha gave the Sūtra known as Counsel to the King, a teaching on the wisdom of ruling peacefully in accord with the Dharma. (NE 215: 4 folios)

आर्यरत्नाकरो नाम महायानसूत्रम्

།འཕགས་པ་དཀོན་མཆོག་འབྱུང་གནས་ཞེས་བྱ་བ་ཐེག་པ་ཆེན་པོའི་མདོ།

T

Ārya-ratnākara-nāma-mahāyāna-sūtra Near Saketa, in the grove of Kṛṣṇa, the Buddha gave the Sūtra known as The Mine of Jewels at the request of Mañjuśrī and other Great Bodhisattvas. In this teaching the World-honored One described the inconceivable Buddhafields and the compassion of the Tathāgatas to the assembly of bhikṣus, sixty-two thousand Arhats, and eighty-four thousand Bodhisattvas. (NE 124: 159 folios, 7 bampo)

पञ्चशिक्षानुशंसासूत्रम्

།བསླབ་པ་ལྔའི་ཕན་ཡོན་གྱི་མདོ།

T F

Pañcaśikṣānuśaṁsā-sūtra In Gargara, in the Medicine Forest on the Mountain of the Crocodiles, the Buddha gave the Sūtra known as Benefits of the Five Trainings, a teaching on the five precepts appropriate to householders, for the benefit of the householder Phaṇakula and his wife Manakulā. (NE 37: 11 folios)

आर्यमैत्रेयपरिपृच्छा नाम महायानसूत्रम्

།འཕགས་པ་བྱམས་པས་ཞུས་པ་ཞེས་བྱ་བ་ཐེག་པ་ཆེན་པོའི་མདོ།

T C

Ārya-maitreya-paripṛcchā-nāma-mahāyāna-sūtra While residing in the Bargana Mountain Forest, the Buddha gave teachings on the Bodhisattva path requested by the Bodhisattva Maitreya and answered Ānanda's questions concerning the activities of the Bodhisattva on behalf of sentient beings. This teaching, known as The Questions of Maitreya, was given to an assembly of five hundred bhikṣus including the venerable Kauṇḍinya, ten thousand Bodhisattvas including Maitreya, and a multitude of other beings. (NE 85: 25 folios, 1 bampo)

वज्रसमाधिधर्माक्षरः

།རྡོ་རྗེའི་ཏིང་ངེ་འཛིན་གྱི་ཆོས་ཀྱི་ཡི་གེ།

T C

Vajrasamādhidharmākṣara On the Mountain of the Fortune-tellers (near Rājagṛha?), at the request of the bhikṣu Agasta, the Buddha gave the Sūtra known as The Diamond Samādhi, an instruction on the one vehicle, to the assembly of ten thousand bhikṣus including Śāriputra, Maudgalyāyana, and Subhūti, two thousand Bodhisattvas, and eighty thousand men of the highest nature, together with a multitude of gods, nāgas, and other beings. (NE 135: 45 folios, 2 bampo)

आर्यवज्रमण्डा नाम धारणी महायानसूत्रम्

།འཕགས་པ་རྡོ་རྗེ་སྙིང་པོའི་གཟུངས་ཞེས་བྱ་བ་ཐེག་པ་ཆེན་པོའི་མདོ།

T C

Ārya-vajramaṇḍa-nāma-dhāraṇī-mahāyāna-sūtra While residing in various places near the Snow Mountains together with one thousand bhikṣus, the Blessed One entered the samādhi called The Sameness of All Samādhis. Then, by the power of the Buddha, the gods of the highest realms, including Indra and Brahmā, together with thirty-two thousand devaputras, came to where the Buddha was meditating. At that time the Enlightened One revealed numerous emanations. The Great Bodhisattva Mañjuśrī entered samādhi, filling all with joy; Maitreya entered samādhi, and all were made tranquil. After each of the Great Bodhisattvas had entered samādhi, the Buddha smiled, and, in response to a question by Mañjuśrī, set forth the Vajramaṇḍa Dhāraṇī. (NE 139: 24 folios, 1 bampo)

आर्यलोकानुवर्तनं नाम महायानसूत्रम्

།འཕགས་པ་འཇིག་རྟེན་གྱི་རྗེས་སུ་འཐུན་པར་འཇུག་པ་
ཞེས་བྱ་བ་ཐེག་པ་ཆེན་པོའི་མདོ།

T C

Ārya-lokānuvartana-nāma-mahāyāna-sūtra On the mountain of the king of the sages, at the request of the Great Bodhisattva Mañjuśrī, the Buddha spoke of the qualities of the Tathāgatas and the reasons why they accommodate themselves to human conceptions. This teaching, known as Serving the World, was heard by a large assembly of Śrāvakas and Bodhisattvas. (NE 200: 11 folios, 111 śloka)

दशचक्रक्षितिगर्भो नाम महायानसूत्रम्

།འདུས་པ་ཆེན་པོ་ལས་སའི་སྙིང་པོའི་འཁོར་ལོ་བཅུ་པ་
ཞེས་བྱ་བ་ཐེག་པ་ཆེན་པོའི་མདོ།

T C

Daśacakrakṣitigarbha-nāma-mahāyāna-sūtra On Khaladeya Mountain in the land of many great sages, the Buddha gave the Sūtra known as The Ten Wheels of Kṣitigarbha, a teaching on the ten perfections and the virtues required of the Bodhisattva, to the assembly of innumerable bhikṣus and Bodhisattvas. (NE 239: 284 folios, 10 bampo)

आर्यपरिणतचक्रं नाम महायानसूत्रम्

།འཕགས་པ་ཡོངས་སུ་བསྔོ་བའི་འཁོར་ལོ་ཞེས་བྱ་བ་ཐེག་པ་ཆེན་པོའི་མདོ།

T C

Ārya-pariṇatacakra-nāma-mahāyāna-sūtra On Vajraratna Mountain, the Buddha gave the Sūtra known as The Wheel of Blessings, a teaching on the Bodhisattva's nature and practice, for the benefit of the Bodhisattva Vajraratna and the assembly of Great Bodhisattvas. (NE 242: 7 folios)

धर्मसमुद्रो नाम महायानसूत्रम्

།ཐེག་པ་ཆེན་པོའི་མདོ་ཆོས་ཀྱི་མཚོ་ཞེས་བྱ་བ།

T

*Dharmasamudra-nāma-mahāyāna-sūtr*a On Mt. Talaka (= Potala?), a hill upon a small island in the ocean, the Buddha, at the request of the Bodhisattva Lokeśvara, gave to a group of Bodhisattvas the Sūtra known as Ocean of Dharma, a teaching on the ocean of virtues and the advantages of a religious life. "When Bodhisattvas abide in pure loving-kindness, then they obtain liberation." (NE 255: 7 folios, 80 śloka)

आर्याकाशगर्भो नाम महायानसूत्रम्

། འཕགས་པ་ནམ་མཁའི་སྙིང་པོ་ཞེས་བྱ་བ་ཐེག་པ་ཆེན་པོའི་མདོ།

T C

Ārya-akāśagarbha-nāma-mahāyāna-sūtra On Mt. Khalatika, in the land of the great ṛṣis, the Bodhisattva Śaṅku bowed to the Blessed One and requested teachings. In response, the Buddha gave the Sūtra known as The Heart of Space, an instruction on the nature of form and Bodhisattvas, to an assembly of bhikṣus and Great Bodhisattvas as numerous as the sands of the Ganges. (NE 260: 40 folios, 1 bampo)

आर्यसम्यक्चर्यावृत्तगगनवर्णविनयक्षान्तिर्नाम महायानसूत्रम्

། འཕགས་པ་ཡང་དག་པར་སྤྱོད་པའི་ཚུལ་ནམ་མཁའི་མདོག་གིས་འདུལ་བའི་བཟོད་པ་ཞེས་བྱ་བ་ཐེག་པ་ཆེན་པོའི་མདོ།

T

Ārya-samyakcaryavṛttagaganavarṇa-vinaya-kṣānti-nāma-mahāyāna-sūtra In the land of ascetics called Windhorse, on the mountain Increasing Luster near the city of Anavila, the Buddha gave this teaching on the nature of existence and the best conduct of the wise to an assembly of 1,250 bhikṣus and a multitude of Great Bodhisattvas including Maitreya. (NE 263: 240 folios, 11 bampo, 3,300 śloka)

आर्यसप्तबुद्धकं नाम महायानसूत्रम्

།འཕགས་པ་སངས་རྒྱས་བདུན་པ་ཞེས་བྱ་བ་ཐེག་པ་ཆེན་པོའི་མདོ།

T C

Saptabuddha-nāma-mahāyāna-sūtra The Buddha was residing in the land of the long-lived gods on the peak of Mt. Kailāsa, together with five hundred bhikṣus and five hundred Bodhisattvas including Maitreya, Ākāśagarbha, and Samantabhadra. In a nearby forest, a demon caught hold of a bhikṣu, lifted up its hand, and shouted. Hearing this cry, the Bodhisattva Ākāśagarbha paid homage to the Holy One and said, “Bhagavan, in the sky there are great moans and whispers.” Learning that these were portents of illness, Ākāśagarbha asked the Blessed One to teach the mantra that repels all demonic forces. This teaching is known as the Sūtra of the Seven Buddhas. (NE 270: 9 folios, 105 śloka)

महासन्निपातान् महायानसूत्रात् तथागतश्रीसमयो नाम महायानसूत्रम्

།འདུས་པ་ཆེན་པོ་ཐེག་པ་ཆེན་པོའི་མདོ་སྡེ་ལས་དེ་བཞིན་གཤེགས་པའི་དཔལ་གྱི་དམ་ཚིག་ཅེས་བྱ་བ་ཐེག་པ་ཆེན་པོའི་མདོ།

T C

Mahāsannipātān mahāyānasūtrāt tathāgata-śrī-samaya- nāma-mahāyāna-sūtra In the Place of the Sages, at the request of Śrīmahādevī, the Buddha gave the Sūtra known as The Venerable Vow of the Tathāgatas, a teaching on the nature of the Tathāgata’s vow and the means of arriving at supreme perfection, to an assembly of innumerable bhikṣus and Bodhisattvas. (NE 230: 63 folios, 3 bampo)

आर्यचन्द्रगर्भपरिपृच्छासूत्रे बुद्धशासनस्थितिविनाशघटनानिर्देशः

།འཕགས་པ་ཟླ་བའི་སྙིང་པོས་ཞུས་པའི་མདོ་ལས་སངས་རྒྱས་ཀྱི་བསྟན་པ་གནས་པ་དང་འཇིག་པའི་ཚུལ་ལུང་བསྟན་པ།

T

Ārya-candragarbha-paripṛcchā-sūtre Buddhaśāsanasthitivināśa-ghaṭanā-nirdeśa While the Buddha was abiding on Mt. Kartirtak, light from his brow illuminated the four continents, clearly revealing Mt. Meru, the forests, and the fields of all lands. From this light streamed colored rays bearing innumerable images of the Buddha. Viewing this wonder, Bodhisattvas from the ten directions and many Arhats, gods, nāgas, and other beings asked for what purpose the light was shining. The Buddha replied, "After my Parinirvāṇa, images, relics, and scripture which I have taught on the four continents will stream forth in just this manner. " (NE 356: 10 folios, 1 bampo)

आर्यपञ्चविंशतिकाप्रज्ञापारमितामुखं नाम महायानसूत्रम्

།འཕགས་པ་ཤེས་རབ་ཀྱི་ཕ་རོལ་ཏུ་ཕྱིན་པའི་སྒོ་ཉི་ཤུ་རྩ་ལྔ་པ་ཞེས་བྱ་བ་ཐེག་པ་ཆེན་པོའི་མདོ།

STE

Ārya-pañcaviṁśatikā-prajñāpāramitā-mukha-nāma-mahāyāna-sūtra The Twenty-five Doors to the Prajñāpāramitā, spoken on Mt. Meru, the night abode of the gods, was given for the benefit of the Great Bodhisattva Vajrapāṇi, great master of secret knowledge, and many hundreds of thousands of billions of Bodhisattvas, 1,250 bhikṣus, gods, devaputras, and many other beings. (NE 20: 3 folios, 25 śloka)

आर्यप्रतीत्यसमुत्पादो नाम महायानसूत्रम्

།འཕགས་པ་རྟེན་ཅིང་འབྲེལ་བར་འབྱུང་བ་ཞེས་བྱ་བ་ཐེག་པ་ཆེན་པོའི་མདོ།

S T

Ārya-pratītyasamutpāda-nāma-mahāyāna-sūtra In the Trāyastriṁśa Heaven, the abode of the thirty-three gods, at the request of the Great Bodhisattva Avalokiteśvara, the Buddha gave this teaching on pratītyasamutpāda (interdependent cooperation) for the benefit of the gods and a large assembly of great Śrāvakas and Bodhisattvas. (NE 212: 2 folios, 13 śloka)

आर्यत्रयस्त्रिंशत्परिवर्तो नाम महायानसूत्रम्

།འཕགས་པ་སུམ་ཅུ་རྩ་གསུམ་པའི་ལེའུ་ཞེས་བྱ་བ་ཐེག་པ་ཆེན་པོའི་མདོ།

T

Ārya-trāyastriṁśat-parivarta-nāma-mahāyāna-sūtra In the Trāyastriṁśa Heaven, the abode of the thirty-three gods, where the Blessed One was teaching the Dharma out of consideration for his mother, the Buddha gave the Sūtra known as the Teaching in the Heaven of the Thirty-Three, an instruction on the theory and practice of Bodhisattvas, to an assembly of hundreds of thousands. Spoken at the request of the devaputra Candra (NE 223: 75 folios, 3 bampo)

आर्यचतुर्धर्मनिर्देशो नाम महायानसूत्रम्

།འཕགས་པ་ཆོས་བཞི་བསྟན་པ་ཞེས་བྱ་བ་ཐེག་པ་ཆེན་པོའི་མདོ།

T F

Ārya-caturdharma-nirdeśa-nāma-mahāyāna-sūtra While abiding in the Trāyastriṁśa Heaven, abode of the thirty-three gods, the Buddha gave the Sūtra known as the Teaching on the Four Dharmas, an instruction on the four attributes by which Bodhisattvas suppress and destroy the karmic accumulation of all unfavorable actions. This teaching was given for the benefit of the assembly of five hundred bhikṣus, upāsakas, and many Great Bodhisattvas including Maitreya and Mañjuśrī. (NE 249: 2 folios, 13 śloka)

आर्यज्ञानकसूत्रं नाम बुद्धावदानम्

།འཕགས་པ་སངས་རྒྱས་ཀྱི་རྟོགས་པ་བརྗོད་པ་ཤེས་ལྡན་གྱི་མདོ།

T

Ārya-jñānakasūtra-nāma-buddhāvadāna While teaching the Dharma in the Trāyastriṁśa Heaven for the sake of his mother, the Buddha gave the Sūtra known as the Story of Jñānaka for the benefit of the god Jñānaka, who, terrified of being reborn in the animal realms, had sought the Blessed One's protection. (NE 344: 6 folios, 15 śloka)

आर्यघनव्यूहो नाम महायानसूत्रम्

།འཕགས་པ་རྒྱན་སྟུག་པོ་བཀོད་པ་ཞེས་བྱ་བ་ཐེག་པ་ཆེན་པོའི་མདོ།

T C

Ārya-ghanavyūha-nāma-mahāyāna-sūtra In the palace Pure Moon in the Buddhafield of Akaniṣṭha, the Buddha taught the Sūtra known as The Auspicious Array for the benefit of the Bodhisattvas who had completely transcended the objects of the three worlds. (NE 110: 109 folios, 4 bampo)

आर्यात्ययज्ञानं नाम महायानसूत्रम्

།འཕགས་པ་འདའ་ཀ་ཡེ་ཤེས་ཞེས་བྱ་བ་ཐེག་པ་ཆེན་པོའི་མདོ།

T

Ārya-atyayajñāna-nāma-mahāyāna-sūtra When the Buddha was teaching the Dharma in the palace of the king of the gods of the Akaniṣṭha Heaven, the Bodhisattva Akāśagarbha asked the Bhagavan how to direct the mind at the time of death. In response, the Blessed One gave the discourse known as Knowledge Gone Beyond. (NE 122: 1 folio, 10 śloka)

आर्यसर्वतथागताधिष्ठानसत्त्वावलोकेन बुद्धक्षेत्रनिर्देशव्यूहो नाम महायानसूत्रम्

།འཕགས་པ་དེ་བཞིན་གཤེགས་པ་ཐམས་ཅད་ཀྱི་བྱིན་གྱི་རླབས་སེམས་ཅན་ལ་གཟིགས་ཤིང་སངས་རྒྱས་ཀྱི་ཞིང་གི་བཀོད་པ་ཀུན་དུ་སྟོན་པ་ཞེས་བྱ་བ་ཐེག་པ་ཆེན་པོའི་མདོ།

S T C E

Ārya-sarvatathāgatādhiṣṭhāna-sattvāvalokena-buddhakṣetra-nirdeśa-vyūha-nāma-mahāyāna-sūtra While dwelling in the Potala, Avalokiteśvara's palace, with five hundred bhikṣus and many Bodhisattvas, gods, nāgas, and other beings, the Blessed One manifested one hundred thousand forms, purifying even the most obscured among the assembly. Rays of light shone forth into all the realms of the world, bringing sight to the blind, health to the infirm, strong bodies to the crippled, and joy to all sentient beings. All the gods left their blissful realms for the joy of listening to the Sūtra known as The Array of Teachings on the Buddhafields Where All Beings are Viewed with the Blessings of the Tathāgatas. (NE 98: 41 folios, 2 bampo)

आर्यश्रीमहादेवीव्याकरणम्

།འཕགས་པ་ལྷ་མོ་ཆེན་མོ་དཔལ་ལུང་བསྟན་པ།

T

Ārya-śrīmahādevī-vyākaraṇa In Sukhāvatī, the paradise of the Buddha Amitābha, the Buddha spoke the Sūtra known as The Prophecy for Śrīmahādevī, predicting Śrīmahādevī's future attainment of Buddhahood and teaching the Dharma for her benefit. This teaching was heard by the assembly of bhikṣus, the Great Bodhisattva Avalokiteśvara, and all the Great Bodhisattvas of the Golden Aeon. (NE 193: 10 folios, 100 śloka)

आर्यसंधिनिर्मोचनं नाम महायानसूत्रम्

།འཕགས་པ་དགོངས་པ་ངེས་པར་འགྲེལ་པ་ཞེས་བྱ་བ་ཐེག་པ་ཆེན་པོའི་མདོ།

TCEF

Ārya-saṁdhinirmocana-nāma-mahāyāna-sūtra In the Crystal Palace arrayed with the supreme brilliance of the seven precious substances, the Buddha gave the Sūtra known as Comprehending (Buddha-wisdom) to an assembly of innumerable Bodhisattvas including Mañjuśrī and Maitreya, together with innumerable Śrāvakas, devas, nāgas, yakṣas, gandharvas, asuras, garuḍas, kinnaras, and mahoragas. Responding in turn to the questions of ten Great Bodhisattvas, the Buddha gave this teaching on the nature of phenomena, conditioned and unconditioned dharmas, the compounded and ultimate realms, the wisdom of the Bodhisattva, the nature of phenomena, provisional and definitive meaning, the definitive meaning of yoga, the ten stages of the Bodhisattva, and characteristics of the Dharmakāya, (NE 106: 109 folios)

आर्यबुद्धभूमिर्नाम महायानसूत्रम्

།འཕགས་པ་སངས་རྒྱས་ཀྱི་ས་ཞེས་བྱ་བ་ཐེག་པ་ཆེན་པོའི་མདོ།

TC

Ārya-buddhabhūmi-nāma-mahāyāna-sūtra At the request of a Bodhisattva, the Buddha gave the Sūtra known as The Stages of Buddhahood, a teaching on the great perfections of Tathāgatas and their infinite wisdom, to the assembly of bhikṣus whose aspirations for enlightenment were fully awakened, and to Indra, Brahmā, gods, nāgas, and the world-protectors. Spoken in the Crystal Palace. (NE 275: 18 folios, 200 śloka)

आर्यसिंहनादिकं नाम महायानसूत्रम्

།འཕགས་པ་སེང་གེའི་སྒྲ་བསྒྲགས་པ་ཞེས་བྱ་བ་ཐེག་པ་ཆེན་པོའི་མདོ།

T C

Ārya-siṁhanādika-nāma-mahāyāna-sūtra In the palace of Vijetā, in the place of the sun and moon, the Buddha gave the teaching known as The Roar of the Lion, recounting the story of the Bodhisattva Vijaya, who went to another realm to pay homage to the Tathāgata Dharmaśrī. This teaching was given to the assembly of one hundred billion bhikṣus and Arhats. (NE 209: 9 folios, 1/3 bampo)

आर्यधर्मसंगीतिर्नाम महायानसूत्रम्

།འཕགས་པ་ཆོས་ཡང་དག་པར་སྡུད་པ་ཞེས་བྱ་བ་ཐེག་པ་ཆེན་པོའི་མདོ།

T C

Ārya-dharmasaṁgīti-nāma-mahāyāna-sūtra In a multistoried palace manifested by the miraculous power of wisdom and merit, in the very center of the expansive and undifferentiated Dharmadhātu, the Buddha gave the Sūtra known as The Song of Dharma, an instruction on the perfections and virtues practiced on the gradual path to enlightenment, to the assembly of 1,250 bhikṣus, a vast multitude of Bodhisattvas, gods, and nāgas, and many hundreds of thousands of other beings. (NE 238: 198 folios, 7 bampo)

आर्यधर्मतास्वभावशून्यताचलप्रतिसर्वालोकसूत्रम्

།འཕགས་པ་ཆོས་ཉིད་རང་གི་ངོ་བོ་སྟོང་པ་ཉིད་ལས་མི་གཡོ་བར་ཐ་དད་པར་ཐམས་ཅད་ལ་སྣང་བའི་མདོ།

STCE

Ārya-dharmatāsvabhāva-śūnyatācalapratisarvāloka-sūtra Seated on the throne of wisdom in the temple of Mṛgarāja, the Buddha perceived that each of the beings in the assembly of Bodhisattvas, humans, gods, and demigods had a different concept of the Buddhadharma. Sending forth rays of light to illumine the understanding of each being present, the Buddha imparted the teaching known as The Appearance of All Things from the Openness that is the Nature of Dharmatā. (NE 128: 8 folios)

आर्यलंकावतारो महायानसूत्रम्

།འཕགས་པ་ལང་ཀར་གཤེགས་པའི་ཐེག་པ་ཆེན་པོའི་མདོ།

T

Ārya-laṅkāvatāra-mahāyāna-sūtra At the request of the nāga king who ruled the ocean-encircled land of Laṅkā, the Buddha gave the Sūtra known as The Descent From Laṅkā, an extensive teaching of the Third Turning containing the doctrine of all the Tathāgatas, to a great gathering of bhikṣus, Bodhisattvas, nāgas, and gods including Indra and Brahmā, all of whom had assembled from various Buddhafields. Spoken on Mt. Malaya on the isle of Laṅkā. (NE 107: 272 folios, 9 bampo)

आर्यतथागतानां बुद्धक्षेत्रगुणोक्तधर्मपर्यायः

།འཕགས་པ་དེ་བཞིན་གཤེགས་པ་རྣམས་ཀྱི་སངས་རྒྱས་ཀྱི་ཞིང་གི་ཡོན་ཏན་བརྗོད་པའི་ཆོས་ཀྱི་རྣམ་གྲངས།

T C

Ārya-tathāgatānāṁ buddhakṣetra-guṇokta-dharmaparyāya In the monastery of Bodhigarbha, the Great Bodhisattva Prabhācintyarāja, inspired by the Buddha, gave the Dharma teaching known as Proclaiming the Qualities of the Buddhafields of the Tathāgatas, an explanation of the nature and perfections of the realms of Amitābha, Akṣobhya, Vajragarbha, and other Great Beings. (NE 104: 3 folios)

आर्यसागरनागराजपरिपृच्छा नाम महायानसूत्रम्

།འཕགས་པ་ཀླུའི་རྒྱལ་པོ་རྒྱ་མཚོས་ཞུས་པ་ཞེས་བྱ་བ་ཐེག་པ་ཆེན་པོའི་མདོ།

T C

Ārya-sāgaranāgarāja-paripṛcchā-nāma-mahāyāna-sūtra In the nāga king Sāgara's palace in the great ocean, the Buddha gave the Sūtra known as The Questions of Sāgara, King of the Nāgas, a teaching on the nature of existence for the benefit of the nāga king and the assembly of eight thousand bhikṣus, together with Bodhisattvas who came from the ten directions, Indra, Brahmā, the four world-protectors, and many gods and nāgas. (NE 154: 15 folios, 200 śloka)

आर्यसागरनागराजपरिपृच्छा नाम महायानसूत्रम्

།འཕགས་པ་ཀླུའི་རྒྱལ་པོ་རྒྱ་མཚོས་ཞུས་པ་ཞེས་བྱ་བ་ཐེག་པ་ཆེན་པོའི་མདོ།

T C

Ārya-sāgaranāgarāja-paripṛcchā-nāma-mahāyāna-sūtra In the nāga king Sāgara's palace in the great ocean, the Buddha gave a Sūtra known as The Questions of Sāgara, King of the Nāgas, a teaching on the four dharmas, for the benefit of the nāga king, the assembly of 1,250 bhikṣus, and a vast multitude of Great Bodhisattvas. (NE 155: 2 folios, 12 śloka)

आर्यानवतप्तनागराजपरिपृच्छा नाम महायानसूत्रम्

།འཕགས་པ་ཀླུའི་རྒྱལ་པོ་མ་དྲོས་པས་ཞུས་པ་ཞེས་བྱ་བ་ཐེག་པ་ཆེན་པོའི་མདོ།

T C

Ārya-anavatapta-nāgarāja-paripṛcchā-nāma-mahāyāna-sūtra In the nāga king Sāgara's palace in the great ocean, at the request of an assembly of many hundreds of thousands of beings asking about the attainment of Buddhahood, the Blessed One gave the teaching known as The Questions of the Nāga King Anavatapta. This Sūtra was given for the benefit of King Anavatapta, sixty-eight thousand other nāga kings, and forty thousand nāga princesses. (NE 156: 96 folios, 4 bampo)

आर्यमहामेघवायुमण्डलपरिवर्तसर्वनागहृदयं नाम महायान-सूत्रम्

།འཕགས་པ་སྤྲིན་ཆེན་པོ་རླུང་གི་དཀྱིལ་འཁོར་གྱི་ལེའུ་ཀླུ་ཐམས་ཅད་ཀྱི་སྙིང་པོ་ཞེས་བྱ་བ་ཐེག་པ་ཆེན་པོའི་མདོ།

T

Ārya-mahāmegha-vāyu-maṇḍala-parivarta-sarvanāga-hṛdaya-nāma-mahāyāna-sūtra On the peak of the storied palace in the middle of the great ocean, the Buddha gave the teaching known as The Great Cloud and Wind Maṇḍala from the Sūtra called The Heart of All Nāgas, imparting mantras and prayers for obtaining rain. This Sūtra was given to one thousand nāga kings including Nanda and Upānanda. (NE 234: 10 folios, 1 bampo)

आर्यमहामेघः

།འཕགས་པ་སྤྲིན་ཆེན་པོ།

S T C E

Ārya-mahāmegha While residing in the palace of the nāga kings Nanda and Upānanda, the Buddha was accompanied by large assemblies of bhikṣus, bhikṣuṇīs, Bodhisattvas, and a host of nāga kings attended by eighty-four hundreds of thousands of millions of krores of nāgas. At that time the supreme king of nāgas honored the Buddha and asked, "How, O Venerable One, may all the troubles of all the nāgas be ended, that they, blessed and made happy, can send forth the rains in season, for the benefit of the people of Jambudvīpa?" In response, the Buddha gave the nāgas efficacious prayers, delighting the nāgas and ensuring rain for the beings of Jambudvīpa. Among men and nāgas alike, this teaching became known as The Great Cloud. (NE 235: 26 folios)

आर्यषण्मुखा नाम धारणी

།འཕགས་པ་སྒོ་དྲུག་པ་ཞེས་བྱ་བའི་གཟུངས།

S T C

Ṣaṇmukha-nāma-dhāraṇī When innumerable Bodhisattvas had assembled in the courtyard in the middle of the sky filled with the seven precious objects, the Blessed One addressed these great beings saying, "Noble sons, in order to bring joy and benefit to all living beings, take up the Dhāraṇī of the Six Doors." With these words, the Buddha began this teaching to the assembly of Bodhisattvas. (NE 141: 3 folios, 18 śloka)

गाथाद्वयधारणी

།ཚིགས་སུ་བཅད་པ་གཉིས་པའི་གཟུངས།

T F

Gāthādvaya-dhāraṇī In order to cut off all harmful actions, all forms of disrespect to the Buddha and to the Dharma, all laziness and grasping, desire and pride, and all other obscurations, the Buddha taught the Dhāraṇī of Two Verses, from which great benefits arise. (NE 143: 1 folio)

भगवतो महोष्णीषतथागतगुह्यसाधनार्थप्राप्तिहेतुः सर्वबोधिसत्त्वचर्याशूरंगमे दशसहस्रपरिवर्त्ते दशमः परिवर्त्तः

།བཅོམ་ལྡན་འདས་ཀྱི་གཙུག་ཏོར་ཆེན་པོ་དེ་བཞིན་གཤེགས་པའི་གསང་བ་སྒྲུབ་པའི་དོན་མངོན་པར་ཐོབ་པའི་རྒྱུ་བྱང་ཆུབ་སེམས་དཔའ་ཐམས་ཅད་ཀྱི་སྤྱོད་པ་དཔའ་བར་འགྲོ་བའི་མདོ་ལེའུ་སྟོང་ཕྲག་བཅུ་པ་ལས་ལེའུ་བཅུ་པ།

TCE

Bhagavato mahoṣṇīṣa-tathāgataguhyasādhanārtha-prāptihetu-sarvabodhisattvacaryā-śūramgama-daśa-sahasra-parivartte daśamaḥ parivartaḥ The golden form of the Tathāgata, pure like the pristine mountains, went forth from the lion throne of the Dharma and left there an image. Then, from this image came words to Nanda and the assembly: "All of you, disciples and Pratyekabuddhas, aspire to produce the mind of the Bodhisattva; yet I have explained the Dharma, and you have yet to understand." (NE 236: 49 folios, 2 bampo)

महोष्णीषनवमगुच्छादुद्धृतः कश्चिन्मारपरिवर्त्तः

།གཙུག་ཏོར་ཆེན་པོ་བམ་པོ་དགུ་པ་ལས་བདུད་ཀྱི་ལེའུ་ཉི་ཚེ་ཕྱུང་བ།

T

Mahoṣṇīṣa-navamagucchād-uddhṛta-kaścinmāra-parivarta The Blessed One said, "Ānanda, may you realize that, by abiding in the mandala of Bodhi, one purifies all compounded things: This is the abandonment of perceptions. Thus is the essence of all appearance transmitted." (NE 237: 25 folios, 2 bampo)

धर्ममुद्रा
།ཆོས་ཀྱི་ཀྲུ་མོ།

T C F

Dharmamudrā All the sons of the Buddha folded their hands in prayer as they meditated on the explanation of the great moral practice of all the Buddhas. "Listen. Once you understand that you have transgressed, make a complete confession, and joy will come. If you do not confess completely, profound harm is produced. You fortunate ones, and you laymen and laywomen who support the Dharma, take heed. Be respectful and ethical, generous and vigorous." With these words of counsel begins the teaching known as Gesture of Dharma. (NE 256: 35 folios, 2 bampo)

बुद्धनामसहस्रपञ्चशतचतुः त्रिपञ्चदश
།སངས་རྒྱས་ཀྱི་མཚན་ལྔ་སྟོང་བཞི་བརྒྱ་ལྔ་བཅུ་རྩ་གསུམ་པ།

T C

Buddha-nāma-sahasrapañcaśatacatur-tripañcadaśa Homage to the Omniscient One. This teaching, known as the 5,453 Names of the Buddha, offers salutations to each of the names of the Blessed One. (NE 262: 177 folios, 8 bampo)

आर्यमहासमयवैपुल्यसूत्रम्

།འཕགས་པ་རྟོགས་པ་ཆེན་པོ་ཡོངས་སུ་རྒྱས་པའི་མདོ།

T

Ārya-mahāsamaya-vaipulyasūtra Great Bodhisattvas gathered from the ten directions, paid homage to the Bhagavan, and said, "By the blessings and power of the Buddhas of the ten directions, you have come into the world. We have seen the Blessed One and heard the Mahāyāna teachings. Hereafter you will pass into Parinirvāṇa. Please explain to us the teachings you have taught for so long in gardens and temples, stūpas and cemeteries, monasteries and cities, on mountains in all directions. You have taught even those in unfavorable states of being the way to be free, closing the doors of hell. Having received merely one word of these teachings, the gods rejoice." In response, the Buddha gave the teaching known as the Extended Sūtra of the Great Vow. (NE 265: 48 folios)

साक्षिपूर्णमुद्रकं नाम

།དཔང་སྐོང་ཕྱག་བརྒྱ་པ་ཞེས་བྱ་བ།

T

Sākṣipūrṇamudraka-nāma "Homage to the most precious beings, all the Buddhas and Bodhisattvas who travel and abide in the three times, throughout the boundless and limitless worlds of the ten directions. Homage to the Tathāgata Ratnākara, Buddha of the East. Homage to the Tathāgata Nirvāṇaśrī, Buddha of the South. Homage to the Tathāgata Jinendra, the Buddha of the North." Following these opening salutations are homages to numerous Buddhas and Bodhisattvas, exhorations to virtue and the accumulation of merit. (NE 267: 8 folios)

आर्यबुद्धानुस्मृतिः

།འཕགས་པ་སངས་རྒྱས་རྗེས་སུ་དྲན་པ།

T

Ārya-buddhānusmṛti "The Buddha is the victorious one, the Tathāgata, who possesses pure awareness and bliss. The Tathāgata is the learned one, the subduer of all beings, the exalted one, the teacher of gods and men. Because of the merit of the Tathāgatas, the roots of virtue are never exhausted and steadfastly spread. The Tathāgatas are the ground of the treasures of virtue." With these words begins the teaching known as Holding the Buddha in Mind. (NE 279: 2 folios)

धर्मानुस्मृतिः

།ཆོས་རྗེས་སུ་དྲན་པ།

T

Dharmānusmṛti "The Holy Dharma is beautifully spoken, auspicious in the beginning, the middle, and the end. Its meaning is good and its words are crystal clear, completely perfect, completely pure. The Dharma is the good word spoken by the Tathāgata in order to teach beings: It is well-received, truly healthy, timeless, and full of meaning. Completely harmonious and well-grounded, the Dharma leads beings to become Bodhisattvas." With these words begins the teaching known as Holding the Dharma in Mind. (NE 280: 2 folios)

संघानुस्मृतिः

།དགེ་འདུན་རྗེས་སུ་དྲན་པ།

T

Sangānusmṛti "The Holy Sangha is good: The Sangha abides correctly, abides harmoniously, abides mindfully, abides rightly, abides agreeably, and abides purely. It is suitable to pay homage to the Sangha, for its quality is completely pure. It is proper to make offerings to the Sangha; it is proper to give all gifts to the Sangha." With these words begins the teaching known as Holding the Sangha in Mind. (NE 281: 1 folio)

आर्यत्रिस्कन्धकं नाम महायानसूत्रम्

།འཕགས་པ་ཕུང་པོ་གསུམ་པ་ཞེས་བྱ་བ་ཐེག་པ་ཆེན་པོའི་མདོ།

T

Ārya-triskandhaka-nāma-mahāyāna-sūtra "The Buddha abides in the temple of the Dharma, through the great wisdom of the Buddhas of the past, the present, and the future, equal with all the Buddhas, abiding in the non-dual Dharmakāya. The Holy One wears the diadem of the Dharma, without any grasping, completely unstained. His speech is melodious, showing complete awareness." With these words begins the teaching known as the Three Aggregates. (NE 284: 41 folios, 530 śloka)

आर्यसर्वाशयपरिपूरणं नाम परिणामना

།འཕགས་པ་བསམ་པ་ཐམས་ཅད་ཡོངས་སུ་རྫོགས་པར་བྱེད་པ་
ཞེས་བྱ་བ་ཡོངས་སུ་བསྔོ་བ།

T

Ārya-sarvāśayaparipūraṇa-pariṇāmanā "I pray to gain the true realization of the Bodhisattvas who have entered the highest stage, and of the Buddha who abides everywhere. In whatever birth, whether as a householder or as a monk, not seeking the end of rebirth, may I be free from desire, hatred, and ignorance in body, speech, and mind, and may I always meet with a virtuous spiritual teacher." With these words begins the Buddha's teaching known as The Prayer for Accomplishing All Intentions. (NE 285: 6 folios, 50 śloka)

आर्यसर्वजगत्परित्राणं नाम परिणामना

།འཕགས་པ་འགྲོ་བ་ཐམས་ཅད་ཡོངས་སུ་སྐྱོབ་པར་བྱེད་པ་
ཞེས་བྱ་བའི་ཡོངས་སུ་བསྔོ་བ།

T

Ārya-sarvajagatparitrāṇa-pariṇāmanā "I pray to the Buddhas and Great Bodhisattvas, and I confess all my wrongdoings. Rejoicing in all merit, I pray to the Buddha and dedicate my merit so that all beings may obtain the clear understanding of unexcelled omniscience. By truth and by words of truth, may I dedicate everything in the same way as the Bhagavan." With these words begins the Buddha's teaching known as The Prayer for the Deliverance of All Beings. (NE 286: 5 folios, 40 śloka)

अभिनिष्क्रमणसूत्रम्

།མངོན་པར་འབྱུང་བའི་མདོ།

TF

Abhiniṣkramana-sūtra The Bodhisattva abided in the Tuṣita Heaven for many kalpas before entering upon his final birth. This Sūtra, which recounts the life of the Buddha and the history of the Śākya clan, among other teachings, begins with extensive homages to the one about to become a Buddha: "Homage to the Peaceful One who teaches the Dharma, to the exalted Buddha who inspires joy; his brilliant visage is like the lotus in full bloom, royal and full of light. Homage to the Dharma of the Tathāgatas, sole bridge across the ocean of unending pain; breaker of samsara's bonds, leading past the fearfulness of lower states of being. Homage to the Sangha, the eight great Noble Ones, praised by the Tathāgata, to whom the smallest offering becomes the greatest gift. Listen as the Teacher expresses the Dharma." (NE 301: 248 folios)

विमुक्तिमार्गंधौतगुणनिर्देशो नाम

།རྣམ་པར་གྲོལ་བའི་ལམ་ལས་སྦྱངས་པའི་ཡོན་ཏན་བསྟན་པ་ཞེས་བྱ་བ།

TE

Vimuktimārga-dhautaguṇa-nirdeśa-nāma This teaching on the qualities of the path of liberation begins with these words of wise counsel: "Desiring to achieve the pure yogic ability of moral practice, one must intently develop the qualities of yogic practice such as having few desires, being content, and making effort. One must wear the proper Dharma clothing and sustain the body in appropriate ways." (NE 306: 16 folios)

चैत्यप्रदक्षिणगाथा

།མཆོད་རྟེན་བསྐོར་བའི་ཚིགས་སུ་བཅད་པ།

T C E

Caitya-pradakṣiṇa-gāthā After the Buddha, the One of Great Wisdom, had turned the Dharma Wheel in the world, the wise one Śāriputra humbly asked, "What are the results that come from circumambulating a stūpa? May the Guide of the supreme universe of this great kalpa please advise me." The perfect Buddha, supreme among beings, the Enlightened One, then gave this teaching known as Verses for Circumambulating a Stūpa. (NE 321: 5 folios, 70 śloka)

एकगाथा

།ཚིགས་སུ་བཅད་པ་གཅིག་པ།

T

Ekagāthā "Leader of Beings, there is no one like you in the world of men or in the heavens of the gods." This salutation is known as The One Verse. (NE 323: 1 folio)

चतुर्गाथा

།ཚིགས་སུ་བཅད་པ་བཞི་པ།

T

Caturgāthā "Homage to the Conquerors who possess the thirty-two marks of excellence, the most perfect Buddhas, who have reached enlightenment, turned the Wheel of Tranquility, and completely transcended sorrow." This salutation is known as The Four Verses. (NE 324: 2 folios)

नागराजभेरीगाथा

།ཀླུའི་རྒྱལ་པོ་རྔ་སྒྲའི་ཚིགས་སུ་བཅད་པ།

T

Nāgarājaberī-gāthā While abiding in the place of the Tathāgata, the Buddha gathered the bhikṣus around him and said, "You have left the inharmonious householders' life and have now become bhikṣus. You have entered the Dharma, which brings lasting joy. For the sake of all sentient beings, you have meditated on harmlessness and have taken the Bodhisattva vow. Bhikṣus, listen! Men who have wisdom, listen! Cast away nonvirtue and strive for the Dharma, for in this way you will find realization and bliss." (NE 325: 9 folios, 100 śloka)

पूर्णप्रमुखावदानशतकम्

།གང་པོ་ལ་སོགས་པའི་རྟོགས་པ་བརྗོད་པ་བརྒྱ་པ།

S T F

Pūrṇa-pramukhāvadāna-śataka Gathered here are the histories of Pūrṇabhadra and Yaśodharā, accounts of the Laggard and the Captain, and other accounts, each illustrating as aspect of the Dharma. (NE 343: 571 folios, 22 bampo)

उदानवर्गः

།ཆེད་དུ་བརྗོད་པའི་ཚོམས།

S T C E

Udānavarga A collection of the Buddha's essential teachings, beginning with the words, "May happiness abound! As the Jina taught, so will I explain his teachings, in order to clear away sleep and darkness and produce a joyful mind." (NE 326: 109 folios, 4 bampo)

आर्यखक्करसूत्रम्

།འཕགས་པ་འཁར་གསིལ་གྱི་མདོ།

T C

Ārya-khakkhara-sūtra The Buddha gave this Sūtra on the Mendicant's Staff to the assembly of bhikṣus, saying, "Bhikṣus, you must always carry this mendicant's staff. If you ask why, it is because the Buddhas of the past all have carried the mendicant's staff; the Buddhas of the present carry the mendicant's staff, as will the Buddhas of the future. This staff is a staff of wisdom, a staff of good qualities, and a reminder of the Buddha and the Buddhadharma." (NE 335: 7 folios)

खक्करधराचारविधिः

།འཁར་གསིལ་འཆང་བའི་ཀུན་དུ་སྤྱོད་པའི་ཆོ་ག།

T C

Khakkharadharācāra-vidhi "To take up the medicant's staff in the proper manner, you should go before an honored one, kneel, and say: 'Reverend One, I request this of you: I wish to take up the mendicant's staff.' After repeating this three times, you should produce in your mind the thought of developing enlightenment and of taking up the staff for the sake of living in accordance with the Dharma." With these words begins the Buddha's teaching known as Honoring the Taking Up of the Mendicant's Staff. (NE 336: 3 folios)

आर्यद्वाचत्वारिंशत्खण्डसूत्रं नाम

།འཕགས་པ་དུམ་བུ་ཞེ་གཉིས་པ་ཞེས་བྱ་བའི་མདོ།

T C E F G

Ārya-dvācatvāriṁśat-khaṇḍa-sūtra The Bhagavan, who was peaceful and without desire, had obtained unexcelled enlightenment and abided in samādhi. Having conquered all demons, the Buddha turned the Wheel of the Dharma to liberate all sentient beings. In this Sūtra of Forty-Two Sections are compiled teachings given in various places and collected from many different Sūtras. (NE 359A, 16 folios.)

आर्यमहाकरुणापुण्डरीकं नाम महायानसूत्रम्

།འཕགས་པ་སྙིང་རྗེ་ཆེན་པོའི་པད་མ་དཀར་པོ་ཞེས་བྱ་བ་ཐེག་པ་ཆེན་པོའི་མདོ།

T C

Ārya-mahākaruṇāpuṇḍarīkā-nāma-mahāyāna-sūtra In the Sāla Grove near Kuśinagara, as the time of his Parinirvāṇa drew near, the Buddha said to Ānanda, "The Tathāgata passes into Parinirvāṇa at the final watch of night. Ānanda, I taught the supreme Dharma to bhikṣus and Brahmins, to demons and gods, to Brahmā and to others. To anyone who asked three times, I taught the Dharma. So that the stream of the Buddha's teachings should flow undisturbed in the future, I have given the teachings to the Bodhisattva Mahāsattvas." The Buddha then gave the Sūtra known as The White Lotus of Great Compassion for the benefit of the disciples and the Great Bodhisattvas. (NE 111: 146 folios, 6 bampo, 1,800 śloka)

आर्यमहापरिनिर्वाणमहासूत्रम्

།འཕགས་པ་ཡོངས་སུ་མྱ་ངན་ལས་འདས་པ་ཆེན་པོའི་མདོ།

T C

Ārya-mahāparinirvāṇa-mahāsūtra When the Buddha was about to enter Parinirvāṇa in the Sāla Grove on the banks of the Hiranyavatī River, he gave his final teaching, The Large Sūtra of the Great Parinirvāṇa. The assembly attending the Buddha included eighty times one hundred thousand bhikṣus headed by Mahākātyāyana, Vakulla, Upānanda, and others, as well as innumerable Bodhisattvas, gods, laymen and laywomen, rich and poor from all classes of society, including Cunda, the blacksmith. This work describes the miracles that happened at the time of the Parinirvāṇa, the lamentation of all beings on the Buddha's approaching death, and the Blessed One's last instructions, and gives an extensive summary of his teachings. (NE 119: 1,360 folios, 56 bampo)

आर्यमहापरिनिर्वाणं नाम महायानसूत्रम्

།འཕགས་པ་ཡོངས་སུ་མྱ་ངན་ལས་འདས་པ་ཆེན་པོ་ཐེག་པ་ཆེན་པོའི་མདོ།

T C E

Ārya-mahāparinirvāṇa-nāma-mahāyāna-sūtra In the third month of spring, at the full moon, the Buddha taught the Dharma out of great compassion for all sentient beings, offering himself as refuge for all the world. In the Sūtra known as The Great Parinirvāṇa, the Buddha predicted the increase, duration, and decline of his teachings in the future. Each being present heard the teachings according to his or her level of understanding and all rejoiced in the Dharma. (NE 120: 300 folios, 13 bampo, 3,900 śloka)

आर्यमहापरिनिर्वाणसूत्रम्

།འཕགས་པ་ཡོངས་སུ་མྱ་ངན་ལས་འདས་པ་ཆེན་པོའི་མདོ།

T C

Ārya-mahāparinirvāṇa-sūtra In the Sāla Grove, the Buddha predicted the future course of his Dharma to the great disciple Ānanda: "Ānanda, one hundred years after I have passed into Parinirvāṇa, the śāstras will flourish. The Śrāvakas will be filled with joy in the doctrine and will possess clear knowledge. Also, Ānanda, there will come forth a very powerful king by the name of Aśoka who will build stūpas far and wide to contain relics of the Parinirvāṇa. Ānanda, two hundred years after the Parinirvāṇa, the Śrāvakas will possess great understanding and will be skilled in teaching." (NE 121: 4 folios, 60 śloka)

आर्यचतुर्दारकसमाधिर्नाम महायानसूत्रम्

།འཕགས་པ་ཁྱེའུ་བཞིའི་ཏིང་ངེ་འཛིན་ཞེས་བྱ་བ་ཐེག་པ་ཆེན་པོའི་མདོ།

T C

Ārya-caturdāraka-samādhi-nāma-mahāyāna-sūtra In the Sāla Grove, shortly before the Parinirvāṇa, the Buddha taught the Sūtra known as the Samādhi of the Four Rendings for the benefit of the disciple Ānanda, explaining the significance of Ānanda's dream of the five signs of the Parinirvāṇa. (NE 136: 70 folios, 3 bampo)

सद्धर्मराजमहायानसूत्रम्

།དམ་པའི་ཆོས་ཀྱི་རྒྱལ་པོ་ཐེག་པ་ཆེན་པོའི་མདོ།

T

Saddharmarāja-mahāyāna-sūtra In the Sāla Grove near Kuśinagara shortly before the Parinirvāṇa, the Buddha, at the request of the Bodhisattva Gaganagañja, taught the Sūtra known as The King of True Dharma, a teaching on the potential for enlightenment inherent in all sentient beings, to the assembly of many hundreds of thousands of tens of millions of living beings. (NE 243: 29 folios, 1 bampo)

आर्यशिलाक्षिप्तसूत्रम्

།འཕགས་པ་རྡོ་འཕངས་པའི་མདོ།

T

Ārya-śilākṣipta-sūtra While staying with Ānanda in the Forest of the Cannibals, the Buddha gave the Sūtra known as The Stone Cast Away, in reference to miracles performed by the Buddha on the road to Kuśinagara, with instructions on the rounds of rebirth and final emancipation. This teaching was given to the assembly of bhikṣus and hundreds of residents of Kuśinagara shortly before the Buddha departed on his final journey. (NE 295: 40 folios, 2 bampo)

आर्यकल्याणमित्रसेवनसूत्रम्

།འཕགས་པ་དགེ་བའི་བཤེས་གཉེན་བསྟེན་པའི་མདོ།

S T C F

*Ārya-kalyāṇamitra-sevana-sūtr*a Shortly before entering Parinirvāṇa, while resting in the Sāla Grove near Kuśinagara in the land of the Mallas, the Blessed One gave to the assembly of bhikṣus the Sūtra known as Having Recourse to Spiritual Friends, a teaching requested by Ānanda on how to distinguish between virtuous and non-virtuous teachers and recognize true spiritual friends. (NE 300: 2 folios)

आर्यसंज्ञानैकादशनिर्देशसूत्रम्

།འཕགས་པ་འདུ་ཤེས་བཅུ་གཅིག་བསྟན་པའི་མདོ།

T

Ārya-samjñānaikādaśa-nirdeśa-sūtra In the Sāla Grove near Kuśinagara around the time of the Parinirvāṇa, the Buddha gave the Sūtra known as The Eleven Perceptions, a teaching on the eleven matters to be considered before death. (NE 311: 2 folios, 11 śloka)

Abbreviations

AA Abhisamayālaṁkāra, by Maitreyanātha. (NE 3786). *Abhisamayālaṁkāra,* translated by Edward Conze. Roma: IsMEO, 1954.

AK Abhidharmakoṣabhāṣya, by Vasubandhu (NE 4089–90). *Abhidharmakoṣa-bhāṣyam,* translated by Louis de La Vallée Poussin. English translation by Leo M. Pruden. 4 vols. Berkeley, California: Asian Humanities Press, 1988–90.

AS Abhidharmasamuccaya, by Asaṅga (NE 4049). *Le Compendium de la super-doctrine (Philosophie), (Abhidharmasamuccaya) d'Asaṅga,* translated by Walpola Rahula. Paris: École Française d'Éxtrême-Orient, 1971. Reprinted 1980.

AVS Arthaviniścaya Sūtra (NE 317). Berkeley: Dharma Publishing. Forthcoming.

BCA Bodhicaryāvatara, by Śāntideva. (NE 3871). *Entering the Path of Enlightenment,* translated by Marion L. Matics. New York: Macmillan, 1970. Another translation: *A Guide to the Bodhisattva's Way of Life,* translated by Stephen Batchelor and Sherpa Tulku. Dharamsala: Library of Tibetan Works and Archives, 1979.

Bu Bu-ston Rinpoche. *History of Buddhism,* translated by E. Obermiller. Heidelberg: Institut für Buddhismuskunde, 1931. (Materialien zur Kunde des Buddhismus 18)

CN *The Changeless Nature (The Mahāyānottaratantraśāstra) by Arya Maitreya and Acarya Asanga,* translated by Kenneth and Katia Holmes. Second edition. Eskdalemuir, Dunfriesshire: Kagyu Samye Ling, 1985.

DB Daśabhūmika Sūtra. (NE 44:32) *Annotated Translation of the Daśabhūmika Sūtra,* by Megumu Honda, revised by Johannes Rahder. New Delhi: International Academy of Indian Culture, 1968. (Śatapiṭaka Series 74). Another translation: *The Flower Ornament Scripture, A Translation of the Avatamsaka Sutra,* by Thomas Cleary. Vol. II. Shambhala: Boston, 1986, pp. 7–123.

DN Digha Nikāya. *Dialogues of the Buddha,* translated by T. W. and C. A. F. Rhys-Davids. 3 vols. Reprint ed. London: Pali Text Society, 1977. See also *Thus Have I Heard, The Long Discourses of the Buddha,* translated by Maurice Walshe. London: Wisdom, 1987.

JOL Dam-chos-yid-bzhin-gyi-nor-bu-thar-pa-rin-po-che'i-rgyan, by sGam-po-pa. *The Jewel Ornament of Liberation,* translated by Herbert V. Guenther. Berkeley: Shambhala, 1971.

LGPW *The Large Sutra on Perfect Wisdom, with the divisions of the Abhisamayālaṁkāra,* translated by Edward Conze. Berkeley: University of California Press, 1975.

LGS *The Legend of the Great Stupa and the Life Story of the Lotus Born Guru,* by Padmasambhava and Yeshe Tsogyal. Translated by Keith Dowman. Berkeley: Dharma Publishing, 1973

LLP *The Life and Liberation of Padmasambhava,* by Yeshe Tshogyal. Berkeley: Dharma Publishing, 1978.

MN Majjhima Nikāya. *The Middle Length Sayings,* translated by I.B. Horner. Reprint ed. London: Pali Text Society, 1975–1982.

MS Mahāyāna-saṁgraha, by Asaṅga (NE 4048). *Le Somme du grand vehicule,* translated by Étienne Lamotte. 2 vols. Louvain: Université de Louvain, 1973. Another translation: *The Summary of the Great Vehicle,* translated by John P. Keenan. Berkeley: Numata Center for Buddhist Translation and Research, 1992.

MSA Mahāyāna-sūtrālaṁkāra, by Maitreya (NE 4020). *Mahāyāna-sūtrālaṁkāra: Exposé de la doctrine du grand vehicule selon le systeme Yogācāra,* vol. II, translated by Sylvain Levi. Paris: Champion, 1911.

MV *The Mahāvaṁsa, or the Great Chronicle of Ceylon,* translated by Wilhelm Geiger. Reprint edition. New Delhi: Asian Educational Service, 1986. First published 1912.

NE *Nyingma Edition of the bKa'-'gyur and bsTan-'gyur.* Berkeley: Dharma Publishing, 1981.

R *The Life of the Buddha and the Early History of HIs Order,* by W. Woodville Rockhill. London: Kegan Paul, Trench, Trübner & Co., 1884.

Tār *Tāranātha's History of Buddhism in India,* translated by Lama Chimpa and Alaka Chattopadhyaya. Simla: Indian Institute of Advanced Study, 1970.

UT Uttarantantra, by Maitreya (NE 4025)

VMK Vimalakīrti-nirdeśa. *The Holy Teaching of Vimalakīrti, A Mahāyāna Scripture,* translated by Robert A. F. Thurman. University Park and London: Pennsylvania State University Press, 1986. Another translation: *The Vimalakirti Nirdesa Sutra,* translated by Charles Luk. Shambhala: Boston & Shaftesbury, 1990.

Index to Sūtra Openings

General Index

Sita-Cintāmaṇi Mahākāla

Tarthang Tulku

About Tarthang Tulku: A Note from the Staff of Dharma Publishing

Tarthang Tulku, creator and general editor of the Crystal Mirror Series, is an accomplished Tibetan lama who has lived and worked in the United States since 1969. Throughout his life, Rinpoche has dedicated his full energy and resources to preserving and transmitting the Dharma. As his students, we have learned to find inspiration in his devotion and profound respect for the Buddha's teachings.

In the early 1960's, while teaching at the Sanskrit University in Vārāṇasī, Rinpoche founded Dharma Mudranālaya and began publishing texts he had brought with him from Tibet. In 1969, soon after arriving in America, he established Dharma Publishing and Dharma Press, incorporated in 1975 as Dharma Mudranālaya. Under his direction, Dharma Publishing has preserved more than 35,000 Tibetan texts by 1,500 Buddhist masters in 755 large western-style volumes, and

Dharma Publishing's books in English, including translations of important Buddhist texts, have been adopted for use in more than five hundred colleges and universities throughout the world.

An active author and educator, Rinpoche has written eleven books presenting teachings for the modern world, overseen translations of traditional texts, and created and edited *The Nyingma Edition of the bKa'-'gyur and bsTan-'gyur* and *Great Treasures of Ancient Teachings,* the first compilation of the Nyingma Canon together with works by masters of all Tibetan Buddhist traditions. He is founder and president of the Nyingma Institute in Berkeley and its affiliated centers, where several thousand students have come in contact with the Buddhist teachings. Rinpoche has also created and guided the construction and ornamentation of Odiyan, a country center for retreats, study, and extended practice.

In the midst of these activities, Rinpoche serves in the traditional role of teacher for a growing community of Western students. Always willing to experiment, he has established a form of practice for his students in which their work on behalf of the Dharma becomes a path to realization. Although many of his students do not have frequent direct contact with Rinpoche, through the institutions he has established they are able to grow in wisdom and understanding, while developing practical skills for making their way in the world.

With so many diverse demands on his time, it has not always been possible for Rinpoche to verify the accuracy of every element of the books we produce under his direction, and the staff of Dharma Publishing assumes full responsibility for mistakes that appear in our publications. We only hope that on balance we have succeeded in transmitting some elements of the Dharma tradition.

Those of us who have had the opportunity to work under Rinpoche are deeply grateful for the example he has set us. His dedication and reliable knowledge, his steady, untiring efforts, his patience and his caring enable us to direct our energy with confidence that despite our imperfections, our work can benefit others, making it possible for us to contribute in some way to the transmission of the Dharma in the West.

Books in the Crystal Mirror Series

1–3. Footsteps on the Diamond Path The writings of great Nyingma masters and modern Nyingma teachings on mind, self-image, and meditation. An inspiring and practical introduction to the Vajrayāna Buddhism of Tibet. (1969–1974)

4. Guru Padmasambhava and Buddhism in Tibet Lives of the Great Guru Padmasambhava and his disciples convey the power and scope of the Dharma transmission in Tibet. Includes the teaching of the fourteenth-century master Longchenpa on the Natural Freedom of Mind. (1975)

5. Lineage of Diamond Light A richly illustrated presentation of Tarthang Tulku's history of the Buddhist Dharma in India and Tibet, with a special emphasis on the masters and lineages of the Nyingma tradition and translations of two central teachings of the great master Longchenpa. (1977)

6. The Three Jewels and History of Dharma Transmission A traditional introduction to the Buddha, Dharma,and Sangha, including the Buddha's teachings and the philosophical schools they inspired. With biographies of 138 masters. (1984)

7. The Buddha, Dharma, and Sangha in Historical Perspective The life of the Buddha, the unfolding of the Dharma, and the growth of the Sangha, framed in the larger sweep of world history. With maps and comparative timelines. (1984)

8. Light of Liberation A history of Buddhism in India from the origin of the Śākyas to the twelfth century, based on traditional sources and modern archeological research. (1992)

9. Holy Places of the Buddha The origin and value of pilgrimage, expressed in accounts of the eight great pilgrimage places and the monuments along the ancient routes across India into Afghanistan. (1994)

10. The Buddha and His Teachings The path and qualities of the Perfect Buddhas, the life of the Buddha Śākyamuni, and openings of the Sūtras preserved in the Tibetan Canon. (1996)

11. Masters of the Nyingma Lineage Biographies of over 350 masters trace the Mantrayāna lineages from the original transmission of the Dharma to Tibet to the present day. With 31 maps and lists of important monasteries and sacred sites. (1996)

ཨོཾ

ཨཱཿ

ཧཱུྃ